Government 2.0

Government 2.0

Using Technology to Improve Education, Cut Red Tape, Reduce Gridlock, and Enhance Democracy

William D. Eggers

ROWMAN & LITTLEFIELD PUBLISHERS, INC.
Lanham • Boulder • New York • Toronto • Plymouth, UK

ROWMAN & LITTLEFIELD PUBLISHERS, INC.

Published in the United States of America
by Rowman & Littlefield Publishers, Inc.
A wholly owned subsidary of The Rowman & Littlefield Publishing Group, Inc.
4501 Forbes Boulevard, Suite 200, Lanham, Maryland 20706
www.rowmanlittlefield.com

Estover Road
Plymouth PL6 7PY
United Kingdom

British Library Cataloguing in Publication Information Available

Library of Congress Cataloging-in-Publication Data

The hardback edition of this book was previously cataloged by the Library of
Congress as follows:

Eggers, William D.
  Government 2.0 : using technology to improve education, cut red tape, reduce
gridlock, and enhance democracy / William D. Eggers
      p. cm.
  Includes bibliographical references and index.
  1. Internet in public administration—United States. 2. Electronic government
information—United States. 3. Internet in education—United States. 4.
Information society—Political aspects—United States. 5. Information
technology—Political aspects—United States. 6. Political participation—
Technological innovations—United States. I. Title: Government two point
zero. II. Title.
  JK468.A8 E44 2005
  352.3/87/02854678—dc22   2004011017
  ISBN-13: 978-0-7425-4175-7 (hardcover : alk. paper)
  ISBN-10: 0-7425-4175-4 (hardcover : alk. paper)
  ISBN-13: 978-0-7425-4176-4 (pbk. : alk. paper)
  ISBN-10: 0-7425-4176-2 (pbk. : alk. paper)

Printed in the United States of America

⊗™ The paper used in this publication meets the minimum requirements of
American National Standard for Information Sciences—Permanence of Paper
for Printed Library Materials, ANSI/NISO Z39.48-1992.

Contents

Acknowledgments

I wrote this book for two reasons. First, because we are in the midst of a once-in-a-century transformation of government, enabled by technological advances. I wanted to describe this development, to take the reader on a journey across the new digital government landscape, and provide a roadmap for navigating the promises and perils of this new age. Second, while several excellent books have been published on individual topics such as e-democracy, privacy, and e-learning, I wanted to write a book that covered the full panapoly of digital government issues in one place and tie them together into a coherent whole. The reader will be the judge of whether I succeeded in this goal.

It should be no surprise that with a book encompassing such a wide range of issues that many people had a hand in the final product. First and foremost, this book was made possible thanks to the generous support of the Manhattan Institute for Policy Research, where I have been privileged to be a senior fellow for several years. Larry Mone, the president of the Manhattan Institute, is one of the country's most successful policy entrepreneurs. At a time when many research institutions have moved away from producing books because they think people lack the requisite attention span, Larry continues to believe that a well-written and argued book has a unique ability to influence policy and spread innovative ideas.

Also indispensable was my former research associate Eve Tushnet. A gifted writer, researcher, and editor, and wise far beyond her years, Eve made substantial contributions to many chapters in *Government 2.0*. In fact, I could never have finished the book without her assistance. Eve's engaging and perceptive writing can be enjoyed each day by clicking through to her spirited blog, evetushnet.com (www.eve-tushnet. blogspot.com).

Other colleagues from the Manhattan Institute were also instrumental in making this book a reality. Henry Olsen, who oversees the Center for Civic Innovation, was a continual source of encouragement and a font of good ideas. Mark Riebling, the institute's book program director, helped me to sharpen the book's introductory chapter, offered pointed advice when it was most needed, and found the book a nice home with a first-rate publisher. Lindsay Young provided top notch marketing guidance. Teri Moore did a superb job editing the book.

Several colleagues at Deloitte also provided helpful suggestions. Greg Pellegrino helped me to see e-government in new and different ways. Bob Campbell imparted insightful advice on several important issues. Jeannie Rhee helped with the research on e-government and economic competitiveness.

My friends at e.Republic, the publisher of *Government Technology* and *Public CIO*, provided me with two wonderful forums to write about digital government. Moreover, the articles and studies produced by the organization have given me inspiration more times than they will ever know. In particular, I am indebted to Dennis McKenna, Tod Newcombe, Cathilea Robinet, Paul Taylor, Jessica Jones, Mark Struckman, and Steve Towns.

I wish I could personally thank all the hundreds of public officials, think tank scholars, politicians, academics, technology experts, and corporate executives interviewed in the course of writing *Government 2.0*. Much of what I know about this fascinating subject I learned from them. Florida governor Jeb Bush showed me the importance of strong executive leadership in transforming government. Stephen Clift helped me to better understand both the benefits and challenges of using the Internet to enhance democracy. Ari Schwartz and Jim Harper were both invaluable in exposing me to privacy-friendly approaches to technology. Peter Samuel, Daryl Fleming, and Bob Poole walked me through the arcana of intelligent transportation systems. Ed Stern educated me on how technology can reduce business compliance costs. Mark Forman showed me how to drive radical reform through a skeptical bureaucracy.

Other friends and colleagues who deserve special thanks for their contributions include Stephanie Sanford, Joinen Ronen, Chris Warner, Steve Kolodney, Jane Fountain, Jerry Mechling, Dan Chenok, Mauro Regio, Linda Hemby, and Donna Arduin.

Christopher Anzalone, the Washington Editor of Rowman & Littlefield, understood from the outset exactly what I was trying to achieve with the book and expertly guided the manuscript to its final form. I was grateful to be in such professional hands. I wish to thank Terry Fischer, Erin McKindley, and Naomi Burns for the production of the book and Jeff Talley for providing the cover design. Thanks also to Virginia Bridges for proofing the manuscript and Rhonda Holland for compiling the index.

Lastly, my family gave me the strength and inspiration to complete this project. My brother Dave was enthusiastic about the book from the very beginning, read immediately whatever I sent his way, and always made insightful suggestions. My other brother Toph could always be counted on to make me laugh in the face of looming deadlines and other pressures. My wife Jennifer felt—probably more than anyone else—some of the side effects of the book writing process. Only the wife of a writer can fully understand the kind of loneliness experienced when their life's companion is sitting in the same room, but actually off in a different world, his mind piecing together paragraphs and chapters. Thank you for your love, patience, and support. I could not have made it through this without you.

William D. Eggers
Austin, Texas

To the memory of Mom, Dad, and Beth,
and to Jen.

Introduction

A century ago, starry-eyed Progressives sought to remake government in the image of a private sector revolutionized by technology. America had transformed herself from a sleepy agrarian nation into a roaring industrial powerhouse. Through mass movement of goods, railroads introduced business-management procedures to corporations run by new managerial classes, who used telephones, telegraphs, and typewriters to master an ever-expanding data flow. The nation embarked on an efficiency campaign led by people like Frederick Taylor, whose "scientific management" advocated finding the "One Best Way" to do everything from growing roses to shoveling coal. Progressives like Teddy Roosevelt and Woodrow Wilson wondered why Americans couldn't apply the new rules of industrial efficiency to government as well. Thus, the government-as-machine metaphor was born.

The Progressives believed that new rules of industrial efficiency could improve the management of the burgeoning administrative state. After all, ideas like interchangeable parts and one-size-fits-all production made cheap Springfield rifles and Model-T Fords possible. Why not apply these principles to bridge-building, public education, and managing the public-sector workforce? Organizational efficiency would reform a public sector plagued by irrationality and cronyism; large, powerful bureaucratic hierarchies would replace toothless, ineffectual federal bureaus. Boss Tweed would become an Organization Man.

Today's governments are relics of that Progressive Era. They are built for an economy and society that have largely disappeared.

1

In the private sector, mass production is giving way to personalization and customization. The "One Best Way" mentality is yielding to individual choice and personalized services. The organization man is being displaced by the free agent.[1]

Public bureaucracies, by contrast, with their vertical information flows, rigid practices, and strict division of labor, are still organized according to the top-down models created for the industrial economy. As government has grown, its procedures, structures, and controls have become ever more complicated and elaborate. Until only recently, the main function of technology in government was to encode outdated procedures in software and run them on huge mainframes.

The "reinventing government" movement of the 1990s was supposed to slingshot our public sector into the twenty-first century. But that movement focused mostly on reforming individual bureaus and agencies. Some limbs of the government body became lithe and supple. Others started pushing for results, rather than simply trying to beef up their budgets. But government as a whole remained creaky, old-fashioned, and disconnected. Even reformed bureaus don't always play well with others.

Government made very little progress at working better, smarter, and more efficiently *across* agencies and levels of government, despite the fact that almost everything government does today involves multiple agencies, multiple levels of government, and the business sector or civil society.[2] Governments still operate as fractious collections of hierarchical, rule-laden, stove-piped bureaucracies, whose modus operandi is fanatical protection of their turf. Explains University of Wisconsin professor Donald F. Kettl: "Government is struggling to use twentieth-century tools to cope with twenty-first-century problems. We have pursued good management through authority and hierarchy for a century. When new challenges emerged, we responded by reorganizing and strengthening the bureaucracy. Today's problems, however, simply don't fit bureaucratic orthodoxy."[3]

In short, a bureaucracy built for the Industrial Age can't adapt to the Age of Information. Transformation requires uprooting our obsolete, century-old systems and replacing them with new models better suited to the twenty-first century. The Machine Age model that's epitomized the public sector for the past one hundred years is in dire need of a makeover. In the parlance of computer software programs, it's time to upgrade from Government 1.0 to Government 2.0. The Progressive Era, "Government 1.0" in this manner of speaking, gave us the civil service system, the city manager, independent public authorities, administrative agencies, and the Federal Reserve. Our own Information Era requires similarly sweeping changes, many of which involve unmaking much of what the Progressives wrought. What such changes would entail—how they should be implemented, and how they can transform everything from education to national security, revolutionize everything from voting to commuting, solve problems from corporate fraud to welfare cheating—is the subject of this book.

NEW WAY OF THINKING NEEDED

In the last years of President Clinton's second term, and during the presidency of George W. Bush, in city halls, statehouses, schools, federal agencies, and at election booths, we began to see the first stirrings of the public sector applying digital technology in innovative ways. Vowing to achieve "friction-free government," Pennsylvania officials used e-government tools to reduce dramatically the number of forms new business owners were required to complete. Florida Gov. Jeb Bush opened an online high school. The New York City Police Department installed kiosks where 35,000 low-risk probationers could use hand scanners to prove that they were still in town, leaving probation officers free to focus on higher-risk cases. By 2001, Americans were conducting twice as many electronic transactions with government as online stock trades. Then, in late 2002, Congress passed the E-Government Act, designed to accelerate the federal government's digitization.

Yet this first stage of digital government, by and large, meant merely putting a pretty face on a slothful, clunky edifice. Most of the public sector has yet to be transformed. The military can differentiate, from outer space, between a civilian target and a military one in the backstreets of Baghdad; but the average citizen still cannot differentiate between the federal government's forty-nine different job training programs, or its ninety separate early childhood programs. Doing just about anything of importance with the public sector still requires navigating an obstacle course of multiple bureaucracies at multiple levels of government, each of which forces citizens to provide the same information over and over again.

Today's technologies can play a crucial role in fixing the problems of modern government, changing how we get to work, how we pay our taxes, how we register our businesses, and how our kids learn. For example, by tying together different computer databases and facilitating the quick exchange of information, technology can help tear down the walls between government agencies. By cutting the operating costs of government—for activities ranging from processing taxes to delivering benefits—e-government can return huge savings to taxpayers. By slashing the costs of regulatory compliance, digital tools such as electronic permitting and reporting could potentially return billions of dollars in lost productivity back to the economy.[4] By opening up the cloistered world of bureaucratic regulation-making, electronic rule-making can offer ordinary people access to a degree of information and individual influence hitherto accessible only to the most powerful citizens.

And while the Internet won't "save" democracy, digital democracy and on-line campaigning do have the potential to bring back democracy's rich history of vigorous public discourse, updating the agora and the town meeting for the digital age (picture online democracy forums where the guy who runs the Jiffy Lube can talk with the mayor about leash laws) and turning your computer into a no-lines, no-bureaucrats government office (or even, someday, a polling place).

None of this will happen, however, without a change of thinking. Existing technologies give us the power to transform everything from how businesses are regulated to how government protects citizens from terrorism. But our thinking hasn't yet caught up with our tools.

Consider education. Millions of computers were dumped into schools in the 1990s without changing the way teachers teach. The computers served mostly as electronic blackboards—distractions from learning rather than conveyor belts of education. E-learning can realize its promise of transforming education—in fact, it can help to end the model of assembly-line education and change the very definition of schooling. But this won't happen until we change the way we think about children (why should they be segregated with only children their own age?), school (is it a building or an activity?), and public education itself (does the community control it or do individual parents?).

Similarly, for technology to truly reduce the costly friction between government and the private sector, public agencies must go beyond merely transferring cumbersome government paperwork and regulatory requirements to the web (a practice that's been dubbed "putting lipstick on a bulldog") and instead use the web as an opportunity to radically overhaul regulatory processes, cull counterproductive regulations, and slash duplicate rules. In fact, government officials should be rethinking how they regulate altogether.

And then there's the matter of using the Internet to open up government to create greater scrutiny by regular citizens. Achieving real transparency is about much more than just slapping a few friendly stats on a public website. People want to see the full picture, the one that includes the recent surge in the rat population and the slacking sanitation crews. This requires a total mindshift—one in which public officials permit successes *and embarrassments* to be both online and searchable. Sound utopian? In fits and starts, it's already happening, as you'll learn in chapter 6.

The failure to fully imagine how to make the best use of new technologies is unique neither to government nor to modern times. Throughout history there has almost always been a lag between the introduction of a new technology and its transformative use. Case in point: the nearly 1,570-year lapse between the Alexandrian Greeks's invention of the steam engine around 200 A.D., and James Watt's 1769 brainwave about what to do with it.

New technologies also don't automatically raise productivity. It took years after electric power was introduced for productivity gains to materialize. More recently, during the 1980s and 1990s economists continually spoke of a productivity paradox: no one could find any evidence that the billions of dollars companies were spending on information technology (IT) was having any affect on productivity. As University of Chicago economist Robert Solow famously quipped: "You can see the computer age everywhere but in the productivity statistics."

It was not until the late 1990s and the early years of this decade when productivity growth from IT investments finally started to materialize, climbing to 3 percent in 2000 and holding at nearly 2 percent during the 2001 recession and then soaring to more than 7 percent in the summer of 2003. The reason for the lag: it takes time for companies to figure out how to reorganize their operations in order to fully reap the benefits of new technologies.

Government has been especially slow to realize the full potential of digital technology. This should come as no surprise to anyone given bureaucracy's inherent resistance to change and the lack of a profit motive in the public sector. Government will never truly realize the transformative benefits of IT until government systems, ways of delivering services, and bureaucratic structures are rethought and redesigned to reflect the realities of the Information Age.

At least one government institution is trying to do this: the U.S. military. The Pentagon has begun to change its thinking in ways that are beginning to bring the affects of new technology fully to bear. Its early experiences demonstrate both the vast potential and considerable barriers in the transition to Government 2.0.

THE NET-CENTRIC MODEL

After the first Gulf War the Pentagon began to adopt a new doctrine, dubbed "network-centric warfare." This doctrine abandons some long-cherished military dogmas in order to harness fully twenty-first-century ITs. In contrast to the traditional chain-of-command model, which epitomized military organizations for centuries, the network-centric model is flatter, less hierarchical. Information-sharing tools are used to create what is officially termed "Total Information Awareness."

Total Information Awareness, or TIA, is a battlefield term that came into use well before its controversial attempted application to domestic-counterterrorism. The phrase designates the goal, or the grail, of the net-centric doctrine: to give everyone from foot soldiers to field commanders access to the same data, so that everyone can react and interact in real time.

Under TIA, "bottom-up" structures convert general information into specific, actionable battlefield knowledge. This networked war-fighting is made possible by sensors, satellite communications, fast and capacious computers, and a robust information backbone. But even more important than the technologies is the changed mind-set embodied by this approach. "What we are seeing in moving from the Industrial Age to the Information Age is what amounts to a new theory of war," explains Vice Admiral Arthur Cebrowski, the head of the Department of Defense's (DoD) Office of Force Transformation and the father of the network-centric warfare concept. "During the Industrial Age, power came from mass. Now power tends to come from information, access, and speed."

The speed of the U.S. advance on Baghdad during Operation Iraqi Freedom revealed the revolutionary potential of total information access. Radio frequency identification (RFID) and satellite tags allowed the DoD to transform its patchy paper-based logistics system, in which troops were forced to go "container diving" through thousands of unlabeled "mystery containers," to one where they had total asset visibility of every item in every container as it moved across the world to Iraq. Mobile computing devices allowed soldiers to view information collected by radar planes. Sensors and Internet-based communications systems, seamlessly linked, gave forces "situational awareness," enabling widely dispersed units to fight with real-time knowledge of each other's movements, as well as the positions and strength of the enemy. (Soon "bionic smart dust," comprised of thousands or even millions of these tiny sensors, will be scattered throughout the air in the battlefield allowing the military to monitor enemy troop movements and detect any intrusions into military bases.) Most impressively, the flow of real-time information allowed the Army, Marines, Air Force, and Special Operations Command—perennial rivals, who have long had trouble working together—to orchestrate stunningly coordinated actions. Proponents of network-centric warfare believe the new technological capabilities, if properly exploited, can result in a revolution in military affairs.

High technology is a defining feature of the much-publicized crusade to modernize and remake the military—and even warfare itself. While the U.S. military has made huge strides in modernizing its operations—more so in fact than nearly any other institution of government—in countless operational areas, from its outmoded financial systems that are unable to obtain a clean audit to its still ponderous supply-chain systems, the military is still light years behind leading companies such as FedEx and Wal-Mart, a fact of which the secretary is well aware. "In an age when terrorists move information at the speed of email, money at the speed of a wire transfer, and people at the speed of a commercial jetliner, the Defense Department is bogged down in the bureaucratic processes of the Industrial Age—not the Information Age," Rumsfeld told a Senate panel in 2003.

Rumsfield is no doubt correct, but it's also true that the extreme difficulty the U.S. military has had trying to secure the peace in Iraq also demonstrates the limits of technology in modern warfare, especially in peacekeeping and preventing the guerilla-style terror attacks so emblematic of America's present-day enemies. As we will discuss in chapter 2, digital technologies can aid in the fight against terrorists by improving intelligence via faster and better information sharing, but in the Wild West atmosphere of postwar Baghdad such capabilities haven't been nearly enough to prevent thousands of civilian and military deaths at the hands of the fundamentalist militants.

RESISTANCE

Rumsfeld's campaign to transform the world's largest institution into a leaner, more high-tech organization encountered massive resistance from the defense establishment. Army generals bitterly fought Rumsfeld's attempts to shift funding from some of their prized heavy artillery systems to more mobile high-tech weapons. Labor unions opposed efforts to end Industrial Age personnel rules. And the Old Guard on Capitol Hill often seemed more interested in protecting military jobs in their districts than improving efficiency and squeezing costs through the application of information technology. "Big institutions . . . are enormously difficult to change," concedes Rumsfeld. "Things at rest tend to remain at rest."

The intense opposition that proponents of military transformation have faced in their efforts to remake the military through technology can be observed across many fronts of the digital government revolution.

Public employee unions—fearing the loss of jobs—have at times been among the noisiest opponents. Teachers' unions have fought efforts to establish public "cyber charter" schools almost everywhere they have been tried—from Pennsylvania to Colorado—arguing that they'll undermine public education and turn teachers into glorified tour guides and children into mouse potatoes. Federal employee unions have testified against certain e-government efforts warning Congress that it will cause the closure of the local offices. Some middle managers in government, fearing that the ability of new ITs to move information up and down an organization will render their jobs obsolete, dragged their feet on modernization initiatives.

Some politicians have also fought digital government efforts. The corrupt ones have resisted the increased sunlight and public scrutiny brought about by the Internet, fearing that it could undermine their power and expose their skeletons. Meanwhile, the world's most repressive regimes have fought back against the online forces of transparency by blocking "controversial" websites (i.e., CNN), monitoring email traffic and chatrooms and forcing Internet service providers to give the government control over the system's backbone.[5]

The resistance is a moving target, coming in all shapes and sizes, with changing allegiances depending on the particular issue. Civil libertarians push for governments to open themselves up by posting more public information online, but at the same time vigorously battle efforts to use digital surveillance technologies to enhance security. Law enforcement takes the opposite tack: opposing efforts to put more government information online because they're afraid it will assist terrorists and criminals, while leading the effort to make greater use of surveillance technologies.

Some of the objections are legitimate—some aren't—but regardless of their merit, they can't be ignored. Achieving the digital government transformation will entail skillfully navigating through a minefield of opposition.

PERILS

Every great shift has unintended consequences, and the transition from Industrial Age to Information Age government is no exception. Even as they promise better, more responsive, and more participatory government, the IT-enabled changes advocated in this book also pose difficult new questions whose answers will likely define life in a twenty-first-century democracy.

Least predictable are the implications of many of today's advanced technologies on personal privacy, a debate that has only heated up as the nation remakes its domestic defenses to combat the terrorist threat. Biometric technologies such as thumbprint, iris, and facial recognition, along with neural network pattern recognition systems and increased government data sharing all offer astounding new law enforcement capabilities—in fact, they are fast becoming the new weapons of choice for the military, the police and intelligence agencies. But these digital tools also raise the prospect of an Orwellian *1984*-style society. Already, 80 percent of America's nineteen thousand police departments are using surveillance cameras; coming soon are robot cams and "Smart Dust."[6]

The dangers to privacy from some of today's technologies are real. Few Americans want to live in a society where government tracks our every movement, in-depth profiles of every citizen reside in giant federal databases, and we're subjected daily to a form of electronic strip search. But the answer shouldn't be knee-jerk opposition to every government attempt to use technology that could potentially be abused.

Take the 2003 congressional ban on the DoD's TIA research program. TIA had sought to improve information sharing in the fight against terrorism by developing "data mining" software that would search through billions of transactions to look for patterns of terrorist activity by linking government databases in real time to one another and to certain private-sector databases to which government investigators already had access.

To be sure, there may be privacy risks in an approach like TIA, but rather than weigh these risks against the benefits to security and then adopt safeguards and restrictions to prevent abuse, Congress chose to bar any and all deployment of TIA-derived technology by any federal agency.[7] This approach, the blunt instrument of a total ban, reflects a failure to update our thinking to correspond to new Information Age realities. We protect our liberties not by prohibiting government agencies from using the latest technologies, but through our system of checks and balances, our Constitution and our Bill of Rights. In our increasingly security-conscious world, the key to protecting our privacy is identifying and promoting the technological, legal, and cultural practices that allow us to reap the benefits of new technologies without descending into a stultifying Big Brother-like world.

The more we rely on cyber-based systems to run our economy, operate our government, and organize our society, the more tempting a target they present to hackers, criminals, terrorists, and others who would do us harm. In movies like "War Games," the target of the hackers and cyberterrorists was always the Pentagon. In reality, when the cyber attacks come they're more likely to be against critical private-sector targets like Wall Street or the electricity grid, making the task of defending our country from cyberwar infinitely more difficult—but not impossible. Like so many of our most pressing national issues, the key to defending ourselves against potentially catastrophic cyber attacks is building collaborative, public-private networks held together by mutually agreed-upon standards, federal leadership, and the ability and willingness to share information across government agencies and between the public and private sectors.

A ROADMAP

Every entrepreneur frustrated by paperwork, every parent who's sick of being surprised by bad report cards, every commuter stuck in traffic, every activist trying to fight City Hall, and every taxpayer who cares about the future has a stake in modernizing government. This book will present both the promises and perils of digital government, offering a road map for navigating the potholes and roadblocks in this emerging world.

But ultimately, this isn't a book about technology. It's about government reform—the transformation of Industrial Age government into Information

Age government. Technology is a key enabler for this change, but will not, in itself, convert today's lumbering, unintelligible governments into sleek, efficient, citizen-centered organizations. Without inspired leaders and an active citizenry that will punish slacker politicians, digital government can't end turf fights between agencies, make bad regulations disappear, or change the irrational bureaucratic incentives that fail to reward good performers or punish poor ones.

But electronic government, electronic democracy and the other reform tools highlighted throughout this book do eliminate all the excuses for *not* changing. With the advent of self-service online transactions, public officials will no longer be able to blame poor customer service on a shortage of public employees. Agencies will no longer have an alibi for not cooperating with each other. And, thanks to digital government, there will be no reason why citizens can't conduct government transactions in the evenings or on weekends; why politicians can't ask for our input before they submit legislation; or why parents can't regularly check up on their children's test scores and homework assignments by logging on to a website.

Of course, defenders of the status quo—the bureaucrats, interest groups, congressional committees, and contractors that have grown accustomed to feeding off this outdated system—will fight every last attempt to update it. But economic, societal, and political pressures will soon force a day of reckoning, as they did at the beginning of the last century.

The subject of this book is complex, but the thesis is simple: By harnessing the power of new technologies, we have the potential to reshape almost everything about government, and many aspects of everyday life. Understanding how and why this process will take place will be essential to charting the political, economic, and cultural future of America itself.

I

SERVING THE TWENTY-FIRST CENTURY CITIZEN

1

"MyGov": Building a Citizen-Centered Government

At family reunions, Anthony ("Tony") Principi's family regale each other with war stories—literally. His father arrived in the country from Argentina during World War II and immediately signed up for submarine duty. Principi the younger followed his Dad into the military and won a Bronze Star and the Navy Combat Action medal for his leadership and bravery as commander of a U.S. Navy River Patrol Unit in Vietnam's Mekong Delta. His two oldest sons are both officers in the Air Force. Even his wife of thirty years is a veteran, having served as a nurse in Vietnam and later as a Navy lawyer.

After his Navy career ended, he worked on veterans' issues for two decades, serving as staff director of the Senate Committee on Armed Services, as Deputy Secretary of the Department of Veterans Affairs (VA) under the first President Bush, and finally as acting secretary of the department in 1992. It would be hard to find anyone in America who has worked harder, longer, and in more senior positions in government on behalf of veterans than Tony Principi. He is, by all accounts, a giant in the veterans' community.

So when he walked into the San Diego VA hospital during the mid-1990s several years after heading up VA to have some stitches removed from a hip replacement operation that he underwent a few weeks earlier in a VA hospital in Palo Alto, he figured he'd be able to breeze in and out of the facility. Not just because of who he was—though he figured that couldn't hurt—but because he had just filled out reams of forms up at the Palo Alto facility.

No such luck.

The San Diego VA hospital had no idea who Principi was and didn't know anything about his recent operation—nor could they find out quickly, because at that time medical records at most VA hospitals were stored on paper. But even if the medical records had been digitized, it wouldn't have mattered much: The computers in the Palo Alto VA hospital couldn't talk to the computers at the San Diego hospital. So like millions of veterans before him, Principi had to spend hours filling out dozens of forms—the same forms he filled out only weeks earlier—just to get a few stitches removed.[1]

The VA is America's largest civilian government agency. The VA and its mammoth operating divisions—the Veterans Benefits Administration, the Veterans Health Administration, and the National Cemetery Administration—run 173 hospitals, 135 nursing homes, 43 assisted-living facilities, 73 comprehensive home-care programs, 22 separate computer networks, and 300 different computer systems. The same kind of problems that contributed to the intelligence failures of September 11, 2001 (9/11)—government stovepipes, incompatible computer systems, inadequate information sharing, poor knowledge management—produced for many years what might charitably be called a "customer service problem" at VA. Every time a veteran moved to a new location, he had to fill out all the same forms all over again because a VA hospital in St. Louis couldn't tap into a database at a VA facility in Phoenix.[2]

"Many times the record got lost in the middle there," explains Glen Giaquinto, associate director of the VA in New Jersey. Losing track of patients' records was "a constant problem." Problems with the records used to happen "every day," he recalls. "A patient walking in has multiple appointments; he goes to the lab, then to his primary care physician, then maybe to a specialist. We tried different ways to have the medical record follow the patient, but frequently it wouldn't happen, so the next time the patient comes in the lab results aren't there. We'd have to track them down, the patient gets delayed and frustrated, it's kind of a snowball effect. We constantly grappled with it."

Even worse was the process for applying for benefits. In the early 1990s, it was taking about six months for the Veterans Benefits Administration to respond to an initial disability claim. In several highly publicized cases, several vets tragically died while waiting for their benefits to be approved. The resulting negative publicity caused Congress to do what it almost always does in such situations: It sloshed more buckets of money at the agency. The Veterans Benefit Administration got an additional $200 million dollars to upgrade its computers. The result: One decade—and several hundred million dollars—later, it was taking the agency *seven* months to respond to a disability claim.

Moreover, every time a veteran sought a new service such as education benefits, housing, or vocational rehabilitation, he was forced to fill out a new set of forms because there was no centralized way to keep track of the data—a problem that banks, utilities, and most other industries solved more than a decade ago.

While all of the VA's troubles are not behind it, many of them are thanks to one of the most successful high-tech makeovers of any government organization in America. In fact, the VA has improved to the point where private hospital chains now regularly look to it for lessons in how to use technology to improve clinical practices.

Thanks to the VA's new computerized medical-records system called CPRS (Computerized Patient Records System), few veterans experience the problem Principi did; all the VA hospitals can now see the same view of the patient no matter which hospital is visited. CPRS can also perform graphing and tracking functions that a paper-based system could not do. Ross Fletcher, chief of staff at the Veterans Administration Medical Center in Washington, D.C., told *Managed Healthcare Executive* magazine that "with the CPRS, every addition to a patient's record is instantaneous and immediately seen by all users, so the error which comes from not knowing that the patient was seen in the emergency room last night—or as importantly, having his EKG taken several days before and being unable to compare it with the tracing in the emergency room—no longer occurs."[3]

Even the familiar X-ray images have received a facelift. The VA has been a pioneer in using digital X-rays. The result: greater precision in close-ups; retests are less necessary, thus reducing radiation exposure; doctors can work from home—if you've got an Internet connection; you've got your X-ray images. In this new "hospital without walls," noted Dr. Eliot Siegel, VA chief of imaging, "We will be able to handle calls in the middle of the night when no radiologist is on site."[4]

The VA has also made significant strides to streamline the benefits application process. The department now allows veterans to apply for benefits online and by combining several health care benefits forms into one it has saved veterans more than 500,000 hours of paperwork.[5]

The man who led much of the VA's ongoing transformation? None other than Anthony Principi, named Secretary of Veterans Affairs by President George W. Bush in 2000. With his new hip working just fine, Principi built on progress made during the Clinton years in his efforts to "reform the way VA uses information technology," "end the stovepipe incompatibility of the computer systems," and strive for "one VA" where veterans will have to register just once with the department and then be able to conduct all their business online without ever having to know which division of the department does what.

PUTTING THE CITIZEN AT THE CENTER

The problems that plagued the VA exemplify much of what we dislike most about government: Its utter incomprehensibility; the way the right hand never seems to know what the left hand is doing; the way the information you need always seems to be buried deep in the bowels of the bureaucracy; the impersonal "you're just a number" manner in which government treats its customers; the way we can't just take our business elsewhere when we're fed up with crummy customer service. The list could go on and on.

The way government treats us, its customers and owners, frustrates us deeply—at times, it even infuriates us. But, mostly we just accept such treatment. Why? Because that's just how government is and will always be. Right?

Wrong.

As the VA's turnaround demonstrates, digital technology allows us to change many of the things we hate about government. We can make government more intelligible to regular citizens by reorganizing it around citizen needs, like paying a parking ticket or registering a business, rather than around the narrow agency prerogatives of brick and mortar government. Public information about businesses, schools, nonprofits, and other organizations—information now collecting dust in government file cabinets—can be packaged and distributed to citizens over the Internet, helping us to make more informed decisions about everything from which airline to fly to where to send our kids to school.

By arming people with useful information about quality, cost, and performance, governments can, in turn, adopt a less paternalistic approach to their "customers" and shift many programs from monopoly to choice-based models. And thanks to the ability of information technology to deliver customized services and information at relatively low cost, providers can more easily tailor services to the needs of different people, and governments or third parties can match people to the providers and information that best meets their needs and preferences. "One-size-fits-all" government—designed by politicians and bureaucrats for the ease of politicians and bureaucrats—can be transformed into "government you design," where everything we want to do involving government can be customized to each individual's interests, location, and needs. The end result of all these changes? A massive power shift from governments to citizens, as we no longer have to rely on bureaucrats to dictate what information we need and what we must do with it. Our point of entry to this transformation begins with public-sector portals.

SIX WAYS TECHNOLOGY CAN TRANSFORM
THE GOVERNMENT-CITIZEN RELATIONSHIP

1. Reorganize government around citizen needs
2. Make choice-based service delivery more viable
3. Provide neutral information to help citizens make important choices
4. Customize services and interactions between government and citizens
5. Allow citizens to complete government transactions anywhere, anytime from a variety of devices
6. Reduce the costs of government

GOVERNMENT WITHOUT WALLS

For years, policy wonks have debated what government would look like in a perfect world. They agree more often than you might expect. There wouldn't be dozens of different federal job-training programs or agencies with incomprehensible names like the "Bureau of Reclamation." You wouldn't get five different answers to your question depending on which bureaucrat you talk to. You wouldn't be endlessly transferred from one department to another. You wouldn't have to go to half a dozen different agencies just to open a newspaper stand. You wouldn't have to wait in line. And you certainly wouldn't have to fill in the same information again and again and again.

Suddenly, thanks to electronic government (eGov), much of this wish list is within our reach. Around the world, public-sector portals have helped reshape, reorganize, and re-create the governments that built them. "In the world of bricks and mortars, enacting this kind of change would take forty years of fighting interest groups," says Alan Dobrin, the former Chief Information Officer (CIO) for the city of New York. "In cyberspace, you just do it." Government websites have been transformed from clumsy digital brochures into full-service virtual clearinghouses that guide visitors to all manner of information and public services.

After the first shock of 9/11, New Yorkers were faced with uncertainty, fear, and chaos. Rudy Giuliani calmed and heartened them in many ways; perhaps one of his most overlooked services was his ability to cut through confusion and provide frightened people with the information and help they needed. He was the city's head public relations officer, city manager, cheerleader, mourner, military leader, and psychiatrist all rolled into one. America's Churchillian mayor was everywhere: sporting an FDNY hat and giving out relief application phone numbers; in an NYPD hat telling residents about modified trash-cleanup schedules; in a FEMA cap announcing school closings and asking commuters to take public transit to work. During his frequent press conferences, no question was too large, or too small; if he didn't know the answer to a question, there was someone standing nearby who did.

But few New Yorkers had the luxury of following the mayor around all day or staying glued to the city's news channels. For many residents, there was only one place to turn 24/7 to get all the vital info they needed about services, traffic routes, subway schedules, and so on: NYC.gov, the city's online portal (motto: "Always Open"). There, one click could find information on missing persons, locating hospital patients, donating to victims' funds, finding temporary shelter, relocation assistance for businesses, school closings, and a host of other issues.[6] Commuters could find out which roads, tunnels, and bridges were closed, learn the rules for entering the Midtown tunnel, and see video of the traffic flow at hundreds of major intersections.

NYC.gov is organized by "intentions"—things you might want to do, such as pay a ticket or renew a license. You don't have to know which department you want, just what you want to do. The "I Want To" section of NYC.gov, for instance, lets New Yorkers conduct dozens of city transactions online: pay a parking ticket, get a birth certificate, schedule a trash pickup, obtain a business license, find a towed car, file a complaint, and so on.

Like Giuliani did during 9/11, NYC.gov cuts through the organizational complexity of city government for the average New Yorker, providing easily understood information from a wide range of departments. "Previously you might have had to deal with five or six different city agencies to get something done," says Giuliani. "Now you can do it in one place, at one time. E-government allows you to bypass the bureaucracy. It's a way to take government and make it what it should be: a servant to the people."

Portals like NYC.gov can be built around many other different "metaphors" or organizing principles, depending on whom a government wants to reach. The important thing is to organize the web presence around terms familiar to regular citizens instead of just to bureaucrats. Singapore's "eCitizen" website, for instance, with more than five hundred online services, was one of the first public portals to be organized around "life events"—birth registries, primary and secondary school services, job search and career services, housing aid, and retirement services—rather than by department. The site has sections called "towns" dealing with elections, library, sports, recreation, and travel. At "Recreation Town," Singaporeans can apply to have parties in parks, check the availability of facilities or register for recreational courses. Washington State's "Access Washington," and Pennsylvania's "PA PowerPort," portals use identities or roles (citizens, visitors, businesses, governments) as their organizing themes.[7] The U.S. federal government's online presence centers on all three roles (citizens, business, and government) and "customer segments" within each role—the disabled, veterans, seniors, students, farmers, small businesses, and so on. Previously, if you fell into one of these categories you had to interact with a baker's dozen of different federal agencies. Parents of the disabled, for instance, have long been forced to interact with a confusing labyrinth of agencies. Now parents can find all the information and services they need, tied up neatly with digital string and delivered on one basic website.

GOVERNMENT AS INFORMATION BROKER

Just as governments can use the Internet to untangle bureaucratic chaos and connect citizens with the specific agencies and services they're seeking, they can also help citizens make more informed decisions by widely distributing the information they collect about the public and private sector.

Trying to decide which airline will get you in on time to make that important sales presentation? The U.S. Department of Transportation ranks airlines based on on-time departure and arrival records and posts the information on its website. Hoping to shave your monthly electricity bill by switching to a new supplier, but have no idea whom to choose? The Texas Electric Choice website provides confused consumers of Texas's deregulated electricity market with neutral information comparing the rates, terms and conditions, and prices of all potential energy suppliers. Looking for the best nursing home for your aging mother? The state of Florida publishes rankings of all nursing homes in the state based on factors like quality of life, quality of care, and nutrition.[8]

This is one of the most vital roles for government in a digital world: providing accurate, easy access to information. Governments usually collect this kind of information anyway; by making it widely available and packaging it in user-friendly ways, the public sector can facilitate markets, protect consumers, and assist citizens in making important life decisions. Explains Harvard professor Stephen Goldsmith: "Government used to view the information it occasionally collected as a means to some other goal: fixing a street or issuing a license. Information itself now is a product. In a complex society, the Internet facilitates government's role in aggregating and distributing information about access, quality, and price."

One of the most successful examples of this is "school report cards." State governments have compiled online report cards with data ranging from average test scores to dropout rates to class sizes. The report cards enable parents to make more informed choices about their children's educational options, and the public exposure has caused low-scoring schools to improve their performance.[9]

Coming soon are public report cards on hospitals. Residents in Arizona, Maryland, and New York can now go on the web and find out how well the hospitals in their state do across ten measures of care, including treating heart attacks, heart failures, and pneumonia. Eventually this information will be collected for every state and be available on the website of the federal Centers for Medicaid and Medicaid Services which already provides such information for many hospitals (www.cms.hhs.gov/quality/hospital/).

Overseas, the government of India placed kiosks connected to the Internet in hundreds of small towns so that rural farmers could get information about crop markets. The information helps the farmers negotiate better prices with middlemen buyers.

Another way to facilitate markets and strengthen accountability is by establishing eBay-like feedback mechanisms allowing consumers of public services to rate various providers and services. For example, if I'm trying to figure out the best nursing home for my grandmother, I would be able to see not only how state inspectors rated the home, but also how the families of nursing home occupants rated it in terms of quality of care, treatment, and livability. The tremendous success eBay has experienced from letting buyers rate sellers and then posting the ratings on the web suggests that these kind of public feedback mechanisms can play a powerful role in building confidence in a market. The eBay sellers go to great pains to please customers—they know that poor ratings from just a handful of disgruntled buyers could bring down their much-prized customer ratings. In the highly competitive eBay auction markets, that could cost them considerable business from future buyers. Similar public feedback systems could have the same effect on public services.

THE RISE OF CHOICE-BASED SYSTEMS

High-functioning markets require good information about price, quality and performance. Unfortunately, for many services funded by the public sector—education, job training, mental health services, health care—this kind of information was previously very difficult to obtain, if not altogether nonexistent. That's one reason why governments took a paternalistic role, entering into contracts with providers on behalf of clients, or providing the services themselves, so citizens wouldn't get ripped off or maltreated. Either way, government bureaucrats, rather than the people who were obtaining the service, were choosing the providers. That's no model for a democratic society.

Fortunately, government's growing role as an information broker effectively demolishes the argument that people lack sufficient information to make these choices themselves. Performance data from government websites, covering everything from nursing home operators to trash collectors to schools, could help citizens weigh the various choices made available to them under choice-based approaches. Once clients are able to go on the Internet and be armed with information about quality, cost, and performance, providers will be more accountable to clients, allowing governments to shift social, health, workforce, and education services from monopoly to choice-based approaches. Recipients of services would be given the freedom to choose from a range of providers, ultimately giving them more control over their lives.

The shift from control to choice would have several important effects. For example, the competition generated by letting people with disabilities choose service providers in the marketplace should encourage a greater diversity of providers, which in turn would allow a better match between the preferences of the disabled and the services they obtain. Choice also offers more flexibility. If an unemployed person likes the service he's getting from a job training firm, he can continue to spend his voucher there. If his experience is unsatisfactory, he can leave and try another provider. Increased competition among suppliers will lead to specialization, as different suppliers focus on meeting different market niches. This would provide a big boost to small, neighborhood nonprofits: They can't really compete for government contracts with the big, plush, influential charity outfits, but neighborhood groups can certainly compete to attract local voucher-holders. Choice systems also can save money by reducing administrative and monitoring costs for the state, which in turn results in lower unit costs of services.

Government's Navigator Role

But choice is only part of the answer. Many of the people needing assistance are emotionally and psychologically disturbed or addicted to drugs or alcohol—sometimes a combination of the above—and therefore unable to make rational choices about which service providers are best for them. For this population, choice without proper guidance could be a disaster. To rectify this, governments, the private sector, and nonprofit groups need to help some people wend their way through these complex social service, health, and education markets, by serving, in essence, as navigators or agents for clients and their families.[10] One rudimentary example is the Department of Health and Human Service Substance Abuse and Mental Health Services Administration's (SAMHSA) website which has an online substance abuse treatment facility locator enabling family members, social service workers, or the clients themselves to search for treatment centers in any part of the country that would best fit their needs. Based on answers to a series of questions (location, public or private facility, type of treatment desired, and so on), the site will suggest several different facilities that meet the characteristics the individual or family member has indicated are important to them.

Electronic matching systems will soon go well beyond the SAMHSA site. Consider an unemployed individual, let's call him Joe, who, battling alcoholism and depression, decides to seek out government assistance to find a job, get sober, and put his life back together. Joe logs on to a secure website and begins keying in some basic information about himself. He's asked a series of questions about his needs, his problems, where he lives, whether he prefers assistance from religious or secular organizations, and so on. Joe says a faith-based program could help supply the spiritual meaning that has been missing in his life; moreover he would prefer entering a program in Smithtown so he can be closer to his brother. Joe's answers prompt further questions tailored more specifically to his situation. Eventually, the software teases out all the information it needs from Joe and supplies him with links to three faith-based organizations that seem to best match his needs. After clicking on to the websites of each, speaking with counselors at the programs and to his social worker, Joe finally makes his choice and is electronically enrolled in the program. After Joe has begun participating in the program, the organization he has chosen gets a voucher for its services.

MY GOVERNMENT, MY WAY

The rise of navigators and choice-based systems are just two examples of government's coming transformation from its twentieth-century assembly line, Industrial Era model to a customized, twenty-first-century Information Era model. This transformation mirrors private-sector trends in which computers and more flexible work processes enable almost infinite customization at little increase in cost. Such "mass customization" has allowed Dell Computers to offer its customers *16 million* possible computer configurations, while Amazon's software imitates the kind of personalized advice you might get from a neighborhood bookseller. The second we click over to Amazon's website, for example, we enter a store designed just for us, where we get individualized book recommendations, a summary of our past purchases, customized messages, lists of recommended books from our favorite reviewers and the ability to purchase almost anything under the sun with just one mouse click.

Why can't government be more like Amazon? Why can't we log on to our local government sites and be greeted with schedules for the latest recreation classes that meet our interests, an email link to our council members, and a profile of the latest crime stats in our neighborhood? Why can't we receive email notifications each time a zoning change is made that could affect our property, a crime is committed in our neighborhood, or a construction project begins that will clog up our drive to work? Why can't government websites have intelligent digital guides that help us identify and solve our problems, rather than endlessly linking us to more and more extraneous information?

They can and are beginning to do this in some places. Virginia has introduced customizable "MyGov" web pages allowing citizens to choose from topics such as public meeting announcements, interactive government services, legislative sites, local government, local media, public schools, lottery numbers, press releases, state government, and traffic information. But mostly, "personalization" in government has so far meant going to a website, filling out a form and then getting content customized to your interests the next time you log on to the site. While well-intentioned, this approach misses the boat. Why? For one thing, most people don't visit government websites enough to make it worthwhile to go through the trouble of filling out the forms. For another, most of the early personalization tools on government websites have been very rudimentary—for example, they almost never involve actually completing any transactions—and therefore provide little extra value for citizens and businesses. The solution, however, isn't to abandon personalized government, but instead to make it more sophisticated and beneficial to citizens and businesses.

It's not enough, for example, for government websites to simply link people to information, offer advice, or answer frequently asked questions. Instead, they should be more focused on solving problems from the citizen's perspective. This entails creating "intelligent digital guides" that know who you are, providing consolidated services and offering content that reflects your interests. Say you need City Hall to clean up the dirty, rat-infested vacant lot next door. Offline, you'd be forced to fill out separate complaints (and then follow up) with the Department of Health, the Department of Sanitation, the Department of Animal Welfare, the Department of Transportation, and so on. Getting anything done could take months. But online, you would fill out a complaint form that would create a "Vacant Lot Agency." This "virtual agency" would exist only at the moment you're filling out the complaint; its job is to assess your complaint and electronically route your problems to all the relevant agencies. You'd then be able to check the status of your complaint at any time, day or night.

This kind of personalization is really just good customer relationship management (CRM). A combination of computer technologies and business process changes, CRM is about dramatically enhancing customer relationships by reorganizing service delivery around customer intentions and desires, rather than the organization's internal structures. "Our breakthrough four years ago," says Sally Jewel, the CEO of Recreational Equipment Inc. (REI), a recognized leader in creating unique customer experiences, "was to shift to being market-driven—paying attention to who these customers are and how we can adapt to the way they want to recreate."[11]

CRM has allowed private firms to manage their relationships with customers on an individualized one-to-one basis. When we interact with private companies today—whether it's the technical support center to help us set up our new computer or the gas company to pay a bill—we expect to be able to complete a given transaction through multiple channels and for each channel to have all our relevant information, whether we're at the store, on the website, or talking to a customer service rep on the phone. We expect that when we call the company back in two days, the person who takes our call will know whether our particular issue has been resolved and, if not, why not.

Rising citizen expectations is forcing governments to focus more time and attention on creating better, more personalized customer experiences. These efforts are still in their nascent stages. Public officials are struggling with everything from how to integrate customer data across agencies without violating privacy protections to how much emphasis to place on e-government capabilities versus improving telephone call centers. While there is considerable debate about the means, few argue with the end goal: dramatically improving customer service in government. Simple things like sending out email alerts when registrations expire or populating online forms with already existing information could add enormous value, especially for citizens and professionals who have frequent interactions with government—doctors, pharmacists, lawyers, contractors, and small businessmen.

Take a hypothetical case of a contractor building a house for a client. Kate, the firm's business manager, logs onto their secure, customized digital gateway in order to obtain all the building and environmental permits they need from the city. The site prepopulates most of the forms with data she has already provided. After answering a series of questions, she's able to complete the initial applications in less than thirty minutes. The house is automatically passed off to the tax rolls and an electronic tax filing account is set up. Three months into the project, Kate gets an email informing her that the legislature recently passed new earthquake regulations that could affect her construction project and suggests possible alterations. In response to a request from the general contractor requesting an inspection, the city sends her an email informing her that a building inspector will be out to see the property the following week.

The closest any actual government website comes to this kind of functionality may be Student Aid on the Web, a powerful portal run by the U.S. Department of Education that takes college prospective students through every step of planning and preparing for college—including matching them to the colleges that best meet their abilities and preferences. After entering some basic information on the website, students can compare colleges for size, cost, and majors offered; be matched to scholarships, grants, and loans; learn how much they should expect to contribute to college based on income and tax information they provide; and learn how much each school will likely cost them based on probable levels of financial aid. Students can also apply for financial aid online and even fill out individual college applications without leaving the website.

More than 35,000 students have built individual personalized profiles on Student Aid on the Web. The department uses information in the profiles, which in addition to financial information includes career aspirations and choice of major, to push customized emails to students.

The portal was the brainchild of Jennifer Douglas, a former college financial aid administrator, who came to the U.S. Department of Education determined to make finding information about student financial aid easier for students, parents, and counselors. "It [Student Aid on the Web] was borne from the sheer frustration in my own experience as first a financial aid recipient and then a coordinator working with families," explains Douglas. "I would see everyday the lack of understanding and knowledge about where to go for information about what kind of aid is available." The website, which along with its sister site FAFSA on the Web receives hundreds of millions of hits each year, takes an extremely complex and disjointed process that can take weeks or months of detective work to navigate and made it intelligible to the average high school senior.

Governments have not yet reached this level of personalization, but slow and sure progress is making government more citizen-centered. Chicago residents now only have to call one number, 311, to be connected into a wide range of city services. Once they reach a customer service rep, which takes on average only thirteen seconds, they can file a complaint, request a trash pickup, report a pothole, or even inquire about whether an upcoming parade will cause their street to be blocked off. And instead of wondering whether their request went into some government black hole, they can go online and track the progress of their service request, as can city administrators, thanks to a sophisticated citywide management information system. Chicago officials use the data generated by the 311 system to evaluate and improve the performance of services and discern patterns that can help them better target responses to community and citywide problems.[12]

BLINK OF AN EYE

On a cold, northeastern winter day in December 2003, Sean Leach was driving along Route 130 in North Brunswick, New Jersey, when he heard the sirens behind him and then saw the police officer motioning for him to pull over. Leach knew immediately why he was being pulled over: his car registration had expired. The renewal form was right there in his visor; he just hadn't gotten around to mailing it in yet. Now his car would be impounded and he'd have to pay more than $100 to get it out—not to mention all the wasted time and hassle. This was going to be a bad day.

Once police officer Jason Zier approached the car, however, the two got talking and Zier mentioned to Leach that he could renew his auto registration online at the New Jersey Motor Vehicle Commission's website.[a] Zier then went back to his patrol car to issue a summons and order a tow. Meanwhile, Leach called a buddy who took his credit card information and access code and renewed the registration for him online. By the time Zier came back with the ticket, Leach informed him that the car was now registered, a fact confirmed by the computer inside Zier's patrol car. The tow car was cancelled. Leach went on to have a very good day.

a. "Motorist Registers during Traffic Stop," *Associated Press*, December 5, 2003.

The Privacy Wild Card

In the private sector, the cardinal rule for successful CRM is "Know Thy Customer," and the value of personalization correlates strongly to how much data the company has about your tastes and preferences. But when it comes to the public sector, privacy concerns will lead many to pass up the added convenience rather than having such an intimate relationship with the state. "We're entering a whole new territory," says Charlie Gerhards, the former CIO of Pennsylvania. "Some citizens and businesses don't want us to get too good at this [personalization] business. How would you like to go online to buy a fishing license from the state and be told you can't buy one because you have unpaid parking tickets?"

Thanks to open records laws and other peculiarities of government, protecting privacy in a world of customized government will require considerable dexterity. One option is "anonymous personalization," where citizens can visit a website anonymously to obtain personalized but neutral advice about their particular situation. Users need only identify a role that specifies who they are—such as a business owner, a teacher, or a prospective college student—for an intelligent guide to have enough information to walk them through the process of solving their problem. An early, and thus relatively unsophisticated, example of this was flexyourpower.ca.gov, a site set up by California in the wake of the state's energy crisis. Californians would go on the site, be interviewed by an "energy brain," and their answers would be used to give them customized advice on how to conserve energy in their home.

Governments could also team up with private-sector websites that would offer businesses and citizens personalized electronic gateways into government. (More on this in the next chapter.) We'll explore privacy concerns more fully in chapter 9 but for now a few commonsense rules can help to prevent many potential privacy objections to personalization. First, don't make it mandatory. Anyone with objections to personalized government should be able simply to choose not to opt in. Second, disclose exactly what information will be collected, what will be saved, how it will be used—and why—and whether it will be shared with other agencies or organizations.[13]

ANYTIME, ANYWHERE

Soon truly friction-free government will mean that for many government services and transactions we won't even have to go to a website to take care of our businesses digitally. That's because we're entering the era of "ubiquitous computing," in which "computers" aren't just the square PCs hogging our desktops, but innumerable devices embedded anywhere imaginable—in spare parts, walls, toys, furniture, automobiles, magazines (yes, even magazines), TVs, appliances, cell phones, clothing, animals. According to the Institute for the Future, "For much of future computing, the computer screen, the mouse, the keyboard—even the entrenched metaphor of windows—will be obsolete . . . replaced by dozens, perhaps hundreds of interfaces, each drawing on different interfaces and each appropriate to a particular situation."[14]

Net-enabled washing machines and air conditioners will control our homes' climate and energy consumption. "Smart dust," comprised of thousands of sand-grain-sized sensors that communicate with each other, will create power-aware buildings and homes, saving billions of dollars in energy costs. Airports will have sensors to measure noise, while sensors located on factory floors will alert workers to potentially dangerous situations. Farm crises like Europe's foot-and-mouth disease could be quelled before they do much damage, thanks to traceable Radio Frequency Identification (RFID) tags implanted on pigs and cattle that will transmit their movements through transportation systems, allowing officials to know the location of individual animals at every moment.

Ubiquitous computing represents a major wave of change. Already thousands of mothers track their children and armies track their soldiers using Global Positioning System (GPS) devices embedded in cell phones or even clothing. School authorities at a primary school in Osaka, Japan, track students' movements via RFID tags implanted on their clothing or school bags. Soon it will make countless transactions—including many with government—almost effortless. For governments, the first step toward ubiquitous computing is wireless government. Virginia residents can use mobile devices to find info on everything from polling places to the locations of state parks. New Yorkers can check out traffic alerts, restaurant health inspections, and public-safety announcements on the go.

But these basic, "first-wave" applications are already being supplanted by more transformative uses of wireless computing by government. A police force in the Midlands in the United Kingdom alerts small companies of shoplifters in their vicinity on a real-time basis by sending out a warning, containing a description of the criminals via a text message. This is less intrusive, quicker, and far more cost-effective than the previous approach of calling every company. In China, when a prisoner escapes from a prison in a populated area, wardens are alerted by text message (SMS) and then images are distributed by multimedia message (MMS) to local residents so as not to scare them with a siren. In the United States, security sensors are being used to track ships and containers, informing the Coast Guard about where they've been and whether any containers have been breached.

Reaching a point where citizens and businesses can access a public-sector front counter wirelessly anywhere will mean devoting serious resources to IT architecture. "You want to make sure that you can get your citizens to wherever they want to be, whether that's a PDA, desktop, Internet television, or the web-enabled medicine cabinet of the future," says Paul Taylor of the Center for Digital Government. "With everything connected to the web, you need to make sure the technology can adapt to the new devices."

THE BOTTOM LINE

What about government's bottom line? Will putting government services online ultimately save taxpayers money? Shouldn't the billions of dollars that governments are investing in technology initiatives result in big-time cost reduction? After all, companies from Oracle to Wal-Mart have realized large cost savings from web-enabling business processes such as purchasing, HR, and supply chain management. Shouldn't similar levels of savings be possible in government? The answer is yes, but so far such savings have largely eluded the public sector. There are a variety of reasons why this is the case—most governments got a later start in implementing web-based technology than the private sector; government has to serve all citizens thus cannot easily close down an expensive channel of service and so on. But the fact of the matter is that taxpayers have yet to see the same kind of windfall from IT-driven productivity advances that shareholders of private companies have experienced. With many governments facing continual fiscal stress, however, interest in using IT as a cost-cutting tool has never been greater.

From license renewals to parking ticket payments to business compliance reporting, nearly all government transactions with citizens and businesses can be done more cheaply over the Net. Technology allows the public sector to automate many routine interactions with citizens and businesses, eliminating paperwork and reducing processing costs, such as sorting, stuffing, mailing, and printing. For example, the cost of processing an e-payment is a mere two cents, compared to forty-three cents for issuing a check.[15] State and local department of motor vehicle offices routinely report substantial savings from moving their citizen transactions online. Arizona's DMV, for example, saves 76 percent from online vehicle registration renewal.

Another area where digitization can save governments substantial amounts of money is in customer service. Providing assistance with farm programs; signing people up for benefits; processing eligibility requests; answering questions about zoning ordinances or thousands of other subjects; these are just a few of the things that millions of government employees located in thousands of field offices and call centers spend most of their day doing. The salaries, benefits, and overhead supporting this extensive network of government field offices costs taxpayers tens of billions of dollars a year.

TEN WAYS E-GOVERNMENT CAN SAVE MONEY

1. Reduced workforce costs
2. Higher employee productivity
3. Reduced paper costs
4. Reduced processing costs
5. Better supply chain management
6. Better prices on goods and services
7. More efficient markets
8. Reduced travel and training costs
9. Reduced fraud and abuse
10. Lower building and property costs

Leading private companies are reaping huge cost savings by shifting millions of such customer calls to self-service web transactions. Oracle saves $550 million annually by letting customers serve themselves, estimating that each customer care call handled by an employee costs $350, compared to about $20 for those done on its website.[16] Similarly, by moving 35 million customer service calls to a web-based self-service environment, IBM saved hundreds of millions of dollars a year.[17]

Letting customers serve themselves through self-service web-based transactions would allow governments to reduce customer service costs and provide round-the-clock availability to customers. Several years ago, the Texas Workforce Commission shifted its unemployment insurance application process from about two dozen local offices to call centers. Later, the service was offered online. By allowing individuals to apply for unemployment benefits over the telephone or the web, the state was able to reduce wait times, offer more specialized services, and save millions of dollars by closing eleven local offices.[18] In Hennepin County, Minnesota, the county government was able to cut the staff of one department in half after building a website that enabled residents to see and pay their property taxes online.[19]

The key to realizing large cost savings from self-service transactions is to actually shift citizens and businesses to the online channel. Otherwise the additional costs of adding and maintaining the web channel, together with the existing costs of supporting physical and phone service channels, could mean that web-enabling a service could actually increase a government's service costs.[20] "Until we can get very high adoption rates, it will slow down our being able to get efficiencies out of electronic government," said Michigan CIO Teresa Takai. Fortunately there are a host of proven strategies governments can use to boost eGov take-up rates.

Ultimately, much of the savings from self-service transactions will come from lower workforce costs. Florida's HR outsourcing and technology enhancement initiative, for example, will allow it to reduce the number of employees delivering HR services by more than one thousand positions. As more citizens take care of their government needs on the web, governments will need fewer clerks to process requests, fewer human resource professionals to fill out personnel forms, and fewer data processors to transfer information from paper to computers. In Nebraska, for example, the state used technology to cut its seasonal tax-processing workforce in half. At the federal level, the IRS announced in January 2004 that it would reduce its processing workforce by 2,400 full-time positions because the growth in electronic filing has resulted in less work for the 15,000 IRS employees who process tax returns.[21] "When you do move to electronic filing, you no longer need to open as many envelopes, you no longer need to do as much daty entry," explains IRS Commissioner Mark W. Everson.[22]

FIVE STRATEGIES FOR BOOSTING EGOV TAKE-UP RATES

Make It Mandatory. The quickest, most surefire way to raise adoption rates is by forcing customers to use the digital channel. The conventional wisdom is that this is never an option for governments due to access and fairness issues. Not true. While governments can't use the mandatory approach for most e-government services, in certain cases, it's perfectly legitimate, particularly for some government-to-business services.

Make It Cheaper. Governments can make it cheaper and easier to complete the transaction electronically than in person or by mail by providing discounts for completing transactions online or raise the costs of using other channels.

Market It. If people don't know a service is available online or can't find it, they're not going to use it. Aggressive marketing can change this. San José sends out press releases, mails out flyers, and even trots out the mayor to do promotional events. The state of Florida does public service announcements.

Form Partnerships with the Private Sector. Partnering with market-savvy private organizations can also increase uptake. These "channel partnerships" can be established with banks and brokerage firms, sporting goods stores, trade associations and other companies or organizations that have trusted relationships with customers governments want to reach.

Change the Culture. Throwing an e-government application up on the web and going about your operations the same way as before will all but guarantee low adoption rates. Agencies that have had the most success with adoption are those that fully embraced digital government, making it a central part of their mission and strategy—rather than just an afterthought.

Technology is also making it easier for the public sector to detect and reduce fraud. Governments waste billions of taxpayer dollars a year on overpayments, errors, false claims, and outright fraud. In 2000, the Inspector General for the U.S. Department of Health and Human Services found that the Health Care Financing Administration (HCFA) paid $20.6 million for Medicare equipment or services provided to beneficiaries after they died. Meanwhile, in the late 1990s, the VA made improper benefit payments to convicts serving prison sentences. Approximately 13,700 incarcerated veterans were overpaid about $100 million.

New technologies have proven highly effective in rooting out the tens of billions of dollars of taxpayer money that's wasted on fraud, abuse, and erroneous payments. "Data brokers" and online eligibility systems, for example, can help reduce fraud by instantly verifying the income and assets of welfare and Medicaid applicants.[23] After years of steep welfare cost increases, the Canadian province of Ontario modernized its archaic, error-prone eligibility process. The results were impressive: the system determined that 17 percent of all welfare recipients were ineligible and another 8 percent were being overpaid. Total cost savings over five years is projected to be $1 billion.

The bottom line? Over time, digitization should result in fewer government field offices and less duplication and overlap. Waste, fraud, and abuse can be sniffed out and eliminated, as linked-up computer systems and advances in artificial intelligence make it harder for dishonest contractors or crooked public officials to bilk the taxpayers. Moreover, thanks to eGov, governments will need fewer people to handle routine tasks like processing license and permit requests or handling mail. Many middle management jobs will disappear as agencies use technology, rather than multiple layers of managers, to pass information through the organization. No one knows how much money all this will eventually save taxpayers; however, simply replicating the private sector's 20 percent average savings from putting processes online could save governments at all levels more than $100 billion a year. In an age of widespread budget deficits, that number should bring a sigh of relief to policymakers and taxpayers alike.

*   *   *   *   *

For too long, government agencies have arranged themselves in ways that are helpful and intelligible to bureaucrats and insiders—but not to regular citizens. With their overlap of functions and jurisdictions, and their arcane rules and procedures, governments can be a confusing maze even for public employees. But for the average citizen or business, government can be downright incomprehensible. Simply finding the right agency to handle your problem can sometimes require painstaking detective work.

With digital government, much of the hassle and frustration evaporates.

Services and information can not only be made more accessible and intelligible to regular citizens, but also customized to meet their particular needs, preferences, and capabilities. Information about the quality of public and private services can be widely disseminated, enabling government to offer citizens more choice for a wide array of public services. The best part? All of this can even potentially cost less than existing Industrial Age government.

While all this is possible today, the biggest benefits to citizens will come when governments find a way to solve a problem that has bedeviled policymakers and academics for decades: coordinating information and services across agencies and levels of government in order to provide truly seamless government for citizens. We explore this vital issue in the next chapter.

TIPS FOR PRACTITIONERS

- Providing accurate, easy access to information is a vital role for government in the digital economy. To fulfill this role, devote more time and attention to how to package government information in a user-friendly fashion.
- Facilitate markets and strengthen accountability by establishing eBay-like feedback mechanisms allowing consumers of public services to rate various providers and services.
- As more and more public services are opened up to choice, help citizen-customers navigate their way through complex social service, health, and education markets by using technology to match people to the most appropriate providers.
- Enhance customer relationships by reorganizing service delivery around customer intentions and desires, rather than according to your internal structure.
- When creating personalized government, disclose exactly what information will be collected, how it will be used—and why—and whether it will be shared with other agencies or organizations.

2

Knocking Down Walls and Building Bridges

Fragmentation, balkanization, turf protection, silo management—whatever you want to call it—is the toughest dilemma facing public administration today. It is pervasive—within governments, across governments and up and down levels of government. It is the chief contributor to waste, inefficiency, and ineffectiveness in our public sector.

—Peter Harkness, publisher, *Governing*[1]

Long lines aren't the only things that make citizens feel like cattle in the government herd. Conflicting, obscure, inscrutable regulations—red tape—also make us feel like subjects instead of citizens. And here too, what we need is a new approach to government.

Lloyd Good's story began innocently enough, with his decision back in 1980 to build homes on ten acres of property along the canals of Lower Sugarloaf Key, Florida. Good was savvy enough about government to know that the first thing he needed to do was hire a law firm to guide him through the bureaucratic maze. What he didn't know at the time was that his bright idea would fizzle out after a twenty-year journey through an endless labyrinth of agencies at every conceivable level of government.

In 1983, after considerable haggling, Good obtained a permit from the Army Corps of Engineers to dredge and fill wetlands on his property. When the county objected, Good scaled back his plans and got a new permit from the Corps, valid for five years but subject to further review. While he was waiting on the Army Corps, though, the county instituted what amounted to a moratorium on all new development. Application denied. After a successful appeal to the Monroe County Commission, however, Good finally had his county permit.

Then, perhaps feeling neglected, the state plunged into the fray. The Florida Department of Community Affairs appealed the county's permit award to another state agency, the Florida Land and Water Adjudicatory Commission, which rejected Good's building plans in 1986.[2] Good schlepped back to court, won his state case, and was granted preliminary approval for his new development plans—six years after filing his application. But then, out of nowhere, a third state agency, the South Florida Water Management District, stepped in. Application rejected. Again.

Meanwhile, while all this was happening, three animals that resided on Sugarloaf Key were being added to the national endangered species list: a turtle, a rabbit, and a rat. This let another federal agency, the Fish and Wildlife Service, join in the fun, producing a study that recommended further construction restrictions on Good's ten acres. Citing the study, the Army Corps reversed its earlier decisions and denied Good's application on the basis of habitat loss for endangered species. Good sued again, but this time he lost. And so two decades, seven agencies, and three levels of government after filing his first permit application, our hero was back where he started.

Now, one can argue about whether or not the government was right or wrong in stopping Good's development. What seems inarguable, though, is that the process he went through is flawed, and not at all unusual. Our fragmented political system is replete with countless agencies with massive overlap in responsibilities. The result? Doing almost anything of real importance in this country, whether you're a multinational corporation or the owner of a single home, requires navigating an obstacle course of multiple bureaucracies at multiple levels of government, none with any significant ability or inclination to cooperate in order to ease your passage through the regulatory maze. Good's saga demonstrates that information technology won't transform government via portals alone; true change must come by seamlessly knitting together different agencies, different levels of government, and, ultimately, private for-profit and nonprofit organizations.

SEAMLESS GOV

If you're a public servant, it matters a lot to you and your career what agency, division, and level of government you work for. And you probably think that these arcana matter to the rest of us, that the average citizen has at least some vague notion of which tasks are performed at various levels of government: for example, that cities do building inspections and states maintain the highways.

Generally speaking, you're wrong. When it comes to government, most businesses and citizens just want to abide by the law with as little expense and hassle as possible. Citizens don't care about or understand the minutiae of how governments are structured. When we visit the local park, we don't know or care whether it's maintained by the city, the county, or the state; we just want it to be clean.

Citizens, businesses, and even other governments should be able to conduct transactions with multiple levels of government in a single place. Poor Mr. Good, for instance, could have saved a lot of grief if he had been allowed to provide all the information about his proposed development just once, in one place, on one website, rather than filling out countless forms and dealing with multiple federal, state, and local agencies. Seamless government, the subject of this chapter, shifts responsibility for navigating the levels of government from the private citizen or business to the public agencies themselves—and provides people with the (generally web-based) tools they need to ease this transaction. Online service centers that integrate transactions from various agencies within one government entity would eventually also cross governmental boundaries.

But the importance of connecting different agencies at multiple levels of government with each other (and even in some cases with private and nonprofit partners) into a seamless network—what the British call "joined-up" government—goes well beyond providing better customer service. When separate entities don't communicate, "cracks" form between them, and everything from poor Mr. Good-type citizens to terrorists to missing children fall through those cracks. Seamless government seeks to bridge those abysses by using technology to link up government agencies with one another, a reform that is critical for much of what government does today, from coordinating disaster response to reducing regulatory burdens on businesses and citizens. In fact, it promises to be one of the most important government reforms of the decade, one that has the potential to fundamentally change how we citizens perceive and interact with our government and how government agencies interact with each other.

For citizen services, success in achieving seamless government could mean that in time we would be able to complete a range of public-sector transactions without necessarily knowing which government agency we're dealing with; what level of government we're dealing with; or even, in some cases, whether we're dealing with government at all. For public safety, the stakes are much higher. Success could mean a matter of life or death. Finding a way for the CIA to share intelligence in real time with the FBI, and for the FBI to share it with local police departments, commercial airlines, utilities, and other critical infrastructure providers could save the lives of thousands of innocent people.

But before any of this can happen, reformers will need to overcome a number of significant barriers—not the least of which is politics.

DISARMING THE TURF WARRIORS

Few people have been as involved for as long, and as deeply, in trying to transform government through technology as Frank McDonough. He headed up the federal government's information technology (IT) policy during the 1970s and 1980s, long before there was any such thing as a government chief information officer (CIO). Before he finally retired in 2003 after more than three decades of public service, he spent his last half-dozen years as deputy associate administrator at the General Services Administration (GSA) on a single-minded quest trying to make seamless government a reality. His initiative, "Government without Boundaries," aimed to provide certain citizen services, such as business registration and recreation, across all four levels of government. If you want to spend two days camping in Virginia's Shenandoah Mountains, for instance, why shouldn't you be able to make campground reservations on your county's website? "A citizen needs to be able to come into government at whatever level they want to take care of their business," McDonough explains.

Despite McDonough's valiant efforts trying to catch the interest of political appointees and convince states to be guinea pigs for the project, Government without Boundaries didn't exactly take Washington, D.C., by storm. For years, it limped along with no dedicated funding, staff, or high-level executive sponsorship, sustained mostly by McDonough and a few isolated true believers at the state and local level. Only toward the very end of his career did the federal government get serious about seamless government (more on this in chapter 11). What was the problem?

The biggest challenges to seamless government projects aren't technological but political. Web-based technology is now sophisticated enough to meet the challenge; the human capital, however, is less prepared. Every decision made at huge government agencies is marked by political infighting and ancient turf fights. McDonough can effortlessly reel off a list of the barriers to seamless government: insufficient funding; distrust and turf battles between different levels of government; lack of leadership; the large number of state/county/federal entities in the United States (and in many other countries); more pressing priorities; and on and on. But they all pale next to problem number one: old-fashioned politics. "There are some 3,700 municipal governments and 3,300 county governments in the U.S., in addition to state governments," McDonough explains. "Each one has a dozen or more elected officials at the top, all of whom think they're God—and, in their environment, they're right."

In the era of seamless government, however, it will be hard to retain that lofty title, as blurring lines between governmental levels will be a frightening proposition to many local deities. Say you're a county tax assessor. You may not occupy a particularly exalted position in the broader political scheme of things, but in your little fiefdom you're a moderately big cheese. Your name is on the window of the local assessor's office, and everyone who wants to do anything from paying his property taxes to renewing his motor vehicle registration has to either pass through your doors or mail in a check made out to you. And that builds name recognition with the voters in your district before the next election.

Now seamless government comes along, letting citizens pay their *county* taxes online at the *state's* website. Good for them, bad for you. For whom among your voters will ever be reminded of your name now—unless something goes wrong with the *state's* website, of course, blocking the transaction and leading everyone to start looking for someone to blame?

When the feds tried to build a user-friendly one-stop shop website for recreation services where you could click on a state and get information about every park in the state—whether it was run by the feds, the state, or local governments—they encountered strong opposition from more than a dozen states. Why? State officials were concerned that the site, www.recreation.gov, would reduce traffic to their own state tourism sites. Two years after the feds launched recreation.gov, it's goal of true one-stop shopping for public recreation sites was proving elusive; only a handful of states had supplied them with the data necessary for users to access information on the state parks.

Or to offer another example, if you're a state legislator, a big part of your job is constituent service, that is, helping the citizens who elected you navigate those nasty government bureaucracies. It stands to reason, therefore, that the simpler their interactions with government become, the less necessary you become. None of this will do, and so there are almost no incentives for the people who run government today to radically reform it.

Despite such obstacles, seamless gov can, and likely will, happen. The stakes are just too high—particularly in the security area—for it to be held hostage to parochial politics. Overcoming the political issues will be critical to success, but not sufficient. Government innovators will also need to achieve quantum improvements in these four areas:

- Tying disparate information systems together;
- Turning information into knowledge;
- Sharing knowledge across governments; and
- Packaging and disseminating joined-up information to the public.

FALLING THROUGH THE CRACKS

"Where are the children?"

That chilling line appears in an internal memo from one caseworker in Florida's Department of Children and Families (DCF) to another. The children in question were three sisters: Rodericka, Randie, and the girl whose name became the symbol of our nation's broken child welfare system, Rilya Wilson. The memo was filed seven months before Rilya was finally reported missing.[3]

As of September 2004, Rilya Wilson had still not been found. The then five-year-old was reported missing a full fifteen months *after* she disappeared, becoming one of the thousands of children who vanish each year from state child welfare systems. Rilya's case gained national media attention and put Florida's DCF in the spotlight, but the problems that led to her disappearance were in no way unique to Florida. At the beginning of 2003, Michigan couldn't find three hundred children. Other child welfare agencies can't even tell you how many children are lost in their states.

The horrific cases that hit the headlines are almost always the result of a long series of missteps and dereliction of duty. But these tragic cases—of children disappeared, children beaten, and children dead—usually also include an element of information failure. Throughout the country, the systems that seek to protect abused and neglected children are uncoordinated, half-computerized, and often unable to communicate with other relevant agencies even within the same state, let alone with other states' agencies or with federal entities. The families that end up in the system often move frequently, making it even more difficult to track children. Parents, children, and other adults living in the home may be hooked up with scores of agencies and organizations—the school system, addiction programs, probation and parole, and many more. The result of all this? In an age in which we can track in real time hundreds of millions of packages across the world each year, we lose track of thousands of children.

When two different states get tangled up with each other, the results can be particularly disastrous. Kadijah and Coretta Reid, two Miami sisters who had been missing from Florida's system for six years (since the ages of two and one), turned up in South Carolina's child welfare system after social workers found that they were being neglected by their mother. But Florida didn't know the kids had been found, and South Carolina didn't know the kids had ever been in care in Florida. The same thing happened to another pair of sisters, ages nine and eight, who were investigated as victims of neglect by Wisconsin social workers while listed as missing in Florida. When the *South Florida Sun-Sentinel* went on a hunt for twenty-four missing children in the wake of the Rilya Wilson case it found that nearly one-quarter of the children "had been investigated for abuse or neglect in other states during the time Florida considered them lost." The newspaper's investigative team found that child welfare databases in scores of states were "incomplete, difficult to access, and seldom used."[4]

Richard Gelles, interim dean of the school of social work at the University of Pennsylvania, told the newspaper, "The nation has about three hundred child welfare systems. It doesn't have one. You have state systems like Florida and county systems like Pennsylvania. The data warehouses and data systems in Florida don't speak to each other, so there would be no reason to think states could." Each state is its own thicket of tangled public and private child welfare groups, people who only investigate criminal charges of abuse and people who only work long term with families in the system, and a hundred other subcategories, each unable to communicate swiftly and clearly with the next. This lack of coordination persists despite the billions of federal dollars that have been poured into states' child welfare computer systems and the scores of commissions and reports that have assailed the same problems year after year.[5]

GETTING COMPUTERS TO TALK TO EACH OTHER

The trials and tribulations of the child welfare system demonstrate that the first problem that must be solved to achieve seamless government is figuring out how to better manage information across governments— capturing it, categorizing it, ensuring its accuracy, determining its relevance, and distributing it to network users who need it. Part of the solution to this problem is technical: getting disparate government computer systems—many of which are custom-built and based on dated technology—to communicate with each other. Until we can figure out a way to more easily tie together seemingly incompatible computer systems, we'll continue to experience massive difficulties managing information flows.

Some progress is being made in state child welfare systems themselves. Most states are in the process of developing statewide, automated child welfare information systems (SACWIS). These are expected to have many benefits, including speeding the pace of child abuse and neglect investigations and enhancing the ability to report child abuse and neglect, foster care and adoption information to the federal government.[6] Florida's HomeSafenet child welfare system, which went live in July 2003 (but has faced a host of implementation problems,) will eventually allow caseworkers to apply universal standards for abuse and neglect, and make it much easier for caseworkers to cooperate. In theory, it will allow a caseworker whose charge's mother is seeking to regain custody to check up on "things like how often Mom moves around and the people she's hung out with," according to Sarasota YMCA case manager Rona Baldini.[7]

But state-specific improvements won't help the interstate problems. There is currently no usable national database for states to check to see if a child missing from one state has turned up in another. The Federal Bureau of Investigation's National Crime Information Center maintains a database with information about missing children, but it generally does not include children missing from child welfare agencies because the agencies take so long to call in the police. Many states do not require agencies to report missing children to the cops; federal law requires states to report children who run away from state care, but not children abducted by parents or other relatives. And caseworkers rarely check the FBI database to see if their children have been listed as missing— even in states where caseworkers *do* use the database to run criminal background checks on caregivers. The National Center for Missing and Exploited Children also runs a missing-child database, which includes children missing from state care; but only two states, Florida and Illinois, require child welfare social workers to report missing children to the center.[8]

Several states are working on systems to fill that gap. Florida's would allow states to exchange digital photographs of missing children as well as other information about the kids. But even a national database that actually coordinates information from all the states would not solve all the child welfare system's informational problems. Florida's experience teaches another harsh lesson: what computer programmers call "GIGO," or "garbage in, garbage out." If the information an agency has on paper or in uncoordinated databases is out of date or full of mistakes, no amount of coordination will magically make that information useful. The files on Rilya Wilson and her sisters listed DCF's goal as "independent living"—a category reserved for older teens nearing age eighteen, not kindergarteners. DCF records included misspellings, and information like birth dates often conflicted with information in police reports. Some children were entered into the state's database twice; other children were missing.

Those kinds of problems cannot be automated away, though again they too can be at least somewhat alleviated by technological advances. In July 2002, Florida began using portable "Live Scan" units that collect children's photographs and fingerprints in digital form. David Lawrence, chairman of the Governor's Blue Ribbon Panel on Child Protection, said the initiative was "born out of the horrors of the Rilya Wilson case. . . . Getting fingerprints and a picture of Rilya Wilson was an immediate snag in the case." Eventually, the state plans to expand the digital system so that it can help with criminal background checks on all relatives and caregivers who live with children under state protection. The fingerprints can simply be forwarded to law enforcement agencies in order to be checked against their records. Having valid fingerprints would be a huge boon to the system, and could help it find even children whose birth dates or other information are mistaken. "If you do manual fingerprints and send them to Washington, sometimes it takes a month or longer to get the results back, which holds us up from licensing child care agencies and foster homes," DCF Broward County administrator Jack Moss explained. DCF is also seeking to purchase mobile scanners, which caseworkers could use on home visits in order to make sure that children and adults in the household are who they say they are.[9]

Pennsylvania's JNET

When Tom Ridge first became governor of Pennsylvania in 1994, he was confronted with a problem in law enforcement very similar to those faced by many states in child welfare: his state's law enforcement system was completely fragmented. Pennsylvania was teeming with fiefdoms of territorial law enforcement agencies that failed to talk to each other and didn't share information. Just as we observed in the child welfare system, information could sometimes take days or weeks to get to the appropriate agencies, some of which were only a few blocks away from each other.

Governor Ridge immediately set about breaking down these walls and building a secure, integrated system. The result is the Pennsylvania Justice Network (JNET), used by more than three thousand law enforcement personnel in hundreds of federal, state, and local law enforcement agencies across Pennsylvania. Instead of building a big new bureaucracy, the state opted to create a network by connecting together scores of previously unconnected databases and computer systems. JNET cuts across myriad levels of government, storing mug shots, tattoo images, drivers' license photos, criminal records, rap sheets, and the intelligence data vital to protecting citizens against crime. In one case, a rapist was apprehended after the victim described the rapist's tattoo to the police. The police queried JNET, and the system searched several databases, identifying the offender within seconds. When United Airlines Flight 93 went down in western Pennsylvania on 9/11, the FBI ran a list of all the passengers aboard through JNET in order to identify and track down suspected terrorists from the flight. Using arrest information and the digital photo search function, JNET quickly identified several of the terrorists.

A major reason why JNET worked where so many other large information-sharing projects have failed is that state officials didn't try to force the hundreds of participating agencies to abandon their current legacy systems and move to a new centralized database. Instead they connected the law enforcement community together by using technologies that could reach into the existing databases and pull out the needed information. Data is converted into a computer language called Extensible Market Language (XML), a variant of the hypertext markup language (HTML), and then using encryption and specialized software called middleware, the databases are linked together.

Acting as both translator and disseminator, the XML-based solution enables users to exchange data even if they use different platforms and languages. This allows computers residing on different servers with different configurations in various Pennsylvania law enforcement agencies to instantaneously share data with other computers in the network.

This technology model also helped to solve a major political issue: control. Many law enforcement agencies have previously been reluctant to share data because they worried that they would lose control over sensitive information. They also often just flat out didn't trust other agencies not to leak it. Pennsylvania officials overcame this problem by allowing each agency participating in the JNET network to control its own data, selecting which information they wanted to share and who would be able to see it.[10]

TIME FOR BUSINESS

In 1997, Australian prime minister John Howard launched a major initiative called "Time for Business" to slash the costs of doing business with government. One goal was to turn registering a business Down Under from a nightmare maze involving a dozen or more agencies that administered more than 6,600 different licenses into a one-stop registration process at the Australian Business Register. The site gives you one "business number" that will identify you to every one of the five thousand different government entities you could encounter in Australia. Businesses also receive a digital certificate letting them conduct over 1,100 secure online transactions with government agencies at all levels of government by going through the country's Business Entry Point portal.

Businesses in Australia no longer have to continually prove their identity to dozens of different agencies at every level of government. When they change their address, for example, they need only notify government once. According to government officials, the Australian Business Register will save business at least $2 billion over ten years.[a]

a. Greg Dark, deputy commissioner, Australian Revenue Office, interview with the author, April 16, 2002.

CONNECTING THE DOTS

Improving information flows across government agencies is critical but not sufficient to realizing seamless government. As data is passed along through the network, at some point it needs to be turned into useful information that can help inform decisions. This is one of the central problems of our time: How do you turn a sea of information into knowledge? While the most vivid example is the failure of the FBI and CIA to piece together all the bits of information they had about the 9/11 terrorists, almost every governmental task requires turning information into knowledge. Traffic control is ultimately a problem of turning data about congestion into usable knowledge for drivers and transportation planners. Measuring how much students have learned requires making sense of information from students' daily quizzes and assessments. Making government more accountable doesn't just mean putting information on the Internet; the info has to be presented in ways that are easily intelligible to busy citizens who don't have the time or inclination to understand the arcana of government finances.

Many of the most promising solutions to this problem of too much data, too little analysis, and too little knowledge, come from advances in machine intelligence. "Expert systems" capture and organize facts and knowledge by "cloning" the knowledge of experts (more on this in chapter 5). Neural networks, a form of artificial intelligence, can sort through millions of transactions a second, detecting credit card fraud or helping the FBI sort and analyze the millions of tips it receives each year. By helping us to better manage, evaluate, and use information, these and other technologies could eventually help us do everything from catching terrorists to giving school-children an effective alternative to stomach-lurching, high-stakes testing.

Sensemaking

One of the most important efforts to improve our ability to turn information into knowledge has been undertaken by the Department of Homeland Security's Information Analysis and Infrastructure Protection Directorate.[11] Though still in an early phase of development, what DHS ultimately seeks to do is use cutting-edge computer technologies to synthesize information from multiple sources, including the National Security Agency, CIA, and FBI. By collating data from every source on a particular subject, such as a particular terrorist organization or a vulnerable government building, the goal of the undertaking is to connect the dots automatically. This effort, notes *National Journal* writer Sydney Freedberg Jr., represents a "new model of organization: a network connecting other existing networks into a greater whole."[12]

A host of other data-mining projects are also underway at the federal level, many of them sponsored by a little-known office called the Advanced Research and Development Activity (ARDA). The purpose of most of ARDA's eighteen or more projects is to predict or preempt terrorist attacks by using advanced technology to comb through reams of data and spot patterns of activity that can lead to actionable intelligence. One of them, "Novel Intelligence from Massive Data," aims to develop computer software that can sift through masses of diverse data and extract patterns of information from databases, text, video, images, and maps. "Our task is akin to finding dangerous groups of needles hidden in stacks of needle pieces," says Ted Senator, a former research manager of the Total Information Awareness (TIA) initiative who is managing a host of similar ARDA data-mining projects. "We must track all the needle pieces all of the time."[13] Such data-mining projects are controversial as we saw in the Introduction to the book in the discussion of the Pentagon's TIA initiative.[14] So far, however, ARDA's initiatives have escaped Congress's wrath.

Several promising sensemaking efforts exist at the state and local level. One such system, Coplink, is used by more than one hundred law enforcement agencies nationwide, including the San Diego, Boston, Minneapolis, and Phoenix police departments. Dubbed "Google for Law Enforcement" by the University of Arizona computer scientist who created it, the software searches through various law enforcement databases—sex offenders, speeding tickets, felonies, and so on—to look for patterns that would help to identify suspects and build cases against them.[15] Such sensemaking technology has been widely used in the private sector over the past decade to try to bring meaning to the vast quantities of data that now deluge today's economy, but has only recently been employed in the public sector.

CONNECTING MINDS

Getting the right information out of different databases and making sense out of it are both vital to making government more seamless. But ultimately, whether it's deciding whether or not to remove an abused child from his home or preventing a terrorist attack on an overseas embassy, we must still rely on human intelligence and human interaction to make most important decisions, hence the importance of finding better ways to connect minds. But how do you tie distinct groups of people together in a way that will allow you to link the right people up with each other at a moment's notice?

One promising approach came about as a consequence of the 1998 U.S. embassy bombings in East Africa. After the bombings, a blue-ribbon commission was appointed to investigate why the United States was unable to prevent the attacks. Their conclusion: Agencies weren't adequately sharing data and information. The solution: a multimillion dollar project called State Messaging, Archiving and Retrieval system, or "SMART." The sophisticated information sharing system, which will effectively replace the State Department's storied cable communications, is designed to link together the Department of State—and potentially other U.S. federal agencies with an overseas presence—into a single, secure online communication, messaging, and knowledge management network. Through real-time communication links enabled by email, instant messaging, and erooms, more than 46,500 state department employees in 260 locations will be able to share knowledge, search multiple databases, and collaborate with colleagues in other agencies and countries in order to improve crisis coordination and policymaking.[16] "We can have thirty people working on the same document from thirty different countries," explains a senior State Department official involved in the effort. The goal: to modernize the way we conduct foreign policy overseas.

Catching Criminals through Yahoo Groups?

Governments don't necessarily have to invest a fortune in fancy technology to better connect people. Through technology as rudimentary as "Yahoo Groups," the Minneapolis Police Department (MPD) managed to weave together a community with similar concerns and goals that previously had little contact with each other into a public–private network that made a real contribution to crime reduction.

It all started in 1999, when the MPD was looking for a way to reduce crime in the busy downtown area. To accomplish this, they knew they'd have to engage the community more in crime prevention. Unfortunately, traditional community-organizing tools, such as block clubs and crime watches, didn't work downtown because most people left the area after work, making evening meetings impractical. So the police turned to cyberspace and created an online forum where cops, security guards, office managers, and property owners could team up to reduce crime in the city's office blocks. In less than a year, the MPD managed to sign up more than four hundred members of this "virtual block club."

A major reason that members joined the club, and the glue that kept them involved, was the speedy information sharing. The MPD sent out crime alerts, traffic advisories, and incident reports, with stats customized according to the type of establishment the reports were being sent to—homeless shelter, parking lot, downtown building, restaurant, or bar. It also posted maps showing crime patterns and locations of serious crimes. "We have a ton of useful information in our system, much of which is public information," explains crime prevention specialist Luther Krueger, who runs the forum for the police department. "The virtual block club lets us get it out to the community." Lots of police departments send out email alerts. What makes the Minneapolis model different is that it's not just one-way communication; everybody gets to talk. Community participants share suspect pictures from security cameras and detailed information about incidents that typically don't get reported to the police.

What impact has the virtual block club actually had on downtown crime? Plenty, says Krueger. Since the block club started, the incident of thefts, assaults, and disorderly conduct in the first precinct where most of the bars are concentrated have dropped significantly, in some cases by 50 percent; parking ramp incidents fell dramatically; and petty theft from office towers and restaurants has plummeted 21 percent. In one instance, an experienced plant rustler was on a rampage throughout the downtown area, stealing expensive plants from office buildings. Nicholas Luciano, the vice president of a firm that provides security for several downtown buildings, posted a description of the robberies to the group. Within minutes, security personnel from other buildings responded with similar reports and nearly identical descriptions of the plant thief. "You could almost follow the guy down the skyway," recalls Luciano. "People were saying things like, 'We just checked him out of my building.' It works that quick."[17] Soon after, the plant burglar was apprehended.

The key to the virtual block club's success was a willingness from all parties to share information, something that police departments aren't accustomed to doing. "You can't hoard your own information," says Krueger. "If you have information that the public needs and wants, our philosophy is that you should make it easier for them to get it."

Krueger is absolutely right. As government improves its "sensemaking" and information-sharing capabilities, it needs to find better ways of publishing and disseminating the information to citizens. This principle should apply in nearly all areas of government, even, in certain instances, to intelligence data. For example, if we could figure out a way to extract intelligence information from within government's classified "Black Box" of intelligence, repurpose it, and disseminate it to affected public and private entities they might be able to play a much greater role in preventing terrorist attacks. Such a policy has proven effective in the United Kingdom, France, Australia, and Canada where domestic intelligence agencies regularly produce intelligence assessments for business and industry.[18]

WALKING THE WALK

When I went looking for an agency that did all of the pieces of seamless gov well—tying together multiple agencies across several levels of government; making it easier for citizens to interact across multiple levels of government; turning a vast sea of government data into information that citizens could use; packaging it up in a user-friendly manner; and then disseminating it to the public at large—the last place I thought I'd end up was in a nondescript office park at the foot of Phoenix's Camelback Mountains talking to a spunky group of environmental activists. The group's name is Engaging and Empowering Citizenship, E2C for short, and it just may be the most impressive example of seamless gov in America.

The year is 2002 and Chris Warner is standing before a projector screen, eagerly demonstrating to Christine Todd Whitman, then administrator of the Environmental Protection Agency (EPA), what an informational backwater her agency is. He's demonstrating his life's passion, Earth 911, an environmental information website run by E2C, which he built from scratch over the past decade. At the moment he's in his site's beach quality section, showing Whitman real-time data for New Jersey's beaches. The data is remarkably current, having been updated earlier that morning by health and environmental officials working in and for New Jersey. Whitman, the state's former governor, flashes a proud smile that soon fades to a noticeably darker mood when Warner links over to the EPA beach quality website and clicks on New Jersey—where the data isn't a few hours but two years old. "She seemed a bit embarrassed by EPA's data," Warner says afterwards.

It wasn't the first time that Warner has embarrassed a senior government official. Earth 911 has succeeded where scores of government efforts have failed: linking a federal agency, fifty state agencies, thousands of local governments, and countless community groups and nonprofit organizations into one nationwide environmental network providing a wealth of information and real-time data on all manner of environmental programs. Log onto www.Earth911.org, enter your zip code, and you can find out everything you could ever want to learn about local environmental issues, from which businesses recycle used oil filters to how you can reduce storm water runoff. "On one page we have information from twenty-six government agencies," says Warner. "The public doesn't care who runs the page, they just want easy access to the information."

What does Earth 911 have that your typical government agency doesn't have? Well, it's got strong name recognition, and it's easy to find even if you aren't yet comfortable with the Internet. Earth 911 has a URL, but also a bilingual 800 number. Its brand name is nearly ubiquitous, appearing on billions of recyclable products, from oil cans and plastic bags to pesticide containers. And Earth 911 stars in countless public service announcements (PSAs). It doesn't hurt that any government partner, from the largest state to the tiniest hamlet, can use Earth 911's virtual PSA library at no cost to create its own localized PSA starring the likes of Steven Seagal, Beau Bridges, Ted Danson, and Julia Louis-Dreyfus.

Those seeking the future of digital government need look no further than Earth 911. There's just one catch: It's not a government operation at all. "We're a chameleon," explains Warner, sitting with his feet up on his desk in E2C's shoebox-sized world headquarters. "We operate like a non-profit; we have the sustainability model of a for-profit; but we're a public service committed to making a difference."

The forty-six-year-old Warner—or "Hurricane Chris," as former California EPA secretary James Strock, calls him—has blond hair, a deep tan, and a cheery persona so brimming with contagious enthusiasm that he can't sleep at night. "Earth 911 is going berserk, it's just out of control," he tells me. After a few minutes, your name becomes simply "buddy." "Warner," Strock says simply, "is a force of nature."

The company's $2.5 million budget, which comes courtesy of gargantuan corporate sponsors like Hewlett Packard and Home Depot, is barely enough to pay the salaries of its young forty-person staff, which includes a Goth guy who dresses in all black and carries a fake sword around. The computer hardware that keeps the network running is donated; the hodgepodge of mismatched desks, chairs, and bookcases—not to mention the ping-pong table that doubles as a conference table—is mostly donated or borrowed. Oh, and during the first fifteen years of the organization's existence, through countless seventy-hour weeks, E2C's founder, architect, and head cheerleader didn't draw a nickel in salary.

Because Warner shares an office with an outfit called Pets 911 (more about that later), his guests are greeted by a rambunctious, tail-wagging, face-licking pack of dogs—mostly mutts except for "Luna," a white Italian greyhound so thin she looks like a porcelain sculpture. The offices are teeming with animals. Soon you're introduced to Sinatra, the blind cat; Kyan, the three-legged dog; and two parakeets named Foster and Sidney.

Herding Cats

Earth 911 is what is known in Internet circles as an "intermediary" or "aggregator." Its basic job is to provide an interface that lets more than 4,200 government employees, along with environmental organizations, submit timely environmental data and information from more than 10,000 local communities, which the small Earth 911 staff somehow manages to publish in a timely and user-friendly package. This spirit of independence and impartiality has been crucial to the project's success. "We said to all our public and private partners, 'You control the database; you're in charge of your own information,'" Warner explains. "That's the only way they will ever trust the veracity of the data."

This kind of coordination doesn't happen with a single phone call to a government official. "The technology, albeit state-of-the-art, is not the hard part," says Warner. "The hard part is getting all those disparate agencies to work together—or as we like to say, play in the same sand-box." Warner and his team had to form hundreds of partnerships to get Earth 911 off the ground. "It was like herding cats," he says.

"The EPA," he says, "told us flatly that it couldn't be done. They said, 'We can't even get four state EPAs to do anything together; there's no way you're going to get all fifty, not to mention all the local governments.' And in hindsight, they were probably right; it was impossible. We were just too stubborn and naïve to know it."

In another case, Earth 911 proposed a plan to put up a comprehensive water quality site using a grant from the EPA. The EPA loved the proposal but denied the grant. They didn't believe Earth 911 could pull the job off within their proposed timeline of eighteen months. They were badly mis-taken. "By the time we got the letter from EPA denying us the grant, we had the site up and running," recalls Warner, who enjoys nothing more than exceeding the expectations of public-sector bureaucrats. "Due to bu-reaucracy, government officials aren't even allowed to pick the color of the website in the time it takes us to get it operational."

So how did Warner's tiny staff pull it off? Precisely, he says, because they were on their own. "Governments have to deal with a morass of proce-dural requirements," says Strock, who championed Earth 911 while head-ing up the California EPA. "The result is powerful limits on their ability to quickly achieve real-time results. Earth 911 is unencumbered by all that."

Another secret of Warner's success was ensuring that the effort was strictly nonpartisan and nonideological. Earth 911 sticks to the 95 percent of environmental information that most everyone agrees on, and assiduously avoids the 5 percent where all the ideological battles are waged. "The key to all this is to eliminate the politics, left/right, Democrat or Republican," explains Warner. "Any politician at any time could have tubed this."

Linking Up

Can Earth 911's remarkable success be applied to other areas like parks, en-ergy, agriculture, child welfare, and public safety? Warner's answer is a re-sounding yes. "This model can be replicated," he says. "In fact, it can be replicated easily." He's already proved it. In 1999, Warner and his col-leagues brought the retail pet supply chain PETsMART a proposition: Give us seed money, and we'll do for pets what we did for the environment. PETsMART agreed. Next thing you know, Warner had eight of the ten largest animal welfare groups in the country setting aside their fierce rival-ries in order to join Pets 911, which allows users to search for or post a lost pet; find out how to adopt a pet; and be connected to low-cost spay and neuter services, emergency veterinary services, and pet licensing centers anywhere in the country. Pets 911 has formed hundreds of partnerships with media organizations to promote their website. More than 1,200 Clear Channel radio stations, for example, regularly run Pets 911 public service announcements. "Ten years' worth of work," he says, "replicated itself in eighteen months."

Characteristically the indomitable Warner isn't stopping there. With the help of the state of Washington, he built a nationwide AMBER alert network to try to engage residents in their communities to help to bring abducted children home safely. When a child is abducted, real-time, up-to-date information about the child is sent out en masse to members of the community so they can be on the lookout for the child and the abductor. Warner even managed to recruit boxing great Sugar Ray Leonard to tape the first ad for the AMBER alert network.

Like a Starbucks or McDonald's franchise, Earth 911, Pets 911, and AMBER Alert 911 offer the best of the local and national worlds: a big-name brand offering numerous advantages over local public or nonprofit agencies, including reach, economies of scale, and the ability to attract celebrity publicity, along with a decentralized structure with a fund of local knowledge, ensuring that its data stays both timely and ideally tailored to local needs.

This model—national scale combined with local control—is also the idea behind Australia's Centrelink, one of the world's largest seamless government integration projects. Centrelink is an agency that has assembled a wide variety of social services from social security to employment, from thirteen federal departments, various state and territorial governments and nonprofit providers, and gathered them all for "one-stop shopping" under one roof. The program offers a combination of office-based, phone and Internet services that produce around 3 billion transactions per year. "Our whole thesis," says CIO Jane Treadwell, "is that there's value in having a national architecture but the major ingredient needs to be local context, local players. We call it linking up."

THE DISTRIBUTED GOVERNMENT FUTURE

In the immediate future, the most sophisticated intergovernmental information-sharing networks are likely to come from intelligence, law enforcement, and national security. That's where the money and political attention are focused. But soon the same technologies will spill over into workaday governmental functions. In fact, we may get so good at exchanging information and operating electronic networks that websites like Earth 911 become the standard, not the exception. We may seldom have to go to a government website at all to take care of many of our government transactions. The same technology that enables government officials to tear down the walls between government agencies also allows governments and enterprising private companies and community groups to knock down the walls between government and the private sector.

One result will be that government services—not just government information—will be accessible on private-sector websites. Thanks to promising new technologies such as "web services" (see box on page 53), private-sector providers and community groups soon may be able to host public-sector transactions and data on their websites, leaving government portals as just *one* channel—instead of *the* channel—for these transactions. Banks and brokerage firms could offer online tax filing. REI.com could get you a fishing license, even as you're buying your camping and fishing gear on their site. Healtheon/WebMD could provide online Medicare and Medicaid benefits registration. Travel websites could offer real-time passport renewal. Charles Schwab.com could supply all the latest Federal Reserve Bank data. Trade associations could offer online business-license renewal, while business portals specializing in trade, insurance, or construction could offer a host of online government services to their members.[19]

Instead of waiting for people to come to them, government would bring services to where people are.[20] A fair analogy in the physical world is the current process of registering a new car with the state. The car dealer handles the entire process of registering the car with the state for the car buyer. Another example is voter registration: anyone from political parties to MTV can register you to vote. Offering e-government transactions on private-sector websites then would simply be a way of extending online an activity that people are already accustomed to in the physical world.

Many Paths

Australia, the United Kingdom, and the state of Iowa are just a few of the governments that have explicit strategies for syndicating their e-government services to the private sector. By mid-2005, the Department of Interior wants campers to be able to reserve campground spaces and sign up for other recreational opportunities on state and private-sector websites like REI.com. The state of Texas has partnered with a handful of companies that provide legal automation services for Texas law firms to host the state's online court filing system. These firms have established relationships with the law firms and can package the online filing application into their other set of services. "We see them acting as our marketing force," explains Phil Barrett, the director of Texas Online.

WEB SERVICES: BUILDING THE
RAILROAD TRACK FOR E-GOVERNMENT

Web services represent a relatively painless way for businesses to integrate e-commerce applications across different computing platforms. Soon, for example, eBay's auction engine will be "callable" as a web service, meaning that other businesses will be able to run eBay auctions on their sites without their users ever seeing the eBay brand. eBay gets a fee for providing the service. eBay's customer avoids the expense of building its own auction engine. Consumers get the auction functionality where and when they want it. Everybody wins. Think of web services as the equivalent of pay-per-view consumption for e-commerce applications.

Some web services are simple, such as looking through the directory of available stock tickers on the web, finding one that fits your needs, dialing up its interface, and plugging the service into your web page or application. Others are much more complex, such as dialing up an entire supply-chain interaction application. Both kinds of applications are poised to transform e-commerce.

What makes web services not just possible but extraordinarily powerful is XML, a more information-intensive variant of the hypertext markup language (HTML) used to code most web pages. Unlike HTML, XML lets web users exchange data between different devices—server, PDA, PC, cell phone—running all sorts of applications, even if they use different platforms and languages.

But XML is just one component of the infrastructure that will be necessary to make web services a reality. The first step to getting MSN, AOL, or Yahoo to develop a given application as a web service is to let the world know the service exists. This is accomplished by registering the service in a universal description, discovery, and integration (UDDI) directory, a centralized repository where companies and governments can describe the service's interface in web service flow language (WSFL), publishing the data to the directory, and wrapping the application in a computer coding called simple object access protocol (SOAP) that allows it to communicate with outside applications. (It's still uncertain whether governments will build their own UDDI directories of government services, use the public UDDI directories, or a combination of the two.)

Mind reeling yet? It actually isn't as complicated as it sounds. Think of it as a railroad track whose common gauge allows different kinds of trains to run on it simultaneously. XML, UDDI, SOAP, WSFL, and all the rest will create a common technical gateway that can connect different platforms and programming languages.

Another reason for forming online channel partnerships with the private sector is the belief that private companies and community groups are often better able to reach many of government's different customer groups in a way befitting their unique characteristics and interests. "Take a customer group like students," explains Andrew Pinder, the former e-envoy of the United Kingdom. "We ought to be dealing with them using a different sort of language than the stiff and bureaucratic way we tend to talk to citizens. Government is not very good about that, so in this, and other areas, it makes sense to use intermediaries."

As illustrated by the success of Earth 911, some of these intermediaries are likely to be tech-savvy nonprofit organizations and community groups. Neighborhood Knowledge Los Angeles (NKLA), an online tool developed by UCLA aimed at improving and preserving the city's neighborhoods, for example, provides a huge collection of data about properties and neighborhoods in decline on its website. The data, from a wide variety of public sources, helps identify the "early warning signs" of properties or whole neighborhoods that are in trouble: things like tax delinquencies, building code violations, tenant complaints, and property abandonment.[21] Citizens and activists can search for these problems in the database and work with owners and housing officials to develop solutions to save the neighborhood.

Government has long collected this information, but previously it had gathered dust because of the difficulty in obtaining and processing the data. In this case, obtaining all the relevant data, formatting it, analyzing it, and keeping it updated was a huge and costly endeavor, something that would have been impossible without the involvement of UCLA researchers, graduate students, and staff. But by publishing this kind of data as a web service, governments could allow any small nonprofit to easily pull it off the web, slice and dice it in order to figure out the assets and liabilities in a community, and integrate them with its own data and research.

One of the most ambitious efforts to make government data more accessible by using web services is the federal government's geospatial one-stop portal. Users can search a virtual card catalogue of metadata on the site and pull down topographic maps, satellite imagery, climate information, and other geospatial data sitting on servers of different government agencies all over the country. Say you're worried about a hurricane hitting on the Georgia coast and want to put together a plan for your community. You can grab data on emergency routes from the Federal Emergency Management Agency (FEMA), transportation data from the city of Savannah, crop data from the USDA and so on. Users can pretty much "make their own virtual map on the fly," says a manager of the project.

As the viability of web services spreads, government's main role becomes providing citizens with as many different pathways into government services and information as possible. To do this, governments will need to shift their attention from endlessly reconfiguring their portals to more fundamental IT architectural issues. Of the technical hurdles that lie before web services, the most difficult involve privacy and security, as government and third-party groups work to simultaneously ensure that users retain their privacy—so that nobody gets inappropriate knowledge of what any given person is doing on a government-related site—and that their identities are verifiable, to forestall benefits fraud and other crimes.[22] None of this will be easy, but it is all eminently possible.

* * * * *

The work that goes into designing the architecture of government web services would also encourage seamless, intergovernmental electronic service delivery because the same technology that private partners use to bundle e-government applications into their other electronic services would let a county government include a state business licensing application with its online county permitting system.

In time entrepreneurial organizations could gain access to e-government services through a web directory and include these among their other services. Instead of having to form countless intergovernmental task forces, secure funding, fight turf battles, and all the other obstacles to seamless government, integrating services across multiple levels of government could work through open technology standards and straightforward business agreements.

If or when that happens, a lot of lines would blur and citizens and businesses would have more time to do what they want to do, as interactions with government become less frustrating and less time consuming. "Government will be much less visible in the future," said Pinder. "At the moment, people regard government as a nuisance. People don't want to have government; they want services, so let's take government out of their face."[23]

Online transactions aren't the only area in which digital government is blurring traditional boundaries. To different degrees, it is also blurring the lines between local and national, national and international, public and private, and home and school. Whether this is a good or bad thing is the subject of considerable debate. Nowhere more so than in the educational arena, where thanks in no small part to the growth of online learning, soon when we refer to the "public education system," we may also be referring to kids schooled at home, at worksite schools. and—as the walls continue to fall—even children taught in private schools. How this phenomenon is coming about and whether it will be a benefit or detriment to students is the subject of the next chapter.

TIPS FOR PRACTITIONERS

- Shift responsibility for navigating the levels of government from the private citizen or business to the public agencies themselves—and provide people with the (generally web-based) tools they need to ease this transaction.
- Formulate a plan to overcome the political obstacles to seamless government before embarking on one of these initiatives.
- Much of the success or failure of a seamless government initiative will depend on how well you manage information across governments—capture it, categorize it, ensure its accuracy, determine its relevance, and distribute it to network users who need it.
- When agencies need to be joined up for policy or management reasons, analyze how technology might enable you to virtually connect them together into a network before deciding to build a big new bureaucracy.
- Unless absolutely necessary, don't try to force reluctant agencies to abandon their current legacy systems and move to a new centralized database. Instead, use technologies that can reach into the databases and pull out the needed and permitted information. This strategy helps to allay fears from agencies that they will "lose control" of their information.
- Pay close attention to privacy issues when deploying sensemaking technologies.
- Publish data, transactions, and services as web services. This allows other government agencies and the private sector to package the services and information into their own service offerings, thereby providing additional pathways into government services and information. In time, this should also allow services to be integrated across multiple levels of government through open technology standards and straightforward business agreements.

II

INFORMATION AGE APPROACHES TO PRESSING PROBLEMS

3

The Infinite Classroom

The large sign on the door reads "Welcome to Our Class, Room No. 12, Teacher, Mrs. Thorpe." Inside this Chester Springs, Pennsylvania, classroom, the walls are covered with children's drawings and colorings, as well as pictures from American, African, and European history. A computer hums in the corner. Children, fidgeting at their desks, work on math word problems and spelling lessons.

While this sounds like just about any other classroom in America, in reality, it isn't like anything we have ever previously thought of as a public school classroom. In this classroom, the student/teacher ratio is only 4 to 1; five-year-olds learn about Harriet Tubman and Lewis and Clark. Sandy Thorpe, the teacher, also moonlights as the Mom of all four of the students; and upon leaving Room No. 12, rather than entering a school hallway, you find yourself in the Thorpe's sprawling kitchen. Sydney, Simeon, Solomon, and Savannah Thorpe, ages six through nine, are all students in a revolutionary new kind of public school where the curriculum, tests, and lesson plans are delivered online to the students and their parent-teachers in the comfort of their homes.

The "cyber charter" attended by the Thorpe children, the Pennsylvania Virtual Charter School (PAVCS), is run by K12 Inc., an online learning company founded by former secretary of education William J. Bennett and financed in part by Michael Milken and his brother Lowell. The curriculum, books, assessments, computers, teacher, and everything else Mrs. Thorpe and her kids need are provided free of charge by the school, which receives money from the state for every enrolled student. In return, the Thorpes must use the school's curriculum, take daily assessments, log nine hundred hours of class time a year each, take thirty-five hours of gym—and, because this is after all a public school, hold the proverbial fire drill once a month.

The PAVCS curriculum allows each of the Thorpe children to go at his or her own pace. Precocious Savannah is a quick learner who read when she was two and a half years old and needs only minimal coaching from Mom. After stagnating in a traditional kindergarten classroom, Savannah is now doing math lessons nearly two grade levels ahead of her age level. Her younger brother, Solomon, on the other hand, has a difficult time with some subjects. He's easily distracted, and learns best when he's able to manipulate objects. To learn time patterns, for example, he and his Mom spent weeks manipulating the arms of a big clock. It took a long time—and lots of patience—but eventually he was able to master the subject. "He would not have learned time in a regular classroom," says Mrs. Thorpe, "because they would have spent a day on it, and he needed weeks."

Each night, Sandy logs onto K12 and reviews the individual lesson plans for each of her children and prints out the assignments. Her kids aren't allowed to move onto the next subject until they've answered all the questions correctly on the daily assessments that follow each lesson. A teacher supplied by the school assists Mrs. Thorpe, serving as a sounding board and problem-solver for the Thorpes and a couple dozen other PAVCS families. When Sandy was having a hard time motivating Solomon and was considering sending him to a brick and mortar elementary school, the teacher suggested putting his day's work on a piece of paper and cutting it into puzzles. It worked. "For Solomon to get a puzzle completed was everything," says Sandy.

How does Sandy Thorpe, the teacher, separate home time from classroom time? "I don't," she explains matter-of-factly. "School is kind of all the time, especially with little kids. We use everything we can as a learning moment. It's not cut and dry that this is a school time and this isn't." During the week, Sandy Thorpe teaches math, reading, writing, and history, music, and art over the weekend, and science is taught each evening by Mr. Thorpe when he comes home from work. Not only do the kids do fun science experiments, but they spend quality time with their father, something which they all look forward to each day.

Some would argue that her kids are being deprived of the socialization needed to function in society. Sandy calls it nonsense. She points out that her kids go on field trips with other PAVCS kids twice a month to places like the zoo, plays, art museums, and an elderly care home. And her children interact with others their age every day after school, whether they're playing in the neighborhood with the two dozen other children on their street or going to ballet, music, or karate classes. As they get a little older, the Thorpe children will participate in the school band and other extracurricular activities at the local public school a half-mile down the road. "I couldn't imagine a better educational situation for my children," says Sandy.

COMPUTERPHOBIA

While parents like the Thorpes may love them, cyber charters, the "place" where the electronic learning revolution is most advanced, have generated fierce opposition from every conceivable entrenched educational interest group—from teachers' unions to school boards to principals. In Ohio, the teachers' unions, the PTA, and the League of Women Voters filed a lawsuit to stop a cyber charter from being funded. In Texas, teachers' associations blasted proposals to launch virtual charters in the state. "This sounds like a scheme to make Texas taxpayers pay for vouchers to fund schools," charged Carolyn Boyle, coordinator for the Coalition for Public Schools. "This is a backdoor way to fund homeschools." Eric Hartman, legislative director for the Texas Federation of Teachers echoed her: "This is a thinly disguised subsidy to homeschoolers."[1] In spite of this antagonism, cyber charters are legal in twenty-five states.

In Pennsylvania, cyber charter opponents pulled out all the stops to block funding and shut down the state's dozen virtual charters serving more than 10,000 students—the largest population of cyber charter students of any state in the country. Scores of school districts defied the law by withholding funds from virtual charters, causing teachers to go without pay for months.[2] The Pennsylvania Schools Board Association likened them to "weeds growing between the cracks in the sidewalk." More than one hundred school districts joined in a class-action lawsuit (which they lost) arguing that they were unconstitutional.

But this came as no surprise. After all, the educational establishment stands to lose a great deal here. Most school districts and school boards quite rationally fight anything that may cause them to lose even a dollar of the tax money that comes with each child. Teachers' unions and other public-education advocacy groups have worked hard to separate public "charter schools" from private (and therefore suspect) "homeschooling." Virtual charter schools blur these distinctions.

But teachers unions and the educational establishment aren't the only opponents of virtual charters, or more importantly, aren't the only critics of the broader concept of online learning. Indeed, the online learning movement has provoked strong, and sometimes fierce, opposition from all corners, from many teachers who worry that computers will turn their jobs into glorified tour guides, to education experts who see children like Sydney, Simeon, Solomon, and Savannah Thorpe as the forerunner of a dystopian future where Net-addicted, sensory-deprived children can't

---

ARGUMENTS AGAINST E-LEARNING

- Kids are chained to computer screens
- Children don't learn important socialization skills
- Technology has a poor return on investment in education
- Computers deprive children of sensory feedback
- Online learning replaces teachers with computers

---

add, subtract, read, or spell, and where schools have sold out to giant technology companies.

Computers: Not Really the Point

Much of the opposition is based on the misconception that online education means a focus on the computer, dragging kids away from books and blocks and xylophones, tethering them to keyboards, and turning them into mouse potatoes whose little minds have fried from spending too much time in front of the computer screen. To support this view, critics often cite Isaac Asimov's 1957 story "The Fun They Had" in which the science fiction writer envisioned a society in the year 2157 where all students studied from home using teaching robots. One of the students, a young girl named Margie, thinks about what it must have been like when students still went to schools together and were taught by teachers in classrooms. "All the kids in the whole neighborhood came, laughing and shouting in the schoolyard, sitting together in the schoolroom, going home together at the end of the day. They learned the same things so they could help one another on the homework and talk about it. . . . And the teachers were people."[3]

Asimov's tale is a compelling read—but it couldn't be farther from an accurate assessment of the changes e-learning is bringing. Instead of diminishing human contact, separating children from adults and other children, e-learning is giving parents more contact and communication with their children, drawing parents and teachers closer together, letting third-graders mingle with fourth-graders and gifted students with remedial students, and helping teachers spend more time with kids and less time with lesson plans. In this way e-learning can break down many of the segregations in contemporary education. Despite appearances, the computers really aren't the point.

Online learning needn't shackle kids to clunky desktop computers. Emerging wireless technologies allow students to work online almost anywhere, whether they're at an art gallery studying Degas or at a pond doing a science experiment. Students in Alan Nakagawa's high school biology class spend much of their class time exploring the many natural wonders of the Big Island in Hawaii, using wireless network technology to test the island's watershed for pollutants, study whales' migratory patterns, and observe threatened sea turtles via video cams—all the while collecting field data and uploading it to a database. "The kids are out doing real science," says Nakagawa.[4]

K12, founded by two early critics of computer-obsessed education, uses the computer as a delivery mechanism rather than as the focus of a child's attention. K12 students spend only about 20 percent of their learning time in front of a computer.[5] The rest of the time is spent with touchable, traditional items to take their hands off the keyboard and their eyes off the screen: books, geometric blocks, paintbrushes, tambourines, fine art prints, seeds for science experiments, clay, blocks, pen and paper, and maps.

Take Kaleb Harwick, an eight-year-old who is a high-functioning autistic with Asperger's syndrome, very bad asthma—and a 145 IQ. Kaleb didn't speak a word until he was three years old; doctors said he'd probably never graduate from public high school. "They thought he was just about retarded," says his mom and teacher Debbie Harwick. She uses online curricula and assessments to help structure her son's education, but Kaleb himself spends very little time on the computer. Like many autistic children, he learns best from being able to touch things, manipulate objects, and see things three-dimensionally. He learned about medieval Europe and kings and queens by building a giant LEGO castle—complete with moats and drawbridges. The kitchen is overflowing with his science projects, including a functioning robot.

Like Kaleb, thousands of physically, mentally, and emotionally challenged children need individualized learning plans in order to progress intellectually. While mainstreaming has enabled them to work alongside children without those disabilities in the interests of social learning, these children need extra help that a traditional teacher may not have time to provide. Online education can help meet this need.

Critics also point to the lack of return on investment from all the billions of dollars spent putting computers in the classroom in the past two decades. President Bill Clinton commendably campaigned for "a bridge to the twenty-first century . . . where computers are as much a part of the classroom as blackboards." After the hype and the money came the inevitable, vigorous backlash. A study of nearly 14,000 fourth- and eighth-graders found that the $5 billion spent each year on educational technology might actually be hurting children because the computers weren't being put to good use.[6] As recently as 1999, William J. Bennett said there "is no good evidence that most uses of computers significantly improve learning."[7] "I saw computers being used mostly as a way of giving kids' brains a break," he recalls.

There is no doubt that much of the technology dumped into schools over the past decade or more was misused—or, in some cases, went unused. Teachers weren't trained in how to use the computers. The computers weren't hooked up to the Net. The quality of education software was mostly poor. Computers were treated as an "add-on," instead of being incorporated into every subject. But the problem wasn't with technology as such. The problems stemmed from the many educators who hadn't yet figured out how to use computers to advance learning, and the administrators who shipped out computers instead of reforming schools. Technology was mostly used to automate, rather than transform, traditional ways of teaching. As MIT professor Seymour Papert notes: "Throwing a lot of computers into an otherwise unchanged school will just leave you with an unchanged school. . . . But the cause of widespread low effectiveness [of computers] is not the technology. It's using digital technology without a vision of a digital world."[8]

Pedagogical Arguments against E-Learning

Computer opponents also deploy more theoretical arguments. Clifford Stoll, in his book *Silicon Snake Oil*, worries that a secondhand, "virtual" world will displace engagement with real objects and people. "Sensation has no substitute," he rightly points out.[9] The real world can offer real, unexpected, and unpredictable encounters; online simulations of that world can only offer the encounters imagined by the programs' designers.

In her book *Life on the Screen: Identity in the Age of the Internet*, Sherry Turkle, a sociology professor at MIT who has studied children using computers for more than twenty years, writes, "Simulations, for example, are built on hidden assumptions, many of which are oversimplified if not highly questionable." Turkle believes this fosters passivity, ultimately dulling people's sense of what they can change in the world. After mastering SimCity, a computer game about urban planning, a tenth-grade girl told Turkle that she'd learned the following rule: "Raising taxes always leads to riots."[10]

These seem like persuasive arguments against computers . . . and books. Every book is a tiny mediated universe, where the reader encounters only those events and objects that the author has imagined. Books are based on the hidden assumptions of their authors. Books try to find, in language, a substitute for sensation. Books are "virtual"—not real.

The conclusion should be obvious: Online curricula, like books, can't provide for every important aspect of a child's education.[11] Educators who try to force computers to work miracles will fail. But that shouldn't cause us to avoid the particular kinds of learning that computers, and specifically the Internet, can deliver. E-learning is about much more than the keyboard and the mouse; it's a tool for delivering curricula, assessing progress, and receiving information, ideas, and suggestions. And it's a tool that more and more students are finding to be an integral part of their learning experience.[12] "Technology should attract no more attention than a clean window through which one looks," explains Bennett. "It should enhance the educational experience, not distract from it. To me, the main role for technology is to eliminate the noise and get the student directly into the subject and the academic content."[13]

"MY SIZE FITS ME" LEARNING

No more teaching to the middle. No more one size fits all. Instead of mass production through assembly lines, its mass customization tailor fit to the student.

—John Bailey, former director, Office of Educational Technology,
U.S. Department of Education[14]

Imagine trying to feed an entire zoo full of animals from the same bag of chow. If the bag is full of raw meat, the lions are thrilled but the hippos are morose. If it's mice, the snakes go wild but the flamingos go hungry. And if it's fish food, nobody's happy.

It's easier than that to teach a classroom full of students, because some individualization is always possible. Teachers can check up more frequently on slow students, give fast readers extra assignments to stretch their brains, or keep a tighter rein on kids with discipline problems. But inevitably, individual differences get glossed over. Teachers try to make sure everyone is caught up, even if that means taking so long on the first math problem that the smartest kid in the class becomes bored and loses interest. Teachers must play to their own strengths, meaning that kids who learn differently may be left out. And too often, teachers, students, and parents are all operating in the dark, without a good sense of where students' strengths and weaknesses lie. At the end of the term, tests shine a harsh spotlight on deficiencies that have lain hidden for months. "We really have been accustomed to batch-processing kids," says education expert Chester E. Finn Jr., a former assistant secretary at the Department of Education who's now president of the Thomas B. Fordham Foundation, an educational research institute. "We've said, 'Twenty-five of you are going to be treated as identical.' We don't really care if you're different unless you're disabled."

How One-Size-Fits-All Learning Fails Our Children

Such one-size-fits-all learning ill serves the vast range of students, from the smartest child to the slowest, and many of those in between. Consider

Gerald Durrell's experience with assembly line education. According to his headmaster, little Gerald was "the most ignorant boy" in school. Durrell, who had been educated at home until age fourteen, spent only a brief and unsuccessful stint in school, where the budding naturalist's obsession with animals did little to endear him to his teachers.

It can't have been easy to teach a boy who, by his own account, spent his time "assembling everything from minnows to wood lice, eagle owls to scorpions, which inhabited my bedroom and my person in ever-increasing numbers."[15] But Durrell's fascination with the animal world spurred his imagination and his love of learning: His first word was "zoo," and he learned basic math through calculations involving insect anatomy.[16] He went on to write thirty-five books on animal life, many of them immensely popular, and helped turn zoos from curio cabinets with beasts behind bars into habitats meant to preserve endangered species.

Durrell is far from the only talented, passionate child whose love of learning didn't exactly blossom in a classroom where the teacher's attention is divided and students all follow the same lesson plan. Thomas Edison famously attended school for only three months, yet by age twelve he was already reading Edward Gibbon's *Decline and Fall of the Roman Empire* and performing chemistry experiments in the family basement.

The geniuses get the spotlight, but "just plain average" kids suffer from lack of individualized attention too. In fact, average kids may be *more* neglected by assembly line education than high or low achievers, precisely because they are average—too advanced for remedial classes or individual tutoring, but not prepared for honors courses or academic team events. Some researchers call these kids "woodwork children," because they can fade into the background of a teacher's attention.

Brian Wennerstrum, an ordinary boy who preferred physical education to academics, didn't make noise—and got ignored until his reading skills were a full year below grade level. Only an after school tutor helped him get back on track. Lori Milligan, his seventh-grade science teacher, admitted, "The high end and the low end of the class can take up all your energies. Then there are the rest—the quiet kids who aren't disruptive, who don't need your undivided attention. Where do they fit in?"[17]

Tailoring Learning to Individual Learning Styles

E-learning won't make those problems disappear, but it can substantially alleviate them, delivering exactly the right food for the wild young mind. Students can get personally-tailored educations without needing special schools or separate classes. Recognizing that children learn in different ways and at different speeds, online learning courses typically offer the student multiple approaches to each topic, so lesson plans can be customized according to what seems to work best for the child—what author Daniel Pink calls the "My Size Fits Me" approach to learning.[18] "One of the advantages to cyber ed is that they can return to the lesson over and over again," explains Bonnie McKenney, a virtual charter school teacher in Pennsylvania. "They have instant review. The three things in education are intensity, frequency, and duration: the lessons are short, they're frequent, and they're very multimedia, very intense, very focused."

Statistics bear out that Detroit puts out more "lemons" on Monday than any other day of the week. This is traced to the fact that many people function much better at some times of the day or week than other times. In traditional school, the sick child who stays home misses the lecture, the child upset over his place in the sometimes harsh society of adolescence is too distracted to listen, and the child who forgets his book cannot do the assignment. E-learning allows for flexibility in schooling to take advantage of the times of a child's greatest concentration, getting more bang for the buck in terms of time spent learning, thereby tailoring education to the child.

One of the most exasperating things for parents is watching their nine-year-old kid master an exceedingly complex, multilevel computer game—and then flunk math class. Obviously their child has an aptitude for learning, an aptitude that the computer game designer, but not the math curriculum developer, was able to bring out. To fully comprehend the ebb and flow of a Civil War battle, for example, some students may need to take a virtual tour of the battlefield, seeing what it was like to look over a hill at an advancing army. Other students will learn best through the kind of real-world problem-solving activities prevalent in online learning. In one e-learning history course, a child can click on seven different buttons to learn about Jay's Treaty; each one lets him learn about the subject through a different medium—video, text, interaction, music and so on. The premise: all kids are gifted learners; they just learn in different ways.

It's even possible now to eliminate much of the guesswork involved in deciding which learning approach works best for the student. Using artificial intelligence, the computer can adapt the pace, complexity, and direction of the learning experience according to the learning styles and attention span of each student. What's the best approach to use to teach Jenny about fractions? Fluids, lines, pies, or groupings? Based on which learning approaches have previously worked best for her in math and other subjects, the computer might recommend "fluids." Technology will also be "presence" and "contextually aware," meaning it will be smart about the person, the device they're using to connect to the Internet, and even who else is online to assist the student's learning session.

The ultimate effect of these changes would be the end of assembly line education. Children in the same classroom could learn different things and in different ways at the same time. Computers would analyze students' learning styles and based on that analysis, schools would enter into learning contracts with each child in which they agree to focus on each student's specific needs, abilities, and learning. Students, teachers, and parents would be able to access learner profiles of every student online from any digital device.[19] Along with all these changes, age segregation could be phased out, as could rigidly breaking up the school day into periods devoted to individual subjects.

EQUALIZING EDUCATIONAL OPPORTUNITIES

E-learning has sparked fears of a "digital divide," but it should be evident that an educational divide already exists; e-learning is actually helping to bridge that gap. Virtual tours may not sound like a big deal, but to students in rural areas, they're important. It's expensive to buy books full of glossy photo-tours of museums and monuments; it's hard to slice days out of the school year for field trips; but it's cheap and quick to take virtual tours and "field trips" to other countries to teach geography, or to other time periods to teach history.

Schools can go on virtual class trips to the White House, their state capitol, or even Paris. In times past, the less lucky schools would have to settle for French classes where "conversational French" meant training students to say, "Concierge, do I have a letter? I am going to the tobacconist." Today, students can gain cultural understanding and practice their conversational skills by asking real French students questions over email. More than 1,300 rural South Dakota school kids had the opportunity to listen to, speak with, and ask questions of some of the best musicians in the world when they connected to the National Symphony Orchestra via the state's Digital Dakota Network. Holly Hester, a senior at Hudson High in Hudson, Massachusetts, found great benefits in having several Buddhist students living in Venezuela enrolled in her online course on Eastern and Western thought. "We can ask them direct questions about Buddhism," she explains.[a]

And the Internet is even helping bridge some of the widest educational divides in the country. The Pennsylvania Virtual Charter School won a $2.5 million federal grant to establish computer centers in the Philadelphia and Pittsburgh inner cities, so kids without home computers could use the online curriculum after school. The centers served five hundred children from public elementary schools.

a. Andrew Totter, "E-Learning Goes to School," *Education Week on the Web,* E-Defining Education Special Report, May 9, 2002, 5.

REAL-TIME ASSESSMENT

"Assessments" are the key tools that allow e-learning to offer more individualized education. Quick, painless, and frequent assessments are like old-fashioned tests, but the purpose of the assessment is not to pass or fail kids; instead, assessments are checkups that let students, parents, and teachers see where any problems have occurred and whether children are ready to move on to the next level. By tapping into these assessments, we can build profiles of each student's performance. Kids who sail through an assessment in one subject can continue making progress in that subject until they get stumped, even if they're still struggling in another subject. The idea is to let kids push their own boundaries—leaping far ahead in subjects where they excel, using the time they would have spent being bored going over material they already understood, instead working on subjects that require more time for them. Janet Thompkins, the mother of two children at Routh Roach Elementary School in Texas, marveled at the difference the Computer Curriculum Corporation's (CCC) SuccessMaker e-learning curriculum had made to her kids: "When my nine-year-old son was in the third grade last year, he went from third-grade math to seventh-grade math. It is incredible—they get to go as far as their minds can take them."[20]

Kids who fail an assessment get a chance to learn the same lesson a different way, perhaps with a greater emphasis on visual aids, word problems, or hands-on models. In this way, many kids who fall off the educational wagon get second or third chances, keeping them learning within the system instead of giving up and possibly becoming discipline problems. Likewise, kids who do not thrive in a competitive environment where they are judged against the progress of their peers may more readily embrace online education with its emphasis on individual progress through assessment.

Assessments could eventually replace grades, since they offer more precise information on a child's strengths and weaknesses, allowing for midcourse corrections. End-of-year computer assessments identify what the child learned during the school year and tell parents where knowledge gaps remain. The program can even automatically generate a summer learning program.

The way we test right now, we can't always tell if course materials are working until the end of the semester or even the end of the year. We sacrifice months of learning before we find out that we've been working with ineffective materials or styles of teaching. That should be unacceptable to every parent, teacher, and principal—not to mention the frustrated students! Online testing tied to sophisticated statistical and evaluation tools, together with quick, frequent assessments, solve the problem. In this way, each child, to some degree, has his own personalized instructor present-ing material at his own pace. The traditional teacher's role changes from being the sole source of knowledge to facilitating each child's individual education—less teacher and more tutor.

No More Guessing

Pat Herr is a Virginia fifth-grade science teacher at Ball's Bluff Elementary School in Leesburg, Virginia. E-learning assessments, combined with newer and tougher state testing standards, forced her to stretch skills formed during ten years of fifth-grade teaching. She began to focus more closely on the differing needs of individual students. "This is my bible," says Herr, pulling out a thick notebook containing reports generated by the school's computerized math program. The reports identify which math skills have been mastered and which haven't, show how far above or behind her grade level each child is in each area, and also catalogue the child's progress over time. The reports might identify, for example, that a child has mastered classifying triangles by sides and angles but needs help with long division. Herr can target where each student needs help. "The reports tell me the individual levels my students are working at, what they're good at, and what they need help with," says Herr.

"Teaching the same way to a whole class of students with varying abil-ities is no longer possible," says Herr. "If Tammy is a half-grade behind in subtraction but Tommy is a grade level ahead, why would I be teaching them the same thing? It would be an injustice!"

The assessments let children feel like they're in control of their educa-tions, rather than being helpless victims of their intellectual weaknesses. Kids learn the virtues of accurate self-judgment; they're not trapped be-tween the false show of unearned self-esteem and the gnawing pain of feeling like a failure. "My kids live for Mondays," says Herr, laughing. That's the day when Herr meets with students one-on-one to go over their previous week's progress on their assessments. "The kids get really ex-cited about the meetings every week, asking, 'What was my gain? Am I doing better at fractions? Where do I need more help?'" In "homework club," eight-year-old Daonte, a bespectacled third-grader, does a little touchdown dance each time he answers a question correctly from his math assessments.

One of the most important advantages of the regular feedback pro-vided by online assessments is allowing parents to verify that their chil-dren are really learning. E-learning emphasizes parental involvement and choice in several ways, but before parents can be involved they need to be informed. Parents often have a hard time keeping up with their child's homework. Even if they know their kid is struggling, they don't always know how to help. "Parents really feel like they're in the dark," explains Pat Petrossian, a second-year teacher at Pyle Middle School in Bethesda, Maryland. "By the time they find out about how their kids are doing, it's often too late, because we're into the next grading period." To rectify this, Petrossian sends his students' parents weekly email updates about class goings-on. The emails include links to his website, where parents can see their child's test scores and check up on homework assignments. "The parents love it," says Petrossian, who answers about twenty emails a week from parents. Petrossian's digital outreach proved so popular with Bethesda parents that he was voted Teacher of the Year.

Regular assessments are also important for evaluating the effectiveness of the cyber lessons. If a textbook isn't working as a teaching tool, usually the best you can do is replace it before the next school year (and even this is rare, due to the huge expense). Online learning, on the other hand, allows continuous fine-tuning of the learning materials thanks to data that details on a daily basis which lessons are working and which aren't. Moreover, "eBay-style" feedback mechanisms can allow parent and students to evaluate the usefulness of each lesson, providing important feedback for the curriculum developers and other parents. Explains Bennett:

> We know every day how students in the aggregate are doing on our lessons. Let's say that most days our students are humming along scoring 90 percent on our math assessments. Then one day we see the results and it's closer to 60 percent. Immediately we know that something is wrong with that lesson. We send in a team of curriculum experts to figure out what happened. They see that some of the instructions are confusing. They fix it and soon we have a brand new math lesson, ready for the next wave of students.[21]

The End of High-Stakes, Year-End Testing?

Not surprisingly, parents, teachers, and students all seem to prefer these richer and more frequent assessment mechanisms to high-stakes, year-end testing. "'What does this mean?' That used to be our school board's reaction when presented with a report of our district's performance on standardized tests," explains South Madison Community School's assistant principal Jim Coyne.[22]

This doesn't mean, however that high-stakes testing should go away. Instead, technology should be used to make the checkpoints smaller and more frequent. Right now, we spend between $30 and $60 billion a year on classroom-based student assessments—quizzes, tests, homework, and so on—yet this data isn't integrated into statewide testing systems, hence the need for end of year tests. However, once schools and online providers use technology to synchronize their internal assessments with

---

IT'S NOT THE DATA, IT'S WHAT YOU DO WITH IT

In exchange for receiving state funds, every school district in the state of New Jersey must supply the state Department of Education with a truckload of data. School districts must report test scores, student expulsions, dropout rates, teacher salaries and benefits, student race/ethnicity, and myriad other things. All in all, New Jersey schools must fill out nineteen different forms, each of which can take days to complete. The laudatory purpose of all these reporting requirements is to track individual school performance and compare it against state averages. Until very recently this used to be hard to do because no one in New Jersey had any idea what happened to all the data once it reached the Department of Education. The state had no central repository, or even a record, of all of its data. No one knew exactly who had what data and school districts charged that much of the information the state collected was redundant.[a]

This is changing in New Jersey and other states as more and more school districts and state education departments adopt "data-based decision making" (also referred to as "data warehousing"). This involves tying together the thousands of different data elements collected by school districts and states into a centralized computer depository that educators can use to look for patterns in the data that could help improve schools. "I think what it does . . . is allow us to move away from voodoo education, where we're just shooting in the dark about what the issues are with students," says an Ohio school superintendent who uses his school district's data warehouse in his day-to-day decision making. Broward County, Florida, was one of the first school districts to establish a data warehouse. Previously, if a teacher wanted to see the past history of one of her students, she would have had to contact the student's former teachers or previous school. Now, a teacher can instantly see the student's academic history, enabling her to better understand the student's strengths and weaknesses. In addition, each year every teacher receives a detailed analysis of how each of her students performed on each part of the state assessment system.

a. Lynn Olson, "Schools Discovering Riches in Data," *Education Week*, www .edweek.org, June 12, 2002.

---

the state standards and they add up to the same whole, then there's no reason why regular online learning assessments couldn't replace the stomach-lurching, high-stakes year-end testing—a development that would make most teachers, parents, and especially students very happy indeed.

A host of formidable challenges must be overcome before we can reach such a state of nirvana. Just getting to universal online testing—never mind the far more complex task of synchronizing internal assessments with state standards—will take years. A two-year pilot online assessment project in Washington State had some encouraging findings but was also plagued with technical glitches, computer compatibility problems, and server troubles. In one school, the servers kept going down whenever the vending machines were plugged in! Related one teacher involved in the project: "Trying to administer the online test was a disaster. . . . The last time I attempted to give the test, about half of the computers were not functioning. This project was an absolute nightmare and I did not want to do it again."[23] While frustrating to some teachers and students, the problems were not surprising, considering that online assessment is still in its formative stages. Eventually the technical problems will be solved because the advantages of online testing—cost savings to school districts, time savings to teachers and nearly instantaneous learning feedback for students— are too great to retreat. "Testing by computer," explains education testing researcher Randy Bennett, "—and in particular, via the Internet—is inevitable."[24] It just might take awhile.

FUTURE TEACHER: EDUCATIONAL ENTREPRENEUR OR COG IN THE EDUCATION FACTORY?

"I was bored silly in school," says Pat Herr, remembering back nearly forty years to when she was the same age as her students. "I would conduct elaborate science experiments in my garage but then flunk science class." Herr's ethnically diverse students are many things—rambunctious, talkative, fidgety—but bored is not one of them. Herr rarely lectures anymore. She's ditched the science textbook ("It hasn't been updated in twelve years, and the kids learn better interactively anyway," says Herr), replacing it with a combination of Internet resources, CD-ROMS, software programs, and beakers and vials. Her students test the hardness or softness of rocks online, learn about how sound travels through a software program called Science Court, and explore the oceans using an interactive CD-ROM program called "The Great Ocean Rescue." The ocean program, in which students play scientists on a limited budget working to solve environmental problems like blast fishing and sewage disposal, incorporates several different lessons: science lessons about geology, oceanography, and marine biology; lessons about how to approach complicated questions; and even lessons about making trade-offs, because nothing in the Ocean Rescue is free.

Herr has become more a facilitator or coach, and less the all-knowing dispenser of knowledge. For math class, she seeks out websites like allmath.com and brainquest.com, in order to challenge the quickest minds in her class. She spends much of her school day walking around the class helping students with their individual problems. "Technology has changed the way I teach," says Herr. "You can stand in front of a room and lecture to kids all day, but children learn better when you facilitate learning by letting kids discover on their own."

Disintermediation?

Almost no one involved in education disagrees with the notion that e-learning is transforming the role of teachers, changing what they do all day and redefining the very nature of their work. The unanimity breaks down, however, when it comes to whether this will ultimately prove good or bad for teachers. One school of thought sees teachers like Pat Herr as eventually being "disintermediated" by online learning, as travel agents have been marginalized by travel websites. Teachers' unions like the American Federation of Teachers say this is already happening in higher education, where the traditional role of the professor is being "unbundled" as online-course creators dole out its parts to technology experts and instructional designers.[25] Some professors fear that the university will offer them a fee to design a course, and then sell the course without letting them profit from it or teach it—handing teaching over to low-paid part-timers. As evidence, they point to the online branch of the University of Phoenix, which employs no full-time professors; its 1,400 "practitioner faculty" aren't eligible for tenure or benefits. At the K-12 level, teachers' unions fear, if every school district contracted with online curriculum providers only a few hundred or thousand great teachers might be needed for the entire country. The rest of today's teachers would be reduced to tutors and teacher aids who help students with the lessons.

This "teachers as cogs in the education factory" scenario is not altogether impossible, but it's highly improbable. The future is not likely to be nearly as grim for teachers as many opponents of online learning would have us believe. Instead of travel agents, a better approximation for how teachers might be affected by the Net is real estate brokers. Brokers used to act as the sole possessors of information about the local housing market—especially if you were trying to purchase a home in a distant community. Today, home buyers can find housing market information on the Net that's almost as detailed as what the brokers possess, making it much easier for them to educate themselves about faraway housing markets. But rather than letting themselves become sidelined by this technology, real estate brokers have embraced it—sending out customized email notifications of new houses on the market, providing virtual tours of the properties, and so on.

Like real estate brokers, teachers will undoubtedly have to get used to playing a very different role than that of the principal content provider.

"The teacher as source of all information has died," says Vicki Durbin, the principal of Yavapai Elementary School in Scottsdale, Arizona. "They're becoming project managers." But this doesn't mean their new role will be any less important or fulfilling than that of "sage on the stage." The teacher as coach and guide can spend more time working with parents, teaching students character, and generally focusing on the personal interactions that technology can't do and contemporary schools don't do enough. And being freed of lesson-plan drudgery will be a godsend to most teachers, who now spend anywhere from fifteen to twenty-five hours a week preparing for class—time that could be better spent working individually with students. "I have no life," says third-year teacher David Hitchcock, a ponytailed twenty-something former restaurant manager, who wakes up at 4:00 A.M. every morning to spend two-and-a-half hours putting together his lesson plans. "I'd love it if someone put together lesson plans for me as long as I could manipulate them to fit my teaching style and the needs of my students."

THE END OF EDUCATION AS WE KNOW IT

I think conventional textbooks—they're pretty much dead.

—Peter Cookson, director of educational outreach at Columbia
University's Teachers College[26]

In 2001, then six-year-old Clayton Sawyer enrolled in the Colorado Virtual Academy, where his mother taught him at home using books and online curricula supplied by K12. Clayton, in other words, was receiving his education from a mixture of public and private sources: from his mother, from a for-profit online national education company, and from a taxpayer-supported virtual charter school. Is Clayton Sawyer receiving a public or a private education? Your Dodge Omni may be manufactured in California, but the manufacturer is owned by a German company and uses Japanese engine design, Taiwanese microprocessors, and Canadian steel. Is it a foreign or domestic car? Do you even know where the line should be drawn? Do we possess the rhetorical tools that would allow us to understand and define the difference?

Many of the issues and controversies concerning online learning come to a head with virtual charter schools, which, of course, explains the ferocious opposition they have engendered. Cyber charters raise the most fundamental questions about what a school is, what a teacher is, what we mean by public, how schools should be financed, and when "public education" is no longer public. Like vouchers, virtual charters threaten the educational establishment because they demolish the wall between public and private. "Public education," in an e-learning model, occurs wherever learning takes place. If public education can take place in the home, there is no reason why it can't take place in a private school. Over time, if the growth of virtual charters continues, it could open the door to vouchers and similarly radical changes in school funding, striking a fatal blow to the public education monopoly. Our century-old centralized educational model would be replaced with a new approach in which online learning is seamlessly integrated with face-to-face learning interactions; public funding goes to learners, not schools; families have a variety of educational choices and learning options to choose from, ranging from custom-tailored, home-based instruction to traditional schools; and providers specialize in serving students with different learning styles and preferences.

Let's imagine a typical family—call them the Moores—with three school-age children in, say, 2010. The oldest, Susan Moore, takes physics, English, and biology classes taught by typical public school teachers in an ordinary classroom setting. Her algebra, however, is paid for by the school but delivered electronically to her and her classmates by a curriculum provider which contracts with nationally-recognized experts to teach the class. (Two teaching assistants in the classroom assist students one-on-one.) Susan's twelve-year-old brother David attends a charter school for most of the day but takes Russian lessons at a Berlitz learning center on school property. Ten-year-old Jill, like millions of other American children, is homeschooled by her parents with the help of online education providers. Like many homeschoolers, Jill supplements her education by taking a class or two at the local public school, where she also plays forward on the soccer team.

The Moore children's daily educational schedules—and the way they, their parents, and the local school system arrived at them—constitute a mixture of public and private sources blurry enough to render today's education debates virtually meaningless. Should tax dollars pay for the "public" aspects of their education and not the "private" aspects? Does it make sense to give a grade-level label to Jill, who's struggling with multiplication tables, but racing through *Johnny Tremaine* and *The Count of Monte Cristo*? What should we call Jill's mix of public and homeschooled education?

Line Blurring

The changes wrought by e-learning will ultimately challenge many of our most deeply held beliefs about education as the lines blur between home and school, teacher and parent, student and teacher, elementary and secondary, and public and private. "There never used to be any gray space between us and public schools. It used to be all black and white," says Mark

Hegener, publisher of *Home Education Magazine*, lamenting the blending of homeschooling and public education.[27] Many homeschoolers fear that if public education provided in the home looks too much like homeschooling that's completely designed and funded by the parents, both kinds of home-based education will be subjected to stringent and ideologically offensive restrictions. Often cited is a case in Alaska, where the state launched a virtual school especially for homeschoolers, called IDEA (for Interior Distance Education of Alaska). Though not a charter school, it does receive public funds. In one instance, the Alaska Department of Education tried to winnow out textbooks from Christian authors—even when those texts didn't deal with religion. Carol Simpson, the department's homeschool coordinator, wrote to one Christian author, "We have been warned several times by a high official in the DOE that we need to be extra careful about the issue of buying 'religious' curricula."

But the public-private blends offer rewards to public schools as well as to homeschoolers. The two groups need cooperation, not conflict, since each has something to offer: the public schools have sports teams and science labs, the homeschoolers have children and the funding those children can bring. As online education continues to blur the public-private lines, homeschool advocates may be marginalized if they don't turn their attention to the protection of home from state rather than the separation of home and state. Explains Colorado's Treon Goossen, who was at the forefront of the 1980s battle for the right to homeschool, "There are those who fear that anything that smells like homeschooling but is regulated will bleed over into homeschooling, but I disagree with that, because we have a statute that protects homeschooling rights, and we're careful to watch for bleed-overs. If a virtual school is the best people think they can do for their family, more power to them."[28]

AFT president Sandra Feldman points out one real problem with e-learning—but it's a problem that can be solved by the very public-private mixing that her union opposes: "Some courses just don't work very well in an online environment, take high school chemistry as an example. K12 claims they can do it with animated beakers and bunsen burners. I'm not sure that's the same as mixing the chemicals, lighting the burner, smelling the sulfur and watching the chemical reaction."[29] When public and private blur, a student can smell the sulfur in a classroom, then head home for the rest of her lessons.

Getting to this point, however, will require major cultural changes in an educational establishment that has traditionally been hostile to such integration. Nick Trombetta, chief administrative officer of the Western Pennsylvania Cyber Charter School had problems trying to get public school administrators to allow children at his cyber school participate in a fundraiser for muscular dystrophy. "Some of these guys won't even let these kids join walks for hunger," he explains. "So you pick up the phone and you say you can't do that. Lucky for us, about 90 percent of superintendents in the state recognize that the kids need extracurriculars offered by traditional public schools."

But when the mixing does happen, then the homeschoolers will likely be correct in their belief that the continued blurring of the lines between public and private and home and school could lead to more regulation of homeschools. But that regulation would likely take the form of testing requirements, rather than detailed, potentially offensive curricular requirements.[30] Statewide assessment tests and statewide monitoring and tracking of students' and schools' progress would be the glue that holds this decentralized system together as a publicly funded area.

But the shift from regulating means to regulating ends should also mean that we'll no longer prescribe the minutes and the hours and the degrees and the credentials and the size of the pad of paper a school needs to use. The central idea of the charter school movement, i.e., to give schools and parent-teachers more freedom in exchange for greater accountability, would accelerate. So if a virtual charter's parents wants to teach their kid religion or communism or French cooking, the state will say "Go right ahead, it's not the state's business because we're not going to test those things, but they do have to learn algebra, reading comprehension, and phys. ed."

Future Schooling

E-learning strengthens the role of parents in education, without isolating children from the larger community. It makes a neglected philosophy of education seem obvious: the philosophy that states that children's first and foremost educators are their parents; that parental guidance is the key to learning and taking responsibility; that familial loyalties precede and strengthen, rather than threaten, civic loyalty; and that children should be integrated into the larger community rather than being walled off among their peers.

E-learning also eliminates physical boundaries. Universities already operate in a borderless world, drawing students from every state and even from other countries. Now that ability to offer an education to faraway students is coming to the elementary and secondary school world. Of the more than 2,090 students who enrolled in Trombetta's Western Pennsylvania Cyber Charter in Midland, Pennsylvania, in the 2003–2004 academic year, only a dozen or more of them were actually from the rural town.

The loss of defined borders will force schools to change. Private schools have already learned to market themselves, making sure that all parents in the area know the schools' strengths. Public schools will have to do the same thing. Schools will have to excel in something, perhaps even specialize, in order to attract students—and they'll also have to make sure people know about their strengths. This need for marketing will be one of the biggest challenges of the borderless world. One solution is a different kind of public-private partnership. "Everyone brings something to the party," says education-technology innovator Ted Fujimoto. "If the university or educational institution has intellectual property that they're trying to distribute, and the private sector is much better at packaging and distributing it, then you'll see that collaboration."

Though it will take a while, age segregation, letter grades, and strict grade-level distinctions could all go away (see table 3.1). Textbooks will also be history, replaced by online learning delivered to the desktop, digital paper and tablet PCs. "I would guess that it would not be unreasonable to assume that the majority of content will be pulled down and reprinted off the Internet [in the future], and it will be contemporary knowledge—it won't be a nine-year-old science book," says former Georgia Congressman Johnny Isakson. "Instead, it will be the most recent, updated information—the teacher pulls it down, hands it out, the kids take it home. You are talking about a tremendous savings in dollars."[31]

By changing how teachers teach, how students learn, how schools are managed, even what schools are, online learning has the potential to alter the structure and system of public education in ways every bit as fundamental, if not more so, than vouchers, charters, national standards, smaller class sizes and other better-known public-school reforms. "Radical education reform has until now focused on shifting the governance arrangements or the flow of funds, but it hasn't shifted the basic technology of

Table 3.1. The Future of Learning

Out	In
One-size-fits-all education	"My size fits me" learning
Physical boundaries	Infinite classroom
All-for-nothing, high-stakes, end-of-year testing	Frequent assessments rolled up into one comprehensive student learning profile
Letter grades	Learning assessments
Age segregation	Children in the same classroom learning different things and in different ways at the same time
Strict grade-level distinctions	A child able to race ahead to seventh-grade math while still taking fourth-grade reading
Textbooks	Adaptive, online learning downloaded to desktops, laptops, and tablet PCs
Teacher as "sage on the stage"	Teacher as facilitator and coach

schooling," says Chester Finn Jr. "With e-learning, we're talking about transforming the technology of schooling in the broadest sense of the word. What could be more revolutionary? That's an invention of flight kind of breakthrough."

Of course, few believed the Wright Brothers would ever fly. Eighteen months before they took to the air at Kitty Hawk, astronomer Simon Newcombe intoned, "Flight by machines heavier than air is unpractical and insignificant, if not utterly impossible." Even four years after that historic flight, British Secretary of State for War Richard Burton Haldane confidently stated, "The aeroplane will never fly."

But they flew, and travel was never the same again.

E-learning is beginning to take off. Soon it will be just as important to schooling as airplanes are to travel.

TIPS FOR PRACTITIONERS

- Use technology to transform, not automate, traditional ways of teaching.
- Technology is just a delivery mechanism. It shouldn't be the focus of the child's attention.
- Blend the best of virtual and real-world learning to create a truly exceptional learning experience for the student.
- Tailor learning to individual learning styles through the use of artificial intelligence-based e-learning technologies.
- Improve education decision making by tying together the different data elements from multiple schools and school districts.
- Use data from regular assessments and "eBay-style" feedback mechanisms from parents and students to regularly recalibrate lesson plans.
- Use e-learning tools to transform the role of teachers from "sage on the stage" to coach and facilitator of a child's learning.

4

Wired Roads

Of all the policy problems we face in the opening years of the twenty-first century, traffic might be the least acknowledged. Few issues affect more people on a daily basis than our congested highways and byways. Traffic delays cost Americans more than $100 billion a year in wasted time and fuel, an increase of over 40 percent since 1990.[1] In Organization for Economic Cooperation and Development (OECD) countries overall, the cost of gridlock equals nearly 3 percent of gross domestic product (GDP), or about $810 billion. In Asia, the situation is even worse. In Korea, for example, the cost of congestion is now about 4.4 percent of GDP.[2] The average commuter now wastes almost an entire work week per year sitting in traffic.[3] Congestion is also a major contributor to air pollution.

For decades, policymakers have tried two different approaches to curbing congestion: building more roads and encouraging public transportation. To be sure, more roads and more transit are necessary, if only to keep up with the increased demand. But, given the enormous expense of both approaches, the skyrocketing number of vehicles expected in the next decade, and the geographical and political difficulty of building more capacity in metro areas, neither will be enough to prevent congestion from getting far worse.[4]

What can be done to prevent a future of four-hour commutes? The Greens have a simple answer: impose draconian restrictions on the use of our beloved cars. But most Americans aren't about to surrender our nearly century-long love affair with the automobile and take up long-distance biking anytime soon. Until flashy, skin-hugging Lycra bike shorts are standard work attire, don't hold your breath waiting for the Green solution. Moreover, drivers and car manufacturers have begun adapting to congestion with features like cell phones, stereo systems, automatic transmission, in-the-back entertainment systems, and mobile Internet access, reducing the incentive to ditch the car. Like Toad of Toad Hall, we'll keep "poop-pooping" away in our motorcars no matter how many well-meaning friends try to make us stop. Some economists aren't very helpful, either, telling us we're just going to have to "adapt" to three-hour round-trip commutes. "Use the ride home as a time to 'decompress' from a stressful day at work before coming home to the spouse and kids," they tell us. Ever try "decompressing" while you're stuck in a Boston traffic jam?

Thankfully, there's a third option that's both more promising and more constructive: using technology to convert roads from inert slabs of concrete into living, dynamic transport networks. Just as digital technology linked up soldiers on the battlefield in Iraq with their commanders and provided both parties with total information awareness on the battlefield, it can link transportation planners with emergency road crews and drivers, providing all of them with real-time information about congestion. This allows drivers to make more informed travel decisions and transportation planners to get more out of existing roads—for example, by pricing roads according to current levels of congestion. The end result would be a more efficient transportation network.

The term used to describe the basket of technologies that will enable these changes is intelligent transportation systems (ITS), a catchall phrase for a mix of infrastructure, communications, and vehicle technologies including adaptive signal control, collision avoidance systems, dynamic message signs, electronic toll collection, intelligent cruise control, mayday systems, virtual weighing stations, ramp metering, route navigation devices, traveler information systems, and more.

Let's just summarize it all as "wired roads, wired cars, and wired drivers." ITS is no panacea. It won't eliminate congestion, and it won't alleviate the need to add lanes, manage demand, and build more roads. However, by increasing roadway productivity (the inefficiency of today's freeway systems costs the economy $1 trillion a year) ITS can play an important role in preventing congestion from getting far worse, while boosting safety and diminishing environmental damage—and doing it all much more cheaply than traditional infrastructure fixes. "Compared to adding capacity and discouraging people from using roads," says ITS pioneer Larry Yermack, the former president of the Intelligent Transportation Society of America, "ITS technology is the easiest and least expensive thing to do, and it offers the highest benefits." A 2001 federal Department of Transportation (DOT) study estimated that nationwide deployment of

ITS between then and 2015 could result in a 42 percent reduction in accidents and 41 percent drop in travel time.[5] While some transportation economists believe these numbers are overly optimistic, there is little doubt that new technologies have the potential to improve safety and ease congestion.

DRIVING BLIND: THE INFORMATION DEFICIT

The key to improving our current transportation system is getting more information into the hands of more people, and doing it faster. Drivers, planners, and engineers all face huge information deficits. Eliminating or reducing them would help tremendously in solving the transportation problem.

Take the people who oversee the system: traffic engineers and transportation officials. These folks have few tools to predict future traffic flows based on different conditions or on actions they might take, and it can take far too long before they even learn where an accident has occurred. As a result, real-time traffic data is spotty at best on most highways and virtually nonexistent on streets.

Drivers are even more helpless. How many times have you found yourself sitting in traffic that you wish you'd known about before you left home, so you could have left earlier or taken a different route? Or been stuck in a traffic snarl on a business trip, wishing there were someone in the passenger seat who could guide you to another route? Overhead message signs flashing the proverbial "Congestion ahead" don't say whether you're better off finding an alternate route—let alone where to find one. "The only time you get information is off the radio," says Mark Hallenbeck, director of the University of Washington's Transportation Center. "And, of course, you only get the radio report two minutes after you had to decide between I-90 or 520. It's no good."[6]

What you really need to know is precisely what you usually can't find out: What's traffic like ahead of me all the way to work? How about the weather up there? How can I bypass the congestion, and what are conditions like on alternate routes? Which parking lot closest to my work still has spaces available?

Drivers armed with such accurate, customized, real-time guidance would likely change their driving behavior by taking alternative routes, delaying departure, or choosing buses, the subway, or trains over cars. These informed choices, in turn, would improve the overall system, reducing uncertainty and spreading out demand on the roads.[7] "It's like any other competitive market," says Professor Moshe Ben-Akiva, who directs MIT's ITS program, "if you give people more information, they can make better, more informed choices. And if they make better choices as individuals, then everyone is better off."[8]

"Help Me Get Out of This Traffic Jam!"

A study conducted by researchers at the University of California at Davis reports that nearly one-half of San Francisco-area commuters would modify their route if they had access to traveler information while in transit—and nearly all would take an alternative route in response to an accident or if they had a long-distance commute.[9] Information shortages, of course, are precisely the problem that computers were designed to correct—and from Singapore to London to Berkeley, a host of companies and government agencies are rushing to supply motorists with just this kind of real-time traffic data. Many governments in metropolitan areas now provide real-time traffic information maps called advanced traveler information services (ATIS) on their websites. Cincinnati's site tells you how long it will take to drive a specified length of highway, while Mobility Technologies collects traffic data through its own solar-powered, radar-based sensors and offers dynamic traffic maps for Pittsburgh, Philadelphia, Chicago, and Dallas. Oregon's TripCheck.com site, which averages about 15 million hits a month, offers up-to-date info about road conditions, incidents, and traffic throughout the state. Drivers can study live video feeds from cameras placed along state highways. And the department, rather than hoarding this cornucopia of traffic data, lets the media and other organizations post it on their own sites.

Such sites are a step in the right direction, but most also have serious limitations. For one thing, they're not much help if you're stuck in a traffic jam and need to know how long you'll be there and how you might escape it. The data on most of these sites isn't always current and most in-vehicle navigation systems provide routes based on static maps lacking current traffic data. What's needed is accurate, timely information that's delivered electronically to a convenient place, be it home or office or the car itself, via PCs, handhelds, or onboard route navigation systems. At the moment, no private company or government agency in the United States does all these pieces well.

It's better overseas. For several years, Londoners have been able to receive real-time traffic info on handheld devices made by Trafficmaster, a British company that's wired the London metro area with infrared detectors. In a joint venture with Motorola, Trafficmaster now offers a dashboard-mounted, Global Positioning System (GPS)-equipped device that reports traffic conditions for the road you're on and suggests alternate routes. In Japan, meanwhile, about half of all new cars possess navigation systems, many offering dynamic route guidance and journey times based on real-time traffic data collected by tens of thousands of overhead sensors (sixteen thousand in Tokyo alone) and transmitted to GPS-equipped vehicle devices.

So what do they have that we lack? What's the largest barrier to American ITS: data—or, more to the point, the lack thereof?[10] Less than 20 percent (some experts say as few as 5 percent) of U.S. highways—and almost no arterial roads—are equipped to capture real-time traffic data, either through buried loop detectors or roadside digital poles, and just 16 percent of freeways are wired in the seventy-five biggest metro areas.[11] American drivers, admits Christine Johnson, former director of the ITS program office at the U.S. DOT, "will continue to be stuck until we have more ubiquitous information about our surface transportation system."[12]

And don't hold your breath for that. At the current pace of installing roadway loop detectors, it will take fifty years to get real-time data for all U.S. highways and even longer for local roads, by which point, one imagines, we'll all have our own flying machines and ITS won't even matter. The question is: How can we get hundreds of millions of miles of existing roads wired a lot faster? And the answer is by wiring cars, not roads.

Turning cars, buses, and cell phones into traffic probes could turn out to be a lot easier than wiring millions of miles of roads with loop detectors. In areas where a high percentage of drivers have signed up for electronic toll collection, traffic flow can be captured from car transponders. Tens of thousands of Houston commuters, for example, volunteered to let traffic engineers study their movement (they're assigned random ID numbers as a privacy measure).[13] Other experts suggest that in the near future, most cars, trucks, and buses will be outfitted with computer sensors that let the vehicles themselves be used as probes.

But perhaps the best near-term opportunity to solve the real-time traffic data deficit lies with cell phones. Thanks to a 1996 federal law dealing with 911 calls that went into effect in 2001, all new cell phones must be "location-aware" at all times. Spurred by this requirement, cell phone companies have developed "location pattern matching" that lets them track even those phones that lack a GPS chip. "There are as many cell phones out there now as vehicles," explains ITS expert Dick Mudge, "and as long as a phone is on, we can find it and watch it move." The phone becomes a data probe, indicating its location and speed, but without violating privacy because the computer is just measuring energy waves emitted by the phone. These data in turn allow cell phone companies to calculate, in real time, mile-by-mile, block-by-block traffic speeds, which makes calculating travel times a snap. Once probe technology solves the data dilemma, a comprehensive info grid will let numerous providers offer accurate, personalized travel applications. A driver could say, "I'm driving from Cincinnati to Miami. Taking into account real-time traffic, incident and weather information and road construction, give me the best route to take and tell me how long it will take to get there over each segment of the trip."

DYNAMIC ROAD MANAGEMENT

One of the best real-time traffic information systems in the United States is the University of California, Berkeley's PeMS (Freeway Performance Evaluation Monitoring System), billed as "the nation's first web-based traffic seer." Drivers who click on an online map to specify the beginning and end of their journey are given predictive travel times for up to fifteen alternate routes. Based wholly on real-time data, PeMS is highly accurate: 90 percent of its travel-time predictions wind up between four to ten minutes of the actual travel time. "The chief benefit is, you can adjust your trip to avoid traffic jams," says Pravin Varaiya, the India-born computer scientist who led the program. "But if you're in a traffic jam already, it'll tell you how long you'll be there."[14] Varaiya predicts that better traffic info and management would save $1.5 billion a year in fuel and motorists' time in Los Angeles alone—not to mention reducing the air pollution caused by stop-and-go traffic.

But helping drivers directly is only one of the PeMS system's aims—and not even the principal one. Varaiya also hopes to aid drivers indirectly, by helping transportation planners and engineers pinpoint congestion causes. PeMS would give them detailed real-time and historical traffic data that let them design measures to alleviate bottlenecks and improve highway productivity. Information technology doesn't just make drivers smarter; it makes transportation planners and engineers smarter, too. "We're now operating our freeway systems at very poor efficiency at the time of greatest demand," he says—at a cost to the economy, he estimates, of over $1 trillion a year.[15]

And that's just the beginning; the productivity gains that integrating IT into America's transportation system would make possible, Varaiya claims, dwarf even the gains from increasing capacity. But to realize these, state highway departments need to see roads not as inert slabs of concrete requiring only occasional repair but as living systems requiring active, real-time management. In short, what's needed is a fundamental change in the culture of every state, local, and federal transportation agency. The kind of change that a traffic engineer named Pat Irwin has brought to San Antonio, Texas.

San Antonio's Smart Roads

In the early 1990s Pat Irwin, operations manager of the Texas Department of Transportation's (TxDOT) San Antonio district office, had a problem;

namely, the technology the state used to keep freeways flowing—twisted
wire to communicate with traffic signals and a few loop detectors in the
roads—was last considered cutting-edge when Truman was president. "I
knew we needed something more dynamic," says the white-haired Irwin
in his thick, Texas drawl, "I just didn't know what it was yet."

Irwin also wanted to cut down the time it took to respond to accidents
and other "incidents"—disabled vehicles, weather, etc.—which together
cause about half of all rush hour congestion.[16] Why does clearing an accident take so long? First, the accident has to be detected and its location
pinpointed. Then you need to create a plan to clear the accident and di-
vert traffic around it, which means accounting for a surprising number of
variables: Whom do you send to the scene? How many vehicles? What
should the overhead message signs say? How far ahead should you notify motorists? The list goes on and on—and every minute it takes to clear
an accident adds about four minutes to the traffic queue. So if it takes
seven minutes to deploy a response plan, you've just added another half
hour to the traffic jam.

So one day in 1991, Irwin and his team of engineers played hooky from
their usual daily job of building and managing freeways and took a two-
hour drive to see the engineering marvels at Houston's NASA headquarters, hoping to learn something useful from one of the most high-
tech outfits in the country about how to integrate IT, infrastructure, and
communications systems.

They weren't disappointed. After giving them the usual tour, their
NASA hosts showed them the restricted situation room where NASA sim-
ulates every possible space flight disaster and preprograms a response;
the operating principle being, "no surprises." And seeing this, Irwin had
one of those light bulb moments: developing a system for highway accidents that mirrored NASA's plan for space flight problems, he realized,
could cut incident response times from minutes to seconds, which in turn
would dramatically reduce the resulting traffic jams. With the help of Al-
lied Signal, a major NASA contractor, Irwin's TxDOT group built such a
system. It contains forty thousand preprogrammed scenarios and can respond to any accident in less than one minute.

But faster accident response is only one component of San Antonio's
TransGuide, possibly the country's most sophisticated traffic management system. Almost one hundred miles of San Antonio freeways are now
wired, loaded with message signs, changeable lane control signals, thousands of loop detectors and road sensors, and hundreds of video cameras
linked by a fiber optic network.

The results can be striking. A dense, soupy fog hangs in the air on my
drive down to San Antonio. The highway is crowded but flowing
smoothly; every few miles overhead message signs tell me how many minutes it should take me to get to the next major interchange. TransGuide's

marble-floored 53,000-square-foot high-tech headquarters—a building bearing a striking resemblance to NASA's operations building—is located in the median between two of the largest freeways. In the operations room, your eyes immediately turn to the giant 60-foot by 11-foot panel of video screens covering the front wall showing constantly changing views of San Antonio highway traffic. The first big accident of the day is an eighteen-wheeler that jackknifed at about 6:30 A.M. on a local highway, causing traffic to immediately slow. Computers wired to loop detectors placed every half mile along the freeway note that traffic speeds are slower than the acceptable range for that time of rush hour and trigger an alarm at Trans-Guide. Video cameras placed along the road, triggered by the warning, instantaneously bring up an image of the incident at the control station of Bill Koerner, the operations manager, who then has five seconds to verify the accident and send it to the operator for action. Along with the camera footage, a screen pops up on Koerner's monitor that asks three questions:

1. What caused the incident?
2. How many lanes are closed?
3. Does the demand exceed the capacity of the road?

This is all the computers need to know to swing into action. Highway message signs eight to ten miles away from the accident tell motorists a truck has overturned and recommend taking alternate routes. Control boxes above each lane move cars from the right lanes (where the accident occurred) to the left lanes. The on-site police dispatcher takes control of the video camera and dispatches a fire truck, EMS, a few tow trucks, a huge wrecker, and a Hazmat unit. And this all happens in less than one minute. "We let the technology do the work for us," says Irwin. The really amazing thing about TransGuide is that any San Antonio motorist can get almost all the same information as the control room engineers—the hundreds of live video shots, the incident locations, and real-time, point-to-point travel times and route guidance—by logging on to TransGuide's website.

Now, these systems don't come cheap—they cost around $1 million a mile to build and deploy—but they're still cheaper than adding a highway lane, and the results are impressive: emergency response time has improved 20 percent, accidents are down 15 percent (real-time info reduces sideswipes, rear-ends, etc.), and delays have fallen by seven hundred hours.

San Antonio's highways are a rare exception, but in select systems in the United States, Europe, and Asia, we can see the first stirrings of fully dynamic road systems. The city of London uses computerized sensors and signs to adjust the speed limit on its 117-mile beltway to ensure a smooth traffic flow. Over four hundred ramp meters manage freeway access on over two hundred miles of freeways in the Minneapolis-St. Paul metropolitan area, cutting travel time, increasing throughput (more cars getting down the road over a given time period), and reducing the number of crashes.[17] All ninety-two miles of Singapore's freeways, along with many surface roads, are wired for electronic data collection and video surveillance and connected to a Star Trek-like mission control room where traffic engineers run the country's expressway monitoring and advisory system.[18] Overall, according to the U.S. DOT, dynamic roads equipped with sensors, cameras, synchronized traffic signals, variable speed limits, message signs, ramp metering, lane signals, signal priority systems, and other technology could potentially cut travel times up to 48 percent.[19]

The Death of the Tollbooth

Does anyone besides tollbooth operators really like tollbooths? They force people to slow down, scan a bewildering array of signs, risk fender benders by merging lanes at the last minute, fumble around for the right amount of cash, stop or slow down and, finally, pay up. Toll plazas are a major cause of congestion; they also harm the environment by contributing disproportionately to tailpipe emissions. "People aren't necessarily opposed to paying tolls to drive on roads," says Robert Poole, director of transportation policy for the Reason Foundation and one of the country's leading transportation authorities. "It's the stopping at toll booths that they really don't like."

Thankfully, these twentieth-century artifacts may soon join eight-tracks and vacuum tubes in the dustbin of history. Already most toll-charging roads, bridges, and tunnels are equipped with electronic toll collection (ETC) technology that allows tolls to be collected at high speeds. And within a decade, most remaining tollbooths will be doomed by "transponders," credit-card-sized cards placed on windshields or in license plates. Antennas mounted above roadways record a given car's road usage by communicating with the transponders, and tolls are debited from the drivers' accounts. Eventually, these vehicle-to-roadside messaging systems (called dedicated short-range communications) will also enable safety warnings, weather advisories, map database updates, dynamic route guidance, and intersection collision avoidance.

Electronic toll collection has enjoyed more early success than any other ITS technology. Just a little more than a decade after its first deployment, about half of all toll transactions are now conducted electronically—a truly remarkable adoption rate. Writes Peter Samuel, the editor of *Toll Roads* newsletter:

> It [electronic tolling] was invented by scientists and engineers in the aero-
> space business, developed by investor-financed companies, designed by

consultants and financed, installed, maintained, promoted and operated by state toll agencies and their contractors. The users, motorists, pay for it. Fully, and they love it.[20]

The best place to observe the dramatic impact of electronic tolling is in the New York City area, where about 71 percent of all toll transactions are conducted electronically through the popular E-ZPass system. The system has been adopted by twenty-one member agencies in ten states in the Northeast, meaning that about 9.6 million E-ZPass-equipped motorists can drive from Maine to Maryland, and from Delaware to the Ohio line, without ever stopping at a tollbooth.[21] In the pre-E-ZPass days, motorists endured horrible backups at toll plazas during commuting hours and holidays, especially if they were trying to get onto the bridges and tunnels that connect New Jersey to New York City. Those half hour waits are now fifteen-second delays, and throughput is way up (in-plaza, lane-based ETC systems can handle two to three times as many vehicles per hour as manual toll lanes).[22] "E-ZPass is the most extraordinarily positive thing that has happened to regional transportation in New York in many decades," exults Michael Ascher, executive director of New York's MTA Bridges and Tunnels. "We used to have legislators sponsoring bills to drop the tolls on heavily traveled holidays. Not anymore, because toll collection doesn't delay traffic."[23]

And the most impressive thing about E-ZPass may be that, because it doesn't physically remove tollbooths themselves, it's already outdated. Today some toll lanes are reserved for E-ZPass motorists who, for safety reasons, still slow down to 10 to 15 MPH when passing through them. Most new toll roads, on the other hand, are built with open-road tolling technology, meaning any tollbooths are off to the side of the road so vehicles with transponders never even have to slow down. The latest trend is to ditch the tollbooths altogether. Regular users of Toronto's 407-ETR, the first tollroad to operate without any tollbooths or toll collectors, have transponders in their cars while a video camera takes a picture of the license plate of any car that lacks a transponder and sends the owner a bill.[24] No human being ever touches most transactions.[25] The technology's adherents are, to say the least, enthusiastic. "It's less expensive to build and operate, and it's better for air quality, noise, and fuel and land consumption," says Daryl Fleming, president of eTrans, the consulting firm that aided the Toronto deployment. "If you're looking at anything but open-road tolling, you're not serving your customers."

Smart Pricing

Cross the Hudson River from Jersey to New York City between 6:00 and 9:00 A.M. on the George Washington Bridge or through the Holland or Lincoln Tunnel and you'll be charged a dollar more than you would at any other time of the day (two dollars more if your car doesn't have an E-ZPass transponder). Welcome to the world of "peak-hour" or "variable" pricing, whose laudable goal is to convince some drivers who can avoid rush hour to do so. So far, the strategy has worked in New York; since peak-hour pricing was introduced in 2001, rush hour use of the bridge and tunnels has fallen slightly (while traffic in the hour before rush hour rose 2 percent), a reduction sufficient to improve traffic flow.[26] The lesson: always pay attention to your customer's bottom line. "People base their travel decisions on out-of-pocket costs," says Poole, of the Reason Foundation. "They really don't take into account the way their use of scarce road capacity imposes costs on others."

"Congestion" or "peak-hour" pricing lets rush-hour drivers choose to either pay the extra fee, choose a different mode of travel, or change their trip time—and convincing even a small percentage of drivers to choose the latter two options can greatly improve traffic flow. If, on the other hand, enough people choose to pay peak-hour charges, this both sends a signal that more capacity is needed and brings in more money to help pay for it. Thus can the laws of supply and demand let transportation systems, like any other marketplace, decide what goods ought to be supplied. "The idea," says Samuel, "is to get market signals for how much motorists will pay to expand capacity. Right now, we don't really know."

Soon we will. On Southern California's I-15 toll lane, for instance, charges vary from hour to hour and even minute to minute, according to how many cars are clogging the road at any given time. A computerized system of sensors measures traffic volume, calculates lane occupancy, determines proper toll rates, and then sends the information to variable message signs. Freeway lanes can even be reversed depending on which direction is carrying the heaviest traffic at the moment. The simple idea here, of course, is to use pricing to keep these roads free-flowing. But once you adopt the principle, the applications that present themselves next are virtually limitless.

Consider high-occupancy toll (HOT) networks, a concept developed by Poole and transportation researcher Kenneth Orski. These are interconnected systems of limited access lanes on urban freeways.[27] The central idea is to transform the patchy and unconnected HOV lanes that exist in most metropolitan areas into HOT lanes and then extend and link them to each other to form regional HOT networks of free-flowing priced roads. Under this system, a driver could use the designated lanes for free if he met the high-occupancy criteria or alone if he were willing to pay the toll. Such a system would provide motorists with "congestion insurance," contend Poole and Orski, because they would be able to completely bypass congestion—as long as they were willing to pay for the privilege.

Meanwhile, in February 2003, the largest and most extensive electronic road pricing project in the world was launched in London. Vehicles entering central London are now electronically charged a flat fee between the hours of 7:00 A.M. and 6:30 P.M. during weekdays. Enforcement of the charge is based on automatic number recognition technology using cameras situated on the boundary and throughout the charging zone. The charge can be paid through several channels including online, the telephone, text messaging, post, and retail outlets. Since the congestion charge went live, it has had a major impact on local gridlock. One year after the program's inception, traffic speeds had increased 37 percent, congestion had dropped 40 percent during charging hours, and round-trip journey times fell 13 percent. These results prompted Paris, Stockholm, Edinburgh, Sydney, and a host of other major cities to explore the possibility of adopting the London model.

Ditching the Gas Tax

Once you start thinking about it, you realize that the same technologies that enable open-road tolling could eventually change the way roads are funded—and replace the hated gas tax with direct road access fees—a switch that transportation economists have fantasized about for decades. "Road systems," says Fleming, "should be priced and run the same way as utilities, with pricing reflecting demand." Until now, this concept was unworkable because the only way to collect road charges was to erect tollbooths on every last highway and street corner—a surefire way to end one's political career.[28] Emerging technology, though, makes supply-and-demand road pricing not only possible but rather simple: just outfit every car with a transponder (in essence, an electronic license plate), then track a given vehicle's road usage by outfitting highways with gantries like the ones used on tollroads (traffic lights could serve the same role on surface

---

FIRST-YEAR RESULTS OF LONDON'S CONGESTION CHARGE

- Traffic levels   25 percent lower
- Congestion   40 percent lower
- Weekday speeds   10 to 20 percent increase in peak periods
- Delays due to traffic   50 percent reduction
- Bus reliability   25 percent increase
- Bus speeds at peak hour   25 percent increase
- Time savings benefits $279M

Source: Transport for London (2004).

streets) or solar-powered infrared beacons mounted on roadside poles. The billing is the same as for electronic toll collection.

Another option is equipping each vehicle with GPS receivers (integrated in new vehicles in the dashboard and retrofitted to existing vehicles as little black boxes) that would track vehicle movements, store historical data about the vehicle's position, and calculate the road usage fee in order to deduct it from the account. This method of pricing will be used in Germany for collecting road use charges for trucks. Beginning sometime in early 2005, truckers in Germany will pay an average of twenty-five cents a mile to drive on the autobahn. The charges are calculated via an onboard unit that uses satellite GPS signals.

A similar system will be in place in the United Kingdom in 2006. The charge will cover all trucks, including delivery vans, and will apply to all roads in the country. The UK government has committed to reducing other fees—most likely duty or tax on diesel fuel—to fully offset the revenues from the truck road user charge. Other European countries are expected to follow. By the end of the decade, electronic road use pricing is likely to be the standard way of charging European truckers for road usage. The United Kingdom is already exploring extending this model out to automobiles nationwide.

Will this ever happen in America? The ingrained power of the political interests that favor the gas tax gives ample cause for skepticism. Still, some analysts believe that eventually the political barriers will give way to fiscal reality. "As we look at the future of fuel taxes, it's clear that they won't be a viable way of paying for the road system," says Reason's Poole.

> Political and economic pressures will demand huge improvements in vehicle efficiency and greater use of alternative fuels—and this in turn will mean less revenues coming in from the gas tax, which will result in a growing mismatch between our infrastructure needs and revenues . . . the only way to solve this conundrum [short of a massive hike in the gas tax, of course], is to phase out the gas tax and take advantage of technology and expand the toll concept to most roads.

Poole, Fleming, and others see a future in which roads are run like utilities, with different providers running different segments of the network and charging for usage the same way today's utilities charge for electricity. And in this way, technology allows for a fairer system, whereby those who use the roads most pay for those roads most. Twenty years ago this would have been considered pure fantasy. Today, wireless communications and the Internet make such a vision not only possible but probable. "Once it gets very inexpensive to collect tolls," says MIT's Ben-Akiva, "and we're getting close—pricing based on congestion is bound to happen." The trick, of course, is to price based on *anticipated* congestion—if you're pricing based on actual congestion, the battle has already been lost!

SMART CARS

One reason flying is so much safer than driving is that pilots have access to sophisticated navigation guidance instruments, warning systems, on-board radar, computerized weather reports, and an autopilot function. Soon small planes will be able to detect all other planes in their vicinity, adjust their course for weather problems or high terrain, synchronize arrival times with other planes, and come equipped with a host of new safety features—including parachutes![29] If the car you buy next week integrated some of these same features into a simple, easy-to-use dashboard, then logic would dictate that driving could be made, if not quite as safe as flying, at least a lot safer than driving today. (In 2002, there were 42,815 traffic fatalities.)

The future is almost here. "In the wake of the computer and information revolutions, motor vehicles are undergoing the most dramatic changes in their capabilities and how they interact with drivers since the early years of the century," writes Cheryl Little of the Volpe National Transportation Systems Center.[30] A century after Henry Ford introduced the Model T, cars and trucks are becoming less and less like that original simple machine and more and more like mobile computers: intelligent, Net-connected vehicles that deliver data, navigation guidance, safety warnings, even a second driver via collision avoidance systems (more on this soon). Already, OnStar, which provides route support, safety and security, and airbag deployment, comes factory-installed in all but one of GM's fifty-four models as well as on certain vehicles manufactured by Acura, Audi, Isuzi, Lexus, and Volkswagon. If you're in an accident, within ten seconds of impact OnStar will ask if you're okay and tell you help is on the way unless you indicate you're not hurt. In the future, cars might look more like Volvo's $10 million Safety Concept prototype car, which is loaded with cameras, sensors, night vision enhancement systems, video display monitors, and microchips. The purpose of all this technology? To radically reduce the number of accidents by giving drivers a much better view of the traffic around them.

As we discussed earlier, accidents cause half of all congestion, and systems like San Antonio's TransGuide can reduce how long it takes to clear them. But the ultimate goal of the smart car, of course, is to keep accidents from happening in the first place. The Society of Automotive Engineers estimates that human error causes 90 percent of all traffic accidents—with inattentive drivers at fault for three out of every four crashes! Want more startling stats? Sixty percent of all intersection crashes and 30 percent of all head-on collisions could be avoided if drivers had just an extra half second to react.[31]

Collision Avoidance Systems

New technology may soon give us that half second, and more. Collision avoidance systems using radio sensors on vehicles' front, rear, and sides alert drivers to potential collisions. Intelligent cruise control adjusts your car's speed to keep you a safe distance from the car ahead, and drowsiness-detection systems use biometrics and neural network technology to warn you when you're about to nod off.[32]

The bottom line? Driving should get a lot safer. The National Highway Traffic Safety Administration believes that adopting collision-avoidance systems could prevent 1.1 million accidents a year in the United States, or 17 percent of all accidents, saving 17,500 lives and $26 billion in accident-related costs.[33] And, of course, reducing the traffic congestion those extra 1.1 million accidents would have caused.

But the first real-world test of whether smart cars actually make roads safer will likely come not from cars but from trucks. Tens of thousands of eighteen-wheelers now roaring down America's highways (more than 15 percent of the nation's commercial fleet) are equipped with collision warning and intelligent cruise control systems manufactured by Kalamazoo, Michigan-based Eaton Corporation. Eaton's VORAD system uses high-frequency radar—like the kind that let Royal Air Force pilots see in the dark during the Battle of Britain—to detect other vehicles in the truck's blind spots and emit warning sounds whenever a truck is close to hitting another vehicle. The Smart Cruise speed control system reduces the truck's speed as traffic slows ahead and speeds it back up as traffic warrants. VORAD-equipped trucks will soon have onboard computer screens for monitoring engine, brake, and tire status and displaying the vehicle's blind spots.

The results to date have been pretty impressive. The eighty trucks in North Carolina-based Cardinal Freight's fleet, for instance, went 4.5 million miles with no over-the-road accidents after installing collision-avoidance technology. "Without a doubt, the system has prevented accidents, and it has improved the overall performance of our drivers," says Doug Gilmer, the company's safety manager.[34] After sixty million miles with collision-avoidance systems, Columbus, Ohio-based Arctic Express's 460 refrigerated trucks reduced accidents by 75 percent. Comcar Industries realized a 66 percent drop in accidents after installing collision-warning systems on many of their trucks. U.S. Express slashed rear-end collisions by 57 percent. Soon, says Arctic Express president Richard Durst, "collision warning systems will be just like antilock brakes and reflective markings on trailers."[35]

You'd think these numbers would make it just a matter of time before collision avoidance systems are installed in cars as well—but so far the U.S. auto industry hasn't fully embraced these technologies. Chrysler says in-vehicle technologies will reduce collisions by as much as 80 percent, while GM is testing the concept at the company's Tech Center in Warren, Michigan.[36] Ford, however, apparently has no plans to deploy collision-warning systems anytime soon. "They give out a lot of false positives," says Gerry Conover, a Ford senior executive and ITS America board member. "They have them in F-111's [fighter planes] and the planes still run into mountains. There's also a great amount of work that has to be done just dealing with driver's reactions. Drivers do dumb stuff."

Besides, they may simply not like the new features. "People don't want their car to beep at them," says Chris Royan, president of Eaton/VORAD. "Drivers who follow too close don't like them because they'll beep at you. They'll beep all day long unless you drive safer." Indeed, some truckers despise VORAD systems and wouldn't use them if they weren't forced to by trucking companies intent on saving money by reducing accidents.

And then there's liability. A car maker that installs equipment explicitly billed as enhancing safety opens itself up to lawsuits if anything goes wrong. For instance, if you hit another vehicle because your collision warning system failed to notify you in time, is the manufacturer liable? To make this work, Congress would probably have to offer the auto industry some sort of temporary amnesty program limiting tort liability in such cases (much like they did the airline industry during the early days of its formation). For these reasons and others, we are likely to be in the latter portion of this decade or later before collision warning becomes a standard feature in vehicles—at least in America. Overseas deployment, however, could come earlier.

Indeed, Europe and particularly Japan are well ahead of the United States in mass deployment of smart cars. The European community is aiming for a 50 percent reduction in collisions by 2010; Sweden has a national target of zero collisions.[37] And the only way these numbers can be achieved is through widespread ITS adoption. Japan's first ITS-enabled vehicles rolled out of the assembly lines in 2003. Linked up to road sensors, they alert drivers to road obstructions through voice messages or dashboard text displays. The Japanese government believes ITS technologies, packed with risk warnings, improved driver perception, better information presentation, and collision-avoidance controls, could reduce accident fatalities by 30 to 40 percent.[38] The aggressiveness of foreign car companies in deploying collision avoidance will eventually spill over to the United States, say some ITS proponents. And despite Conover's skepticism, Ford itself is leading one of the most promising collision avoidance projects in the world. A feature called e-Proximity would enable cars to communicate with each other and automatically deploy countermeasures—such as dipping the nose of the car or extending its bumper—

when sensing impending impact. "We're developing systems so the cars won't collide," says Ron Miller, a Ford safety engineer.[39]

AUTOMATED HIGHWAYS: NO DRIVERS WANTED

In the 1939 World's Fair in New York, General Motors unveiled a "Futurama" exhibit with radio-controlled cars and an automated expressway. The fair also featured a film called "To New Horizons" that claimed that within twenty years cars would go 100 MPH and use radio signals to keep a safe distance from each other. Road congestion and traffic accidents, the narrator promised, would be eliminated.

Thus was born the idea of the automated highway, a concept that captured the imagination of futurists, engineers, and movie screenwriters for decades, from the years after World War II when GM was demonstrating vehicles with hands-off automatic steering, proximity warning systems, real-time traffic communication, and speed control, to KITT, the smart car on the television series *Knight Rider*. Science fiction aside, traffic engineers drool over the idea of automated highways for one simple reason: they can *triple* throughput on the road, improving traffic more than all the other strategies discussed in this chapter put together.

But after a half century and many billions of dollars worth of research, how close are we to driving—or, more to the point, *not* driving—on automated highways? To find out, I ventured out to UC Berkeley's Richmond Field Station to talk with Steve Shladover, a UC Berkeley professor, deputy director of Berkeley's PATH transportation program, and the world's leading authority on (and evangelist for) automated highways. Shladover has spent basically the past three decades figuring out how to make cars drive themselves. Sporting a short-sleeve button-down shirt, thick black glasses, and three pocket pens, Shladover looks like, well, exactly what he is: a geeky, middle-aged engineer. As he shows me the Richmond campus, he admits that progress on deploying automated highways has been slower than he would have thought. "I guess it was just the enthusiasm and naïveté of youth," he says, "but I would have been real surprised if you told me then that thirty years later, in the beginning of the twenty-first century, automated highways would still just be a gleam in the eye rather than a reality."

On the Richmond campus, adjacent to the largest earthquake testing structure in America, sits PATH's automated roadway test track. I was expecting the *Jetsons*. I got the *Beverly Hillbillies*. The "high-tech" on the weed-sprouting track consists of ninety-nine-cent magnets stuck in the road to keep cars on track. It turns out that most of the high-tech in automated highways goes into the vehicles themselves. In half a dozen maintenance buildings on the campus sit an assortment of vehicles ranging from eight

1997 Buicks to a twenty-foot truck rig to a huge snowplow truck, all with one thing in common: they're all loaded with sensors and computers that let them communicate with each other and magnets on the road.

The eight Buicks have cruised, driverless, at freeway speeds on real roads just four meters apart from each other, communicating wirelessly at fifty times a second—which Shladover calls "platooning"—accelerating; decelerating; stopping in total coordination; splitting so other vehicles can enter, then rejoining as one platoon. The occasion for this demonstration was DEMO '97 in San Diego, the first full-scale, multivehicle, smart-highway demo in a real-world setting. Viewing stands were erected so spectators could ogle at all the fancy technology as Carnegie Mellon University and Houston Metro teamed up to demonstrate how fully automated vehicles could operate in nonautomated traffic. A minivan and a Pontiac Bonneville equipped with collision warning, obstacle avoidance, and full automation technology automatically changed lanes.[40] Honda Motors demonstrated both an infrastructure-supported and an independent vehicle approach using two Honda Accords. Ohio State University showed an automated car passing a manually driven car.[41] "It was the best chance we ever had," Shladover says wistfully, "to bring automated highways to fruition."

Then, just a few months later, the federal DOT pulled the plug on funding for automated highways, choosing instead to place its bets on intelligent vehicles, which the department viewed as having better short-term prospects for deployment. The DOT's concerns with automated highways are shared by many ITS proponents. One big problem is the cost. Wiring the roads with sensors costs only $10,000 a mile. Equipping vehicles with the technology they'll need to communicate with those sensors, however, gets pricey—and it's an expense that car and light truck buyers (i.e., you and I) would have to bear themselves. Is it any wonder vehicle manufacturers are in no hurry to install it?

Car companies also wonder whether drivers will ever let a computer run their cars while they're inside. "Volkswagen managers showed their chairman car platooning at three feet apart," says Ford's Conover, " and he immediately shut the program down, saying consumers will be scared to death to give up control." Is he right? Perhaps. On the other hand, we also give up control every time we get on a plane, train, bus, or ferry. Moreover, we wouldn't have to give up driving ourselves altogether; the automated highways would mostly be targeted at commuters in congested urban areas.

Lastly, there's that nasty (and very American) litigation issue again. If you get in an accident today, you can't sue the car manufacturer unless you can prove the accident is a direct result of equipment malfunctions. But what if you get in an accident while the computer is driving? And who's liable if the accident is caused by the sensors in the road? These and any number of other questions need to be worked out before we'll find ourselves sitting back and enjoying coffee, a Danish, and the morning paper while our cars drive us to the office. "We can resolve them," says Shladover. "They're not nearly as unsolvable as people want to make them out to be."

At the very least, we can sketch a semirealistic timeline. The first real-world deployment (and here's one you won't see coming): snowplows. California has installed pavement magnets in a 1.5 mile stretch on Interstate 80 to help guide snowplows in a snowy mountain pass during periods of low (or no) visibility. It is in a developmental phase and not yet a standard. Next will come automated, driverless buses, which in fact are already shuttling passengers at a Tokyo theme park, an office complex in Rotterdam, and a park in London. Europe's CHAUFFEUR automation project has implemented "electronic tow-bar" operations for heavy trucks, in which a lead truck, driven by a human, is followed by a second truck under automated control using radar-sensing vehicle-to-vehicle communications. California is funding pilot projects to use similar technology to create the equivalent of "bus and truck trains." And cities like Boston are setting up Bus Rapid Transit (BRT) systems providing service throughout the city in dedicated tunnels and roadways: operations similar to, but much cheaper than, light rail. In time, these could be converted to automation.

Another possibility is automated truck-only lanes on interstate highways. Five years from now the majority of trucks are likely to come already wired with adaptive cruise control, collision avoidance, and the like; equipping them for automation wouldn't take that much more work. What makes transit buses and trucks particularly attractive as automation pilots is that they're both under professional maintenance regimes, so you wouldn't be dealing with the maintenance uncertainties of the general public.

The closest passenger cars are likely to get toward automation within the decade will be low speed automation systems that will take over vehicle control in congested stop-and-go traffic. And moving in parallel to projects aiming to increase the number of "driver-free" vehicles on the road are projects aiming to give us former drivers something to do while we're kicking back with that aforementioned coffee and Danish. "Telematics" providers are rushing to fill up drivers' in-car "dead time" by offering a host of digital, mobile services. Soon, your car will be able to give you information ranging from the location of the nearest amenities (such as gas stations, parking facilities, and restaurants), to real-time traffic information integrated with mapping data, to news, music, and audio books that are personalized according to your particular tastes and preferences.

THE FUTURE: TRANSPORTATION AGENCIES AS INFORMATION PROVIDERS

What do all these ITS innovations have in common? A relentless focus on improving the life of the average citizen. The performance of transportation departments, for instance, has historically been judged largely on two factors: 1) How many roads they build; and 2) How fast. "State and county DOTs really don't have a great self-interest in solving problems," says Samuel. "In terms of hard budget numbers, the worse the problem, the larger the likely budgetary allocation. The more the traffic problem is solved, the less their likely budgets. It's perverse incentives."

But those incentives are changing, because we're running out of space to build new roads and because taxpayers and legislators are wising up. "We won't keep on measuring performance simply by the number of miles built," says San Antonio's Irwin. "We'll need to squeeze more performance from the network through active management."

ITS will manage that trick by giving us, for the first time, accurate measures on a block-by-block basis of system performance on issues that directly affect drivers: how long it takes to clear accidents; travel time reliability; accuracy and thoroughness of traveler information. "Future DOTs," says Gaven McGill of the Oregon DOT, "will be judged more and more as information providers." It's a lesson that everyone involved in ITS—indeed, anyone involved in any aspect of transforming today's government—can never allow themselves to forget.

TIPS FOR PRACTITIONERS

- Squeeze more performance from the transportation network through active management. Roads should be viewed not as inert slabs of concrete requiring only occasional repair but as living systems requiring real-time management.
- Drivers, planners, and engineers all face huge information deficits. Eliminating or reducing them would help tremendously in solving various transportation problems. What's needed is accurate, timely information that's delivered electronically to a convenient place, be it home or office or the car itself, via PCs, handhelds, or onboard route navigation systems.
- One of the biggest barriers to providing real-time traffic data is that only a small percentage of roads are equipped with the infrastructure to capture the traffic flow. The solution to this problem is to wire the cars, not the roads. Turn cars, buses, and cell phones into traffic probes that can be used to capture real-time traffic data.
- Reduce congestion through the use of "peak-hour" pricing, which lets rush-hour drivers choose to pay the extra fee, choose a different mode of travel, or change their trip time. Convincing even a small percentage of drivers to choose the latter two options can greatly improve traffic flow.

5

G2B: The eGov Invisible Hand

Wired roads, wired cars, and wired drivers are neat—and we'll need them if we want to stave off massive traffic congestion—but it's not the only area where we should be able to reap tremendous economic benefits from digital government. A huge economic windfall will come from easing the government-to-business transactions that today eat up so much of businesses' time and resources.

Today's economy is complex, dynamic, and highly unpredictable. One minute Enron is the seventh-largest corporation in America, the next minute it's a bankrupt flame-out. In this environment, businesses value speed (so they can move products quickly to market) and certainty (so they can plan ahead while doing so). Unfortunately, these are two things they can seldom count on from government—though, as we will see, electronic government has the potential to radically improve both. How do you comply with a particular regulation? It depends which bureaucrat you happen to be talking to. Planning ahead? Public servants from Congressmen to state legislatures to regulators will invariably muck up your best-laid plans by changing the rules of the game overnight.

The costs to the private sector of public-sector red tape come in many forms: paperwork; attorney's fees; extra equipment; endless training seminars on health, safety, and sensitivity; wasted executive time; fees for the armies of consultants whose careers consist of telling companies how to comply with the latest EPA regulation or maneuver a building permit application through City Hall. In 2002, Americans spent about *8.22 billion* hours responding to government requests for information.[1]

Economist Thomas Hopkins has spent much of the last three decades calculating how much federal regulations cost the economy. He has held senior positions in the Ford, Carter, and Reagan administrations, including serving as deputy administrator for the White House office overseeing federal regulations. Now the dean of Rochester Institute of Technology's Business School, Hopkins estimates that the cost of federal laws alone exceeded $843 billion in 2000—or more than $8,000 per household![2] These costs, of course, hit small businesses the hardest. Firms with nineteen or fewer employees faced an average regulatory burden of $6,975 per employee, compared to $4,463 per employee for businesses with five hundred or more employees.[3] Adding state and local regulations brings the costs of regulation to nearly 17 percent of U.S. national income, or one out of every six dollars produced in America.[4]

Carrying such huge costs while trying to earn a profit is like running a marathon while wearing ten-pound ankle weights. Instead of focusing on satisfying customers, businesses—especially smaller ones—end up spending huge amounts of time and energy making sure they meet government's endless requirements. "Last year there were thirty-seven new federal and state regulations that affected small businesses," says Andrew Cory, president of Cory & Associates, an employee leasing firm. "It's a nightmare. You have to hire advisors and CPAs to help you. Then you have to pray they make no mistakes."[5]

Businesses interact with government in a variety of ways. First they have to register their company, obtain licenses and operating permits, renew them on an annual basis and, of course, pay taxes. Next, if you want to build anything, expand operations, or bring a new drug to the market, they'll need new permits and authorizations from a host of local, state, and federal agencies. Lastly, ordinary day-to-day operations mean complying with literally thousands of regulations of all stripes and variations and reporting on compliance to various government agencies.

But what if we could digitize all these processes and by doing so make transactions (paying fees, obtaining permits) easier; simplify and streamline reporting requirements and reduce the number of forms businesses have to fill out. "Conservatively," says Hopkins, "of my total regulatory estimates, you might be able to knock off 20 percent of the costs of compliance." That amounts to tens of billions of dollars in potential savings before you even factor in web-enabling state and local government regulatory processes. And it's state and local governments that have the greatest incentive to cut costs, because they compete against each other to attract companies. With capital, including human capital, more mobile than ever before, companies and individuals unhappy with their current situation can vote with their feet and move to a jurisdiction that will better address their

---

**FIVE WAYS DIGITAL GOVERNMENT
CAN EASE COMPLIANCE COSTS**

1) Provide information in one easy-to-access location.
2) Simplify and streamline reporting requirements.
3) Reduce the number of forms to fill out.
4) Make transactions (paying fees, obtaining permits) easier.
5) Help businesses understand what regulations apply to them, and how to comply with them.

---

needs. The cost of doing business in a given jurisdiction is one of the most important factors influencing a company's location choice—and the jobs and tax revenues that go with it.[6] Cities and states that provide a climate congenial to wealth creation will flourish; those that don't will languish.

One critical area of economic competitiveness where governments play a defining role is regulatory compliance. Governments can exercise numerous strategies to ease regulatory compliance burdens, including conducting cost-benefit analyses before issuing the rule change, subjecting regulations to periodic sunset reviews, making compliance less prescriptive and more performance-based and ending or reducing the regulation altogether. One of the least understood—but most powerful—weapons available for reducing compliance costs is information technology (see box). In time, the amount of government business that can be done online will be a key factor for a business deciding where to locate—or relocate. They'll want to get all their permits and licenses from one online location; spend less time filling out paperwork; file and pay taxes online; get emails informing them of legislative changes affecting their industry; obtain online regulatory compliance assistance; and so on. "Governments [that] learn to use technology to facilitate speed—those that become friction-free—will see their state prosper," says former Pennsylvania governor Tom Ridge. "And those that hinder it will stagnate."[7]

STARTING A BUSINESS

When Tom Ridge first became Pennsylvania's governor in 1995, the state government was bloated and inefficient; taxes were high; the IT systems were archaic and inadequate; and it was one of only two states lacking even a homepage. The Keystone State was about as tech-unfriendly as you could get.

Ridge set about changing this by appointing a blue-ribbon streamlining commission, cutting taxes, enacting workers' compensation reform and making technology a top priority of his administration. "It is clear to me," he said early on, "that technology will be the driving economic force in the new millennium."[8] Within a few years, the state went from being a digital laughingstock to being awarded *Government Technology* magazine's "Best of the Web" among state websites.

How did Ridge do it? For one thing, he set wildly unrealistic deadlines for putting services online—usually to the deep consternation of the agencies and IT department who had to implement them—and then held their feet to the fire to get it done. It didn't hurt that the 6-foot 3-inch, massively built Vietnam vet was an extremely imposing presence. "There's nothing like an order from the governor to focus the mind," said one of Ridge's former top aides.

On a hot August day in 1999, Ridge's cabinet received just such a directive: the state would be the first in the nation to create a single, integrated online entry point for new businesses. Ridge's goal was simple: "Make it easier to start a business in Pennsylvania than anywhere else." All well and good, but in the public sector, such a directive would typically be accompanied by a lax multiyear timeline for getting it done. Ridge gave his team a month. "The Governor's philosophy is that you don't give work groups lots of time to wring their hands about every little detail," said Charlie Gerhards, Pennsylvania's CIO at the time. "You get a test site out there, prove the concept and improve it later."

For any entrepreneur trying to start a business, deal with a network of vendors, or do business with a state or federal agency, navigating the bureaucratic backwaters of government regulations can dim even the brightest dreams. One of the biggest headaches is wading through the hundreds of separate license and permit categories issued by dozens of city, county, state, and federal agencies just to get permission to open your doors. No one knows how many would-be entrepreneurs give up rather than attempt to negotiate this regulatory maze involving anywhere from twenty to twenty-five different steps. In most states, even registering a business on the web would involve scores of searches, numerous telephone calls, visits to dozens of websites, and, if you're lucky, filling out a half-dozen or more forms you download from the web.

But such hassles are now ancient history in Pennsylvania. "PA Open4Business" was up and running thirty days after Ridge's announcement—and then upgraded six months after that. Since then it's been significantly enhanced under Governor Ed Rendell. Would-be entrepreneurs go through an automated interview process that asks questions like: "What is your business structure?" "What is your business activity?" "What are the names of your officers?" and so on. After the program has the data it needs, they're invited to register their business and pay the required fees by entering their credit card info. That's it. No standing in line at various agencies or waiting on hold; no filling out multiple forms and no entering the data again and again. A process that once took days or weeks now takes an hour or two at most.

Indeed, doing things faster for the customer has been the cornerstone of Pennsylvania's approach to digital government. Believing that speed-to-market is often the single most critical factor in determining which companies succeed and which companies fail, state leaders have made speed a key part of their economic development strategy.

The strategy worked. PA Open4Business averages more than 1.25 million hits a month. Over 25 percent of the state's businesses are registered users, and many visit the site after normal business hours—Sunday night is one of the more popular times—reinforcing the value of providing 24/7 service. The average entrepreneur saves hundreds of dollars by using the website to save time—which is money, after all. Multiply this by the state's 350,000 businesses and you're talking a serious chunk of change. Pennsylvania businesses can also log onto the site and view their records, change an office address or add a sales location. Eventually businesses will do all their state transactions on the site, including tax payments, permits, license renewals, and providing compliance information. Companies won't even need to know which agencies they're dealing with, and they'll never have to enter the same data twice; all their previous transactions will be stored in electronic briefcases.

PA Open4Business demonstrates digital government's potential impact on business formation: a nightmarish process of dealing with government made almost as easy as opening a bank account. It's the kind of high-impact, commonsense reform that should be replicated by every state and local government in the country.

SPEEDING PERMITTING: STREAMLINING BUSINESS EXPANSION IN SILICON VALLEY

Brian Moura, Assistant City Manager of San Carlos, California, had been through this before, but that didn't make it any easier to swallow. It was the mid-1990s and he and the city manager of neighboring Sunnyvale were being called to the carpet by one high-tech business executive after another for how long it took to get approvals for new facilities and business expansions in Silicon Valley. It wasn't that San Carlos and Sunnyvale were any worse than other nearby cities; they were just unlucky enough to be the only public-sector representatives at this meeting of "Joint Venture: Silicon Valley," a regional partnership of local businesses and

---

"IF YOU WOULD LIKE A TIME REBATE, PRESS 5 . . . "

The late 1970s saw the launch of a tax revolt sparked by California's Proposition 13. Similarly, the first decade of the twenty-first century may see the emergence of a *time* revolt, as people grow increasingly frustrated with standing in line to get their driver's license renewed or waiting on hold to talk to the IRS.

The old saying that "time is money" has never seemed truer. In the midst of time-saving technologies, people feel their day is stretched thinner than ever. Marianne Lewis, the Associate Dean for Innovation at the University of Cincinnati, calls it a "vicious cycle." Says Lewis, "The more we supposedly save time, the more we intensify the need for speed. We're constantly intensifying." Ironically, technology is sometimes seen as the villain in the time wars, as consumers of some of the poorly designed commercial and government electronic services chafe at how long they spend completing seemingly simple transactions.

Just as government has faced the demand for tax cuts by issuing tax rebates, government may now need to address a growing public desire for a "time rebate"—a single-minded focus on cutting down the time it takes to comply with government regulations and complete transactions by improving their quality. The challenge is to employ technologies more widely and more effectively by looking at government systems and processes from citizens' and businesses' point of view.

---

twenty-seven Valley cities. "There was lots of finger-pointing," Moura recalls. "The tech companies explained to us rather forthrightly that the delays were costing them millions of dollars and competitive advantage in the marketplace." One Intel executive stood up and said the delays were costing his firm three-quarters of a million dollars a day in lost revenue. "They almost begged us to find some ways to standardize and streamline the process," says Moura. Other observers described it more as an ultimatum: "Fix the problem or we're moving to more friendly environs."

After all, this was the mid-1990s. The tech boom was moving at warp speed. Silicon Valley firms couldn't expand fast enough to meet the demand for software, hardware, and anything else they could bring to market. Competition was fierce. Product cycles were down to as little as eight weeks. Chips, disk drives, software, routers, switches—all the stuff driving the American economy to record levels of growth—was being developed here. At the time, it seemed that nothing could slow the pace of growth, innovation, and product development in Planet Earth's famous and most prosperous valley.

Nothing, that is, except City Hall. Though the Valley was the world's digital nerve center, the revolution hadn't yet hit its governments, most of which were years behind the private sector. A few cities were still using index cards to keep track of building permits.

One well-gnawed bone of contention was that it took about nine weeks just to get architectural plan checks approved on construction projects. "The market was so competitive that we couldn't stay alive if we continued to be in plan check for the same length of time as our product cycle," said one manufacturer. "There was a huge amount of pressure to get things done faster."

Lessons Learned

Eventually, all the jawboning paid dividends; Silicon Valley: Joint Venture launched an unprecedented, eight-city effort to overhaul the Valley's building permit process.[9] The undertaking, christened "Smart Permit," began by unwriting much of the uniform building code, which was anything but uniform. Permit forms and processes across the region were standardized, so companies with multiple locations didn't face a maze of contradictory building rules. Next the permit process went online, to eliminate the countless wasted hours that architects, developers, and contractors spent enduring bumper-to-bumper traffic to reach City Hall, then waiting in line, paying for permit applications and driving back to work.

Each participating city put a different piece of the permit process online in order to maximize lessons learned. San Carlos, for instance, lets users check the status of their permit applications, view land parcel information, request inspections and submit comments on proposed developments all on the city website. Moura estimates that putting these four services online diverted about one-third of the calls that once went to staff.

Sunnyvale spent millions on a sophisticated site that lets homeowners and contractors obtain simple permits online. The city was so proud of its software that it went into business with a private company to market it to other cities. Then the city sat back and waited for the mad rush of architects, plumbers, electricians, contractors, developers, and homeowners that would surely take advantage of the new online services.

The rush didn't happen. Why not? "We didn't market to them," admits Shawn Hernandez, Sunnyvale's CIO. Three years after the service was launched, the adoption rate was still an anemic 6 percent. The lesson: If you build it—but don't market it—they won't come. "You can't just unveil something and expect everyone to know about it and use it," says Moura. "You have to publicize it, market it, do press releases. The problem is all this runs counter to the way many cities do things."

Well, not always. San Jose unveiled a full-blown marketing campaign for its online self-permitting application. Flyers were mailed to likely users; press releases were issued; the mayor did a press event at a local business. The city even came up with its own version of the Internet free-bie: Giving digital certificates worth $40 a pop to contractors who shifted to electronic permit applications. (There are lots of other ways govern-ments can market e-government services—even on a very low budget. The state of Florida does public service announcements. Michigan asks business and professional organizations to run advertisements about the e-government services in their newsletters.)

The next step is moving the permit counter to the field, something sev-eral Silicon Valley governments are exploring. The idea is to issue permits on the spot from handheld wireless devices. This way inspectors would no longer have to return to headquarters to type up their reports and con-tractors wouldn't have to wait weeks, days, or even hours for the permit. The likely result—more permits issued more quickly—should make the local Chamber of Commerce happy.

But what makes Smart Permit truly unique is that it cuts across gov-ernments. Collaboration of this scope—navigating the competing agen-das and priorities of the member governments and private firms in order to create one building code that applies to everyone, everywhere—is *re-ally, really* hard work; the meetings alone could try even the most dedi-cated public servant's patience. It would have been much easier for each city to go its own way, but that would have been much less valuable for the businesses they were aiming to serve. Ultimately, not pleasing the cus-tomer means not having a customer to please, a lesson the private sector has lived and died by for ages.

Efforts like Smart Permit can substantially reduce business costs. The state of Oregon estimates that its one-stop business process for obtaining approvals for building construction approvals, complete with online per-mitting and reporting, saves the construction industry 10 percent, or $100 million annually, in reduced delays and permit processing costs.[10] If gov-ernments at all levels were to implement digital streamlining initiatives like Oregon and Silicon Valley have done, the U.S. construction industry as a whole could save between $15 to $20 billion per year according to the National Conference of States on Building Codes and Standards.[11]

EASING COMPLIANCE COSTS: PROGRESS AT THE FEDERAL WORRYWART

Like many small business owners, Chris Miltimore works long hours, takes few vacations, and loses sleep worrying about meeting his fifteen-person payroll. Miltimore is the manager of Interstate Batteries, a family-owned, wholesale distributor in Troy, Michigan.

Several years ago, an inspector from OSHA, the Occupational Safety and Health Administration, was driving by the battery shop and decided to pop in for a surprise inspection. It was a visit Miltimore will never forget. "He starts asking me, 'Where's your "right to know" station, where's your emergency evacuation plan,'" explains Miltimore. "I told him 'I haven't the faintest idea what you're talking about.' Wrong answer. That's when he got out his inspection book and started taking notes."

Miltimore was cited for violating a slew of OSHA regulations, none of which he'd ever heard of. The inspector seemed especially exercised—even offended—that the shop lacked Material Safety Data Sheets (MSDS), documents that detail specific substances which may be dangerous, reactive, or flammable. OSHA regulations, Miltimore learned, require a MSDS write-up for *every one* of the four hundred materials his shop uses—even the laundry detergent used to wash employee overalls.

It took Miltimore six months and over 1,500 hours to get "OSHA-compliant." Now he's required to hand each new employee a seventy-page hazard awareness notebook—most employees promptly toss it in the circular file. While Miltimore considers some of the OSHA regulations simply inane, for example he was cited for lacking a written evacuation plan for a shop so small there's an exit within ten feet of you no matter where you stand, what really irked him was that he, like most small business owners, had almost no way of knowing he was breaking any rules until the inspector paid a visit. "There are so many regulations and they're so complex," he says. "It's impossible to know whether you're in compliance unless you're a large corporation with a battery of lawyers and safety specialists."

Created by Congress in 1970 to protect the "safety of every worker to the maximum extent possible," OSHA is the nagging parent to American business. In pursuit of the laudable aim of protecting workers' health, OSHA issues over four thousand detailed regulations covering everything from slippery floors to proper railing height. All in all, America's federal worrywart slaps businesses with about $100 million a year in fines and penalties, half of which are simply for not keeping forms correctly.[12] To be sure, some of what OSHA does is necessary, but the agency had for some time a reputation for being overbearing, overzealous, and overly punitive.[13] In fact, if a poll were taken asking businesses which federal agency they feared the most, OSHA would be topped only by the dreaded IRS. "Our members have a mortal fear that OSHA will come in and shut them down," says Holly Wade of the National Federation of Independent Business (NFIB). "They've all heard stories about OSHA raiding a business; a business getting shut down for having an extension cord under the rug, that kind of thing."

Stories like that of Saul Herscovici, president of Power Engineering and Manufacturing in Waterloo, Iowa, who was fined $2,500 for putting a power cord on a spool and hanging it on a hook. Or of the New Hampshire roofing company that was inspected three times in a single week. After finding no violations on the first two visits, the OSHA inspector returned yet again and recorded an alleged violation holding his home video camera out the window with one hand while steering with the other. Incredibly, it was the business owner, not this fanatical inspector, who was hit with a $10,000 fine. The roofers were just lucky they weren't doubling their pleasure with Doublemint; OSHA's Asbestos Standard bans roofers from chewing gum on the job.

He's from the Government—He's Here to Help

Ed Stern is one of those government "bureaucrats" who business owners like Chris Miltimore believe cause them such grief. Stern has spent most of his thirty plus-year federal civil service career at OSHA. He has a wife and two kids and drives a Buick Century to and from his middle-class home in the Maryland suburbs. He uses lots of acronyms in conversation, speaks of assistant secretaries of federal agencies with the same reverence nonpolitical people might reserve for David Letterman, and apologizes profusely when he can't remember the precise number of a decades-old regulatory statute. In short, Stern is the prototypical federal bureaucrat, except for one thing: for the better part of a decade, he has been on a single-minded quest to convince his agency to fundamentally change its approach toward business.

When Stern first joined OSHA almost two decades ago, it didn't take him long to adopt its worldview. "I quickly absorbed OSHA's culture," recalls Stern; "'We write the rules and it's the people's problem to follow them.' There tends to be somewhat of an antibusiness, pro-enforcement mentality that pervades the agency." Then he had an experience that forever changed his thinking. Stern's counterparts over at the Small Business Administration (SBA) were battling to get OSHA to reduce the billions of dollars a year small businesses were spending complying with government regulatory and compliance burdens. Prodded by the SBA, Stern actually began *listening*—for the first time, really—to the businesses that were forced to comply with OSHA's myriad regulations.

"Some of us began to realize that many businesses don't even begin to know they have health or safety problems," explains Stern. "Most businesses will try to do the right thing, but they don't even know which rules apply to them or how to comply." A bit of a computer geek, he began searching for a technology that could pack all the knowledge of OSHA scientists, engineers, industrial hygienists, doctors, nurses, economists, and lawyers—information that wasn't available to businesses until they got in trouble—into publicly available software. He finally hit on something called "expert systems," an offshoot of the artificial intelligence ma-

TECHNOLOGY FOCUS: EXPERT SYSTEMS

Introduced in the mid-1980s by Stanford scientist Ed Feigenbaum, expert systems are a form of artificial intelligence, meaning the computer makes decisions in real-life situations that would otherwise be carried out by people.

When devising an expert system, you must first break down a decision-making problem into all the small pieces (or facts) that contribute to making the decision. These facts or "rules of thumb" are called "heuristics," which simply means a step in the decision-making process.[a] An example of a heuristic is: "If the red light is flashing, then the car security alarm is on." Via a flowchart-like process, this knowledge is then converted into a series of statements of facts and a conclusion with a defined syntax, termed "rules."[b] An example of a rule is: "If you drive an expensive car and you drive badly, you will pay more insurance."

A piece of software called an "inference engine" then processes the logic, pulls all the rules together and parses through them each time you respond to a question until it gets all the information it needs to draw a conclusion. If there is more than one solution, they can be ordered by *confidence* value or likelihood. The desired result is an interaction with the computer that mimics the interaction someone might have with a real person.

Because they come closer to an actual human interaction, expert systems tend to be much more useful than Frequently Asked Questions (FAQs), or keyword or database searches. For example, expert systems have the ability to rank more than one recommendation based on confidence value. So if there isn't a perfect match, it could give the best match, whereas a database search would simply yield no recommendation.

It's important to make sure to pick the right problems or applications for expert systems. If the knowledge doesn't exist, or if the problem is too big or requires human insight or novel solutions, then an expert system is usually not the right solution. They work best where the problems are manageable and well-defined, and where the knowledge is factual and already exists but just needs to be captured.

A number of Fortune 500 companies can attest to the value of expert systems. Canadian Railways used them for diagnosing diesel locomotive engines. The expert system was able to predict when things would break on the rails—the biggest maintenance expense for railway companies—enabling the company to do preventive maintenance and save an estimated $300 million a year. Dupont Industries used expert systems to disseminate problem-solving knowledge throughout the company. Savings: over $1 billion.

a. Mario DiStasio, Roland Droitsch, and Larry Medsker, "Web-Based Expert Systems for *elaws*," *Failure and Lessons Learned in Information Technology Management*, vol. 3 (1999), 70.

b. There are two main types of inference engines: backward and forward chaining. The backward chaining engine is goal-driven, meaning it has a goal that it is trying to reach or determine to be true or false. A forward chaining inference engine is typically data-driven—the rules are tested based on available data. If the data needed is not already in the system, then the user is asked to supply it.

nia of the 1970s and 1980s. Expert systems provide sophisticated ways of capturing and organizing facts and knowledge by "cloning" the knowledge of experts to provide answers to tricky but routine problems. They seek to mimic intelligent human interaction by asking questions, providing information, and directing the user to the best answers or most appropriate resources based on their responses (see box on page 111 for more information on expert systems). Often, the user may not even realize that he's not communicating with a real person.

Expert Assistance

Over a number of years, Stern and his team built ten expert systems, termed "Expert Advisors," that provide online or downloadable customized compliance assistance for various OSHA regulations. To test the system, I went into OSHA's Hazardous Awareness Advisor and pretended I was a restaurant owner. Based on my answers to a dynamically created series of questions about my hypothetical restaurant, the computer provided me with a summary of hazards likely to be present at my restaurant, along with strategies to control them and a checklist of OSHA standards applicable to my workplace. For example, I was told my fire extinguishers needed maintenance, my workplace needed a hazard communication program, and that I might want to have my employees wear cut resistant gloves when preparing food in order to prevent injuries from sharp knives. The entire process took less than an hour.

Manually going through OSHA's myriad regulations, by contrast, and trying to figure out which ones applied to me—never mind how to comply with them—could have taken days or weeks. "It's like the difference between a medical librarian and a medical doctor," says Stern. "The librarian will help get you a lot of information to read. But when you need expert help, you ask the doctor."

The greatest savings from expert advisors accrue to small businesses; thanks to the software they can forgo the costs of hiring compliance consultants. Businesses would have to spend up to $4,000 for a written equivalent of the reports that the advisors generate in minutes. OSHA estimates savings to small businesses from the Hazard Awareness Advisor alone amount to around $272 million over five years.[14]

The business community's positive response to the Expert Advisors prompted OSHA's parent agency, the Department of Labor (DOL), to build close to two dozen additional advisors on its Employment Laws for Workers and Small Businesses (*elaws*) website, covering topics ranging from the Family Medical Leave Act to Veterans' Employment Preferences.

For each *elaw* application, there are two advisors: one tailored to employees and another to employers. "For years and years," says Roland Droitsch, the now retired thirty-five-year career federal employee who spearheaded the initiative while Labor's Deputy Assistant Secretary for Policy, "I was horrified that we as a huge regulatory agency weren't able to do the first duties of a regulatory agency: Provide easily understandable information to businesses about what they needed to do to comply and then help them comply."[15]

The expert systems solve this problem in a way that can even be better than talking to a "live" customer service representative on the phone. Why? Because with expert systems, information and answers can be tailored to the particular circumstances and characteristics of the firm. And—in contrast to agencies like OSHA or the IRS—expert systems always give consistent answers. "Previously," says Stern, "people were getting different answers from different people, which meant a business might think they were in compliance but [it] really wasn't." What's more, advisor programs are available 24/7; the assistance is based on the combined knowledge of dozens of subject-area experts; and, most importantly, you have a paper trail to fall back on the next time an OSHA inspector comes snooping around your workplace. "It doesn't make the rules go away," says Stern, "but it makes it much easier to figure out how they apply to your actual situation."

Overcoming Obstacles

Getting OSHA and DOL to fully embrace electronic compliance assistance was an uphill battle for Stern, Droitsch, and other supporters.[16] Many OSHA bureaucrats see their mission as enforcing workplace rules against recalcitrant businesses rather than helping them comply with regulations; what fun is working for a regulatory agency if you can't nail malefactors every once in a while? "Our main line to business was always 'We publish the rules in the Federal Register, go look 'em up,'" says Droitsch. "The softies at the agency went out and printed up a pamphlet. That's the extent of the compliance assistance we gave."

Reformers faced another human problem: namely, that the status and authority of OSHA bureaucrats are based on their access to specialized information that's largely inaccessible to the average business. Some inspectors don't like "expert advisors" for the same reasons that many doctors don't like health care websites; leveling the playing field undermines the "expert's" information monopoly. How would you like to be the OSHA inspector whose report is challenged by a business owner armed with printouts based on the accumulated knowledge of dozens of lawyers and economists? "There's always the chance that a compliance officer could be embarrassed," says Stern. "So some people at the agency don't want to put this power into the hands of the public."

Despite the bureaucratic fear factor, the compelling results from early trials mean that nearly all the regulations administered by OSHA and DOL will eventually have their own electronic compliance assistance advisors. An employer will log onto a website, answer a number of questions—the size of his business, the state it resides in, whether it has government contracts, etc.—and the program will tell him exactly which regulations apply to his business, list specific advisors relevant to the firm, and suggest the best order for using them. Any business will be able to get a complete list of all the health, safety, and labor requirements it must comply with, as well as videos and other tools that explain how to do so.

These capabilities, along with many others, will, in time, all be available on the Business Gateway, a Business Compliance one-stop shop portal created by the U.S. SBA. The site, at www.businesslaw.gov, has more than twenty thousand links to federal, state, local, and legal organizations arranged around thirty-nine topics from licensing and permitting to exporting.[17] The SBA estimates the website saves businesses over $526 million by reducing the amount of time and money they must spend finding the regulations that apply to them, understanding their meaning, and then ultimately complying with them (see figure 5.1).[18]

Figure 5.1. Benefits to Business from SBA's Business Compliance One Stop
Source: Small Business Administration.

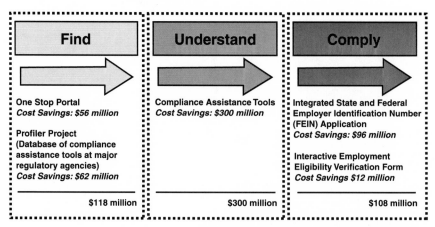

Find

Understand

Comply

One Stop Portal
Cost Savings: $56 million

Profiler Project
(Database of compliance assistance tools at major regulatory agencies)
Cost Savings: $62 million

$118 million

Compliance Assistance Tools
Cost Savings: $300 million

$300 million

Integrated State and Federal Employer Identification Number (FEIN) Application
Cost Savings: $96 million

Interactive Employment Eligibility Verification Form
Cost Savings $12 million

$108 million

ESTIMATED ANNUAL COST SAVINGS $526 million

BUSINESS SAVES MONEY FROM E-COMPLIANCE

Michael Ribaudo, the physician-CEO of Surgical Synergies, runs a $25 million a year company that operates seven surgical ambulatory centers in the St. Louis area. For years, complying with federal regulations, particularly OSHA regulations, had been a major pain in the neck for Dr. Ribaudo. "OSHA training and compliance issues have been getting more complex, not less, over the years," explains Dr. Ribaudo.

Most frustrating to Ribaudo was the cost of compliance. He had to devote a full-time person at each of his seven centers just to manage the compliance process—compiling and updating the material safety data sheets (MSDS), making sure all the employees took the required OSHA classes, and preparing compliance reports. All in all, Ribaudo estimates OSHA compliance was costing his firm about $400,000 a year.

Desperate to reduce these costs, Ribaudo installed a whole suite of customized web-based compliance tools—covering everything from training to process management. The goal: slash the administrative, consultant, training, legal, and paperwork costs involved in complying with government regulations.

The software provided Surgical Synergies with instant access to a continuously updated database of MSDS sheets online. All compliance training at his centers is now done on the web, eliminating the need for offsite training and the travel associated with it. Savings: 98 percent less than the company's previous costs. Ribaudo believes there will be another advantage to web-based compliance tools: increased compliance. "You'll start seeing more compliance because this simplifies things a lot."

TECHNOLOGY AND RETHINKING REGULATION

Electronic government also enables the public sector to fundamentally rethink the way it regulates in certain areas. For example, thanks to the Internet it is now much easier for consumers themselves to obtain detailed and user-friendly information about the quality and safety of a host of services and products than was ever before possible. Evaluations of third-party rating organizations covering everything from nursing homes to consumer products can be accessed on the web. Consumers can tap into the knowledge of other users through eBay-like reviews. In their 2003 book, *The Half-Life of Policy Rationales: How New Technology Affects Old Policy Issues*, Fred Foldvary and Daniel Klein argue that these and other technologically driven innovations have reduced—or, in some cases, all but eliminated—justifications for command-and-control regulation in certain social or economic areas.[19]

Regulation through Sunlight

One implication is that traditional regulatory approaches—detailed pre-scriptive rules and suffocating bureaucratic controls—can, in certain in-stances, be replaced with "accountability through sunlight." Take restaurants. Many state and local restaurant regulations are wholly un-related to the actual cleanliness of the restaurant and often no one even looks at 90 percent of the paperwork the state requires restaurants to fill out each year. Instead of burying restaurant owners in mounds of de-tailed rules, regulations, and paperwork, why not simply post all restau-rant health inspections prominently on the web? Let customers decide for themselves whether they want to carve into a prime rib at a steak-house cited two months earlier for rodents in the kitchen. A failed health inspection grade is a far more effective way to get a restaurant to clean up its kitchen than a $200 fine. The day New York City first posted restaurant Health Department inspections on the web, it received 45,000 hits an hour on its website. Because the inspections are available by wireless devices, New Yorkers can check a restaurant's health inspection right before they decide to sit down for dinner.

A sunlight approach works best in areas where consumers equipped with more information might alter their behavior—for example, by shunning a business—and thereby cause the business in question to modify its behavior in order to avoid losing customers. These con-sumers could also be employees or potential employees, who would factor in the accountability information in choosing one employer over another. Consider workplace safety. As was discussed earlier, OSHA regulations are so numerous and complex that they're practically in-comprehensible to any business lacking a cadre of high-priced lawyers and safety compliance officers. This causes many small businesses to simply ignore most OSHA regulations and hope they won't get caught. With 6.5 million workplaces in the United States and only several thou-sand OSHA inspectors, the odds of getting inspected are about one in one hundred. The upshot is that in millions of workplaces many safety procedures that might actually enhance workplace safety (and even cut workers' compensation insurance costs for businesses) are never adopted. Instead of micromanaging workplace safety, what if OSHA simply published statistics on workplace accidents for every company in the United States, giving each business a safety grade according to a set of agreed-upon standards for each major industry?[20] Workers could see which companies are serious about workplace safety and which aren't, and decide for themselves whether they want to work in a fac-tory that routinely exposes employees to unsafe chemicals. Businesses would be more likely to take safety seriously if they knew that every potential employee could easily compare their safety records with all their competitors.

To be sure, in areas where employment opportunities are very limited, there won't be enough other jobs to go around to make the threat of choosing a different employer credible enough. This doesn't mean, however, that regulation by sunlight wouldn't work. In such circumstances, pressure from existing employees and negative publicity from the local news media could provide the prod needed for the business to clean up its act.

There's one major pitfall to regulation through sunlight. If the information collected doesn't actually tell you much about the company's safety or quality, "sunlight" can obscure more than it reveals. Particularly in the environmental arena, some governments have made the mistake of focusing on inflammatory, but ultimately meaningless, inputs instead of outcomes when crafting sunlight rules. For example, since the late 1980s, companies have been forced to report annual release levels of toxic chemicals into something called the Toxic Release Inventory (TRI). This disclosure requirement, while well-meaning, is mostly based on an output—chemicals released—that may have little or nothing to do with reducing environmental harm or health risks. Moreover, the inventory provides no guidance to help people evaluate relative risks. Governments seeking to replace regulation with sunlight need to figure out whose perspective they should be taking—a potential employee? a potential customer? both?—and focus on the types of information most useful and relevant from that perspective. Otherwise, "sunlight" is just another adversarial, top-down attack on businesses and a misleading and possibly inflammatory source for customers of those businesses.

No More "Mother May I?"

The falling cost and growing ubiquity of sensors and other new detection and metering technologies might also enable governments to rethink regulatory approaches. Currently, whether you want to open a barber shop, expand your factory, drill an oil well, or conduct a host of other commercial activities, in most cases you'll need permission from the government before you do it—or risk a fine and the closure of your business. Michael Williams, the chief regulator of Texas's oil and gas industry, believes technological advances could change this.

The Texas Railroad Commission (TRRC), which (go figure) regulates the state's oil and gas industry, encourages companies to obtain their drilling permits online. Over 15,000 drilling permits are issued electronically each year, saving drillers about $200 per permit, halving the agency's process-ing time, and reducing the average time it takes to get a permit from four days to one. Oil and gas giant Conoco Industries claims the system saves the company $1,350 a month in consulting costs alone.

Williams wants to go beyond web-enablement and use technology to fun-damentally transform the commission's regulatory process. Today, most ac-tions taken by oil and gas companies have to be preapproved by the TRRC after the companies provide reams of data. "Everything an operator does, they have to get permission from us first," says Williams. "It's sort of like a minitrial." Eventually, he believes, the RRC will be able to capture the data it needs in real-time at the oil wellhead and simulate what's likely to happen if a well is drilled. Once this happens, the RRC can move the process from a "Mother may I" model to one in which it lets companies move forward without prior approval, knowing they can be stopped later by the Commis-sion. "We'll allow you to go forward based on your best judgment," explains Williams, "we collect the data, and then we stop you if, for example, you're taking more than your share of natural gas from the ground."

Remote, real-time monitoring like this could in time replace inspection-based regulation in numerous areas. Take air emissions. The federal gov-ernment has called for reducing the time it takes for the public to be noti-fied of a chemical discharge. One way to accomplish this would be by installing monitoring devices that provide continuous, real-time emis-sions information on the fence lines or smokestacks of regulated compa-nies. This would allow environmental agencies to switch to a results-based regulation model: Rather than provide detailed instructions on how to clean up pollution, governments could simply set goals and let compa-nies decide how to meet them—offering expedited permitting, reduced reporting and record-keeping requirements, and fewer inspections to en-courage businesses to install the sensors.[21]

In some areas, there are also strong economic incentives for companies to voluntarily use intelligent sensors. For example, to make workplaces safer and thereby reduce worker-compensation costs, companies could put sensors on factory floors to alert people to slippery surfaces and warn workers to wear hard hats in dangerous areas.

Purge First, Digitize Second

> E-government should not be just about digitizing red tape, but about cutting much of it.
>
> —Vicente Fox, president of Mexico

Online business licensing, e-permitting, and e-reporting, can go a long way toward reducing the costs governments impose on business. For some regulations and licensing requirements, however, there's an even more cost-effective solution: elimination. Governments shouldn't web-enable a license or reporting requirement that shouldn't exist in the first place. "Regulatory burdens will be imposed, hopefully, in a more 'humane' way as a result of web-enabling reporting and monitoring systems, and government will be able to torment employers in a less obnoxious way," says former Indianapolis mayor Stephen Goldsmith. "I don't think, however, that that takes the place of eliminating outdated systems and regulations."

"Eliminate what you can, digitize what you can't" was the approach taken by Florida governor Jeb Bush when he put all the state's 150-odd license renewal transactions on the web. When Bush became governor, one out of every sixteen Floridians had a license with the state's Department of Business Processing and Regulation (DBPR), which issues nearly 1 million licenses annually, covering everything from realtors to plumbers. Back then, the agency had a reputation for dreadful customer service; businesses had to make their way through two hundred phone numbers and hundreds of forms. About one-third of the calls to the department (1 million annually) went unanswered. License renewals took weeks to process and, even paying the agency for licenses was a major hassle. "No one wanted to do business with us," says Kim Binkley-Seyers, then Florida's DBPR secretary. "Our technology, procedures and requirements were all outdated." So Binkley-Seyers set about to reengineer the licensing process in order to create, in effect, one-stop online shopping.[22]

Rather than simply move the current processes online, Florida used web-enablement as a once-in-a lifetime opportunity to completely rethink and redesign the state's business licensing and registration process. All the old job descriptions and positions went away. Why? They were no longer relevant in an environment where the department's primary interface with the business community would be the web. Every employee had to apply for a new position, most of which hadn't previously existed. "I don't understand how people can just implement the technology without redesigning their business processes," says Seyers.

The Florida model is simple. Before you web-enable any state government requirement, you ask two questions. First, do we need to do this in the first place? If the answer is no, the requirement should be eliminated. If the answer is yes, then you ask: What's the least intrusive, most efficient way of regulating this entity or collecting the information or fees?

Take restaurant regulation. Florida has long required restaurants to submit voluminous plans. "The state was asking for staggering levels of information that were wholly unrelated to making sure the restaurant was clean," explains Skip Stitt, one of the consultants who worked on the project. "Moreover, the data they received was never used for anything." Fully 99 percent of the plans were approved without change or comment. Web-enabling the process might save businesses time and money, but they'd still be emailing forms that weren't really necessary. Stitt calls this "doing really stupid things at the speed of light." Instead, Florida is getting rid of many of the requirements altogether, eliminating tens of thousands of business hours' worth of pointless work through that one decision alone.

The state also radically improved on the previously dismal customer service at DBPR. More than 98 percent of all calls in to the department are now answered, and instead of waiting weeks to get their renewal processed by mail or in person, anyone can renew their license in only minutes online. Many Florida businesses have chosen the latter option. In the first year after going online, 60 percent of all real estate and construction licenses were processed on the web.

THE STEALTH REVOLUTION

Electronic government isn't typically the first thing that comes to politicians' minds when they're debating what government can do to promote economic development and create a favorable business climate. It's never going to grab headlines or engender fierce opposition (or defense) from impassioned interest groups. It doesn't usually involve a ribbon-cutting ceremony. But that doesn't make it any less potent as an economic development weapon (see table 5.1).

Just ask Jennifer Griffiths, the safety manager for the Monterey Bay Aquarium. She came to Monterey from Shell Oil in Illinois, where she helped gas stations meet safety and FDA requirements. That meant she was used to keeping up with a crushing load of detailed and changeable regulations. "Many times we'd have to contact our lawyer" to find out which regulations applied in which situations, she said. She estimated that a full 25 percent of her working hours were spent hunting for regulations. She would routinely pay $300 to $1,200 dollars for regulatory reports. "At Shell, maybe one guy would get [the regulations], but he doesn't circulate it to other people," she recalled. In order to find the regs, you had to know the right guy to ask. "Sometimes I found out the guy didn't even work for Shell anymore! It was just going to an empty box." In her seven years with Shell, Griffith picked up snippets of information here, a few useful regulation-hunting tips there—and mostly a realization that it was a major waste of her time.

When she moved to California, suddenly she found that all this information was online. "In California, all I do is go to one website, put in the

Table 5.1. Potential Impacts of Various GtoB Services

Government-to-Business Interaction	Digital Capabilities	Impact	Source of Cost Savings/Benefits
Registering	One-stop shopping	Businesses provide information to government only once instead of many times	Time savings Personnel savings
	Expert systems	Helps businesses understand *what* regulations apply to them	
Licensing	Online licensing applications	Slashes time it takes to get a professional license from weeks to hours	Postage costs Processing costs Time savings
Permitting	Submit permit request online Check status of permit online	Faster processing of permit applications	Speed time-to-market Time savings Personnel savings
		Improved visibility into government approval process	Improve planning
Reporting	Expert systems	Makes it easier to understand *how* to comply with regulations	Reduce professional fee costs Time savings
	Sensors	Provide real-time emission and safety information	Reduce paperwork costs

subject area, and get all the information I need," she noted. In Illinois, state, federal, and local laws often conflicted; California uses its web-enablement process to streamline and coordinate its regulations so there are no such conflicts. A commission meets every time a federal law affecting safety regulation comes out to make sure that California law doesn't clash with federal law. And those $1,200 regulatory reports? Griffith gets them delivered for free over the Net.

The technology-enabled reforms outlined in this chapter are quiet, but they're crucial in creating a legal and regulatory environment that lets markets work faster and more efficiently. They have the potential to save time, money, and headaches for millions of businesses—enhancing the prosperity of all American citizens as a result.

TIPS FOR PRACTITIONERS

- Set wildly unrealistic deadlines for putting services online. Your employees might hate you but the public will love you and the job will get done.
- To help gain outside support for e-government initiatives, quantify the potential business savings from government-to-business transactions.
- Don't assume that "if you build it they will come." They won't—unless, that is, you adopt aggressive strategies to boost take-up rates, such as marketing or offering financial incentives.
- Use the process of web-enablement to transform regulatory processes and even how you regulate altogether. Explore, for example, how technological advances might allow for alternatives to traditional command-and-control regulation.
- When streamlining regulations, ask first "Do we need this regulation at all?" before asking how to make it efficient. Also explore the use of "sunlight" to let the shame factor and potential loss of customers do the regulating for you.

III

DIGITAL DEMOCRACY

6

The Transparent State

A popular Government without popular information, or the means of
acquiring it, is but a prologue to a farce or a tragedy; or perhaps both.
Knowledge will forever govern ignorance; and a people who mean to
be their own Governors, must arm themselves with the power which
knowledge gives.

—James Madison

Freedom, accountability and trust in government institutions all rely
on easy and free access to public information. "Transparency" keeps
government accountable to citizens who know what, how, and why
their government is doing what it's doing. But just making vital information publicly available doesn't mean much if we have to go to great
investigative lengths to find it—and by the time we do find it, it's already out of date. We shouldn't need a lobbyist to navigate our way
around government. We shouldn't be forced to file a Freedom of Information Act request to find out how our government agencies are performing.

In the late 1990s, the Los Angeles-based Reason Foundation undertook a
study of efficiency across twelve service categories in the fifty largest cities.
The study required obtaining detailed but, in theory at least, publicly available budget information from each city. Collecting this information should
have taken just a few months' worth of phone calls and emails. It ended up
taking three years. At great expense, the think tank was forced to send researchers to camp out at dozens of city halls across the nation and practically beg for the information. "We learned that 'public information' does

not always mean 'publicly available,'" explains foundation vice president Adrian Moore, who led the project:

> In some cities, the only public copies of past city budgets were housed at the library, where they were sometimes misplaced or missing. Individual departments often didn't know very basic facts like how many acres of parks or miles of streets are in the city. Even worse were those who flat out refused to give us simple public data, forcing us to go over their heads. The most disturbing thing is that we had these problems even though we knew exactly what information we needed and where it should reside. A citizen less versed in city government structure and operations would likely never even find the right person to ask and give up in disgust.

Horror stories like this still occur, however, they're becoming a little less frequent in some countries thanks to the rise of the web. In the dozen plus years that governments have been posting information online, the Internet has become one of the most important tools in the centuries-long quest for achieving more transparent government. Today's "Netizens" expect important public data to be not only available online but also packaged in a user-friendly format that schoolchildren and their parents alike can easily navigate. And public officials, believe it or not, are taking action, moving from a reactive model of simply responding to freedom of information requests to proactively putting all kinds of government information on the web. The state of Virginia, for example, now offers online access to official public meeting announcements. The Food and Drug Administration's website offers transcripts from its expert drug advisory committee meetings, including presentations from drug companies seeking approval of their products and the FDA's assessment of their claims. A Connecticut government website lets citizens follow arcane state debt financing by tracking every bond dollar spent by the state over a five-year period, learning when, where, why, and how their tax dollars are being spent.

Transparency is moving beyond displaying government documents to giving citizens access to government databases themselves. The Rhode Island Department of Health lets residents search an online database of health licenses of doctors, dentists, other health professionals, hospitals, laboratories, and even restaurants, to view license status and any disciplinary actions taken in the last ten years. Florida's health care agency ranked all 680 of the state's nursing homes based on their history of violations over the previous four years and posted the guide on the web. And it's this level of information distribution that heralds the sort of vast changes that Internet-enabled transparency could bring to the future functioning of American government. Let's consider one important subject: how transparency will affect the way our governments create their budgets.

THE BENEFITS OF SUNSHINE

Few people outside government pay much attention to it, but from a citizen's perspective, the process of putting together a budget is one of the most vital things governments do. The budget is a tangible demonstration of government's intentions and priorities—it's where policy is made and tax dollars are divvied up. But trying to understand the process is, for most lay people, an utterly hopeless task. Sure, any citizen can go to city hall or the state capitol and pick up a copy of the two-volume, phone book-sized documents that constitute her government's budget, but for all her ability to understand them, they might as well be written in Old High Norse. Government budgets are mysterious, unintelligible, jargon-filled, dominated by insiders, and loaded with accounting tricks, sleight-of-hand, and smoke and mirrors.

Nowhere is the inaccessible nature of the budget process more pronounced than in New York State, whose $101 billion state budget is decided behind closed doors by three people: the governor, the speaker of the state assembly, and the senate president. It isn't just the public that's kept mostly in the dark; most state legislators are little more than distant spectators themselves. "They try to minimize any public discussion of the final budget bill," says one longtime Albany insider. "Most legislators don't even see it before they vote on it. The only transparency is after the fact."

For years, Donna Arduin, in her capacity as deputy budget director for New York governor George Pataki, was a key player in New York's secretive budget process. "Few people there knew most of the budget's components," she recalls. "Almost everything was hidden." When she became Florida's budget director, she couldn't have faced a more different environment. Florida's far-reaching "sunshine laws" made it renowned for open government. And Arduin's new boss, Jeb Bush, was committed to making Florida government more transparent and performance-based. (One of Bush's first acts was to start publishing both his and all his cabinet members' daily calendar online.) The combination of Florida's penchant for open government and Bush's penchant for performance management resulted in the first American state budget specifically formatted and designed for the web—what Bush dubbed his "e-budget." The e-budget site offered indexes that let users identify budget data according to functional area and agency. The front page divided appropriations into a few obvious categories, from "education" to "smaller, more effective government." A sidebar let you search the budget, show appropriations by agency, email questions, or surf a glossary and Frequently Asked Questions (FAQ) page. Viewers could also compare the governor's recommended budget with the budget the legislature actually approved. And each policy area came with its own FAQ page; you could find out everything from which agency monitors Florida's lawyers to whether Medicare will cover your fifteen-year-old's braces. Florida is working hard to earn its reputation as the "Sunshine State."

"For our first e-budget, we made decisions based on what we thought people would want to know," says Arduin, now the finance director for California governor Arnold Schwarzenegger. "But for the second one, we linked the site to the budget mainframe system and let the user decide what information they wanted to see, and in what form." Viewers could choose general overviews of state spending in different policy areas, or drill down into detailed data: clicking on the line item "Corrections," for instance, leads you to a longer inventory of subcategories, from inmate health services to probation supervision. Clicking any of these revealed still more details. "Technology," says Arduin, "lets us put the numbers out there and cut them several ways. You can add them across or up and down."

The budget design also allowed users to compare actual results to desired results. The budget for "adult male custody operations," for example, compared the number of prison escapes in a given year with the number desired by the legislature. This degree of openness, of course, entailed certain political risks. "I said, 'Governor, there will be information out there that's ugly. Are you sure you want to do this?'" recalls Arduin. "He cut me off and said, 'We can't be defensive. We need to provide this information. It's our job.'"

Many other Florida government officials and lawmakers weren't as anxious as Bush to shed so much light on the state's budget and performance. "We were hit from all sides," says Arduin. Agency heads didn't like it because it laid bare to everyone—including the much-feared appropriators—every aspect of their departments' performance. Lawmakers, who might be expected to favor the e-budget (if only to use the information to beat up on agency heads), were a mixed lot. Some old bulls feared e-budgeting's democratizing effect could reduce their power, much of which derived from their monopoly on knowledge about the budget's inner workings. "Members who had been here for many years—the only ones who deeply understood the system—weren't too happy about it," recalls Arduin with a mischievous smile. "But the new members loved it. They were so grateful because it let them instantly understand the budget."

Making Citizens Partners in the Policy Debate

When citizens are ignorant of how their tax money is spent, it's much easier for waste, fraud, and abuse to flourish. But when citizens are familiar with the budget and can plainly see not only how their tax dollars are spent, but also what outcomes the government is (or isn't!) achieving from each dollar spent, it forces public officials to be accountable for each

---

FIVE BENEFITS OF INCREASING TRANSPARENCY

- Enhance accountability.
- Increase citizen involvement in government.
- Raise performance.
- Boost government credibility.
- Reduce corruption.

---

funding decision. "It's the combination of technology and systemic reform that matters," says Governor Bush. "Unit costs and performance criteria, combined with technology, let citizens become partners in the policy debate. They can make the process more open and transparent. It isn't just putting it on the web; it's changing how you make it work."

To be sure, only a relatively small percentage of Floridians are likely to spend even a few minutes looking at Florida's e-budget—never mind several hours examining the historical data that shows how funding and desired results match up with actual outcomes. Nevertheless, the small percentage who will go to the website to see how their tax dollars are being spent, together with the scrutiny given to it by the media, government watchdog groups, and trade associations, provides enough oversight to keep public officials constantly on their toes.

It's a fairly simple formula: transparency generates accountability, which in turn generates pressure for improved performance, which in turn generates, well, improved performance. This was the idea, at any rate, when Florida, Texas, Colorado, and other states started posting comparative public school test results online. Giving parents this data, administrators believed, would help them make informed choices about their children's educational alternatives. Parents want to know about the academic performance, teacher quality, safety, and use of taxpayer dollars at public schools. And it looks like such programs may have the desired result. Publication of state "school report cards," says Harvard economist Caroline Hoxby, correlated with improvements on the National Assessment of Educational Progress. "Schools conduct themselves better," says Hoxby, "when their constituents are informed."[1]

Before its test results were published online, fewer than 12 percent of the students at Bessemer Elementary School in Pueblo, Colorado, could meet state literacy standards. Three years after the Colorado Student Assessment Program (CSAP) started putting every school's test scores up on the Net, the percentage of Bessemer students meeting state reading standards skyrocketed to 74 percent, while writing went from 2 to 47 percent. "Before, our teaching of writing was hit-or-miss: a sentence here, a paragraph there," admits Rita Marquez, the school's literacy coordinator. "It was when the CSAP came out that we realized we needed to teach writing."[2]

Like the market economy it serves, government itself responds to competition. As the web provides a more level playing field for government and private-sector information, citizens can compare, for example, public school to private school statistics to better guide their children's education, and these open comparisons in turn force government to survive in the marketplace by working leaner and smarter.

Is it any wonder that in a 2003 Hart-Teeter poll, 28 percent of Americans said holding government more accountable was the most important benefit of electronic government (almost three times as many as selected "convenient services")?[3]

DIGITAL ACCOUNTABILITY

Americans have an agenda for e-government that is more ambitious than just cutting paperwork or time spent waiting in line. They see its potential for giving citizens more information, which gives people the power to hold their government more accountable.[4]

—Hart-Teeter report on citizen attitudes toward e-government

No example in recent years better illustrates the powerful causal relationship between transparency, accountability, and improved performance than the New York City Police Department's widely acclaimed Compstat system. Compstat tracks when, where, and how crimes occur all over the city on a real-time basis, helping the police send a flatfoot to where he's needed most. The keys are timely intelligence, swift resource deployment, effective tactics, unremitting follow-up, and assessment and accountability. "Compstat measures crime every day, distributes it and tells us what time of day most crimes take place in each neighborhood," says former New York City mayor Rudolph Giuliani. "It helps us put police officers in the right place at the right time."

Compstat includes a strong dose of aggressive, in-your-face confrontations. Commanders grill precinct captains when crime goes up in their areas. "We had one of the Compstat meetings every week in a different borough," recalls Giuliani with a twinkle in his eye. "The police department wasn't used to this level of accountability. At the beginning, meetings produced fainting, some fistfights . . . a few police officers even showed up drunk to ease their anxiety."

None of Compstat's accountability mechanisms would be possible, of course, without raw data and powerful analytical tools to make use of it. The Compstat setup at NYPD headquarters—real-time statistics and performance information overlaid on giant, colorful digital maps—looks like something right out of *Dr. Strangelove*. Compstat is an accountability tool, an information-sharing forum, an information-gathering forum, and an educational forum all in one.[5] Agencies with a high shame factor feel pressure not only from the public, but in turn from the top as well.

The results achieved from this information-intensive system, as we've all heard by now, were nothing short of spectacular. Overall crime in New York City went down by over 52 percent; homicides fell 65 percent; auto crime plummeted 70 percent. At Riker's Island, the democratic world's largest prison, inmate violence dropped 95 percent during a time period when arrests rose 454 percent. This immense success prompted Giuliani to do two things. First, he deployed Compstat-like systems—confrontations, accountability, pin mapping, no excuses—throughout other troubled areas of city government, including welfare, child welfare, and corrections. Second, he put the same statistics that his department heads were using to batter or praise their managers out on the web for every New Yorker—including journalists—to see. "It's important to use this information not only as an internal tool," says the former mayor, "but to take it to the next step and make the information transparent to the public." A few mouse clicks let visitors to NYC.gov see the most up-to-date crime statistics in their neighborhood, right down to the hours and days that have the most shootings. You can see if welfare caseloads are rising or falling; whether the Child Welfare Agency is meeting its monthly performance targets; how your neighborhood bistro did on its last health inspection. The long-term effect on the attitude of New Yorkers toward their government could be quite dramatic. "People no longer see New York City as ungovernable or unmanageable," says Giuliani. "E-government allows us to make this permanent."

Baltimore Mayor Martin J. O'Malley uses a data-driven, information and management system modeled after Compstat, called "Citistat," to publicize and diagnose everything from potholes to police responsiveness. At O'Malley's Citistat meetings, Baltimore officials pore over rat-trap stats, pothole stats, drug treatment stats. Good workers get personal notes and Orioles tickets from the mayor; slackers get unwanted publicity. Citistat makes everything public on the city's website, preventing territorial bureaucrats from hiding embarrassing data and giving equally deserved attention to innovative supervisors. In 2002, thanks in part to Citistat, Baltimore's homicide rate fell to a ten-year low,[6] and the city saved more than $40 million through the middle of fiscal year 2003, mostly by slashing abuses of leave and overtime.[7]

The real-time performance transparency represented by government information management systems like Compstat and Citistat will have a cathartic impact on the relationship between citizens and their government.

Politicians won't be able to hide behind a charismatic personality, a political party, or a popular name anymore. Citizens will expect—in fact, demand—hard, documented results in return for their votes. Refusal to use available technology to show the public the workings of government will be interpreted as having something to hide. Nonperforming programs and agencies will find it harder and harder to survive the constant glare of public scrutiny of their performance. All these things will make government more accountable, but first we have to convince our elected leaders to take the plunge to e-transparency.

A MORE HONEST DIALOGUE

> No government is perfect. One of the chief virtues of a democracy, however, is that its defects are always visible and under democratic processes can be pointed out and corrected.
>
> —President Harry S Truman

If you're an incumbent governor, mayor, or county executive, increased transparency isn't just a valuable boon to the commonweal; it could be a terrifying threat to your future political viability. If crucial numbers go up when they're supposed to be going down (or vice versa), and it's all on a public website, your administration's very transparency could provide opposition research for your next election opponent, not to mention an always attack-ready media. Mexican president Vicente Fox found this out the hard way when, soon after being elected president in 2000, he decided to put his expense accounts online as part of an effort to clean up Mexican government.

His reward for his first foray into transparency was "Towelgate," which hit the headlines when a Mexican newspaper examined the expense reports and found a bizarre outlay of more than $400 each for embroidered towels and at least $1,500 for a fancy set of sheets for two presidential cabins whose overall decoration costs totaled a whopping $400,000. Fox immediately ordered an investigation, which led to the resignation or suspension of seven administration employees. The fact that Fox's government had made the information public in the first place didn't stop the bad publicity; the newspaper that uncovered the graft ran an editorial praising Fox for his quick response to the scandal, but other newspapers, and Fox's political opponents, weren't so quick to let the president off the hook.

Given stories like this, why would any politician want to risk putting any performance data online unless it's absolutely required by law? Politicians, after all, generally feel they gain power by controlling information. Traditional political power among insiders is still based on the spigot model: those in power let little drops of information out at specific times to help them achieve specific goals. I posed the question to Giuliani, who, needless to say, had his share of good and bad publicity over the years. The performance-obsessed former mayor clobbered the question the way one of his beloved Yankees would knock a hanging curve out of the park. "If you want to make the people who work for you accountable, you have to be willing to be accountable yourself," he argued. "If you're willing to set out objective measures then you can have a much more honest dialogue with your citizens."

We moved on to other issues, but it turns out he wasn't done yet. "I want to return to your question on transparency," Giuliani said.

> Putting all your performance statistics on the web creates a more realistic set of expectations for the public. You don't have to pretend that everything is perfect. The public expects a good-faith effort to improve things. As long as you've done this, the public will accept it if some statistics go in the wrong direction. It creates a more honest basis for building political support. It all comes down to how you define your role as governor or mayor: Are you trying to deliver better results or just trying to spin your constituents?

President Fox, whose term is over in 2006, must feel the same way, because his transparency campaign continued despite Towelgate. "My government's reports will be transparent, clean and in simple language," said Fox at the time.[8] Just a few years later, he had fulfilled at least part of that promise: on June 12, 2003, Mexico's first open-records and open-government law went into effect.

One benefit of a more informed public, Fox believes, is a public more willing to pay its taxes.[9] "The distrust comes when there are governments which are not honest, which are not transparent," said Fox, "and hence the people are unwilling to pay their taxes."

Despite the passage of the freedom of information law, Fox's transparency crusade faces high hurdles in a country with little previous experience with open government. A 2000 study of public access to information by Iberoamericana University in Mexico City found that Mexico ranked 182 out of 189 countries in making government documents public—beating only Cuba, North Korea, Iran, Iraq, Qatar, Libya, and China. "So ingrained is the government's attitude of not answering to ordinary people," said the report, "that farmers complain of being hung up on by the National Meteorological Service when they call to ask when a storm is coming."[10]

Corruption flourishes in such darkness; countries where the weather report is classified information aren't likely to be forthcoming about where tax money goes or which public officials are using their positions to line their pockets. Is it any wonder that many Mexican officials have come to expect a bribe (a "mordida," or "bite") in order to do their job? Mexico has more than two thousand government licenses of various types, many of which are a magnet for mordidas, as Mary Anastasia O'Grady relates in the *Wall Street Journal*:

> A friend here recently told me about the terrific difficulty he had in securing a government permit to do some work on a building. After almost a year of chasing about for yet another "required" document or being assigned an additional bureaucratic procedure, he finally paid a bribe and got his permit. "I didn't want to do it," he told me, "but I could see that I wasn't going to get permission without it."[11]

A Transparency Mexico survey found that the average mordida was only 109.50 pesos ($12) per transaction. But the little bites add up in a country that averages more than 200 million shakedowns a year—two for each citizen. The total cost of Mexican bribery (counting the higher insurance costs, legal costs, currency risks, lost productivity, foreign investors scared off by corruption, and other indirect costs) amounts to a whopping 9.5 percent of the country's gross national product (GNP), or $52 billion dollars a year, according to the former Mexican anticorruption czar Francisco Barrio.[12] Even worse than the economic costs are the societal costs. Corruption warps and debases people.

Protransparency Mexican politicians hope that shifting many transactions online—thereby letting citizens apply for public permits without facing bureaucrats with their hands out—will marginalize the mordida. "We want to use e-government to beat and combat corruption in government," said Fox. Several Mexican states followed his lead. Enrique Martinez, governor of the Mexican state of Coahuila, published all his government's accounts and contracts online. "Previously there was a taboo about revealing information concerning public works, who was doing the job, how much it cost, etc.," he says. "Nowadays all of that is on the Internet, from the smallest to the largest job."[13] Other states are beginning to follow suit.

How much does this matter in a country where only 10 percent of the population has Internet access? More than you might think. Cybercafes are flourishing in Mexico; the Mexican press can publish the fruits of Internet research for their readers; and the Mund market research firm has found that many people in rural areas actually pay for computers and Internet access even before indoor plumbing.[14]

CORRUPTION BUSTER

> Information is the natural enemy of corruption. Corruption thrives on ignorance, not information. It needs secrecy, not transparency. It seeks darkness, not light.
>
> —Former vice president Al Gore[15]

E-government, needless to say, is hardly a silver-bullet for the problem of crooked officials, which typically involves complex cultural, economic, and governance issues. However, the Internet does allow citizens to scrutinize the political process like never before, and that scrutiny acts as an important check on corruption. A number of Latin American countries actually post information online about public officials' assets in order to discourage them from taking dirty money while in office. "People who get a public office without any assets have amassed great fortunes when they leave office," explains a representative from the Dominican Alliance against Corruption. "This information must be in the public domain so everyone can see it and watch for signs."[16]

Sunlight is the best disinfectant for corruption. In general, the more digital and transparent the government is, the more difficult it is for corruption to flourish. Chile, Latin America's most corruption-free country, also leads the region in electronic government.[17] Its portal is organized in a customer-friendly fashion, offering easy-to-find birth and marriage certificates. Permitting, licensing, taxes, fees, and procurement—all areas where corruption thrives in emerging economies—are all now web-enabled. Permits issued by over twenty different Chilean agencies and departments can be obtained online. The country has been moving all government purchase of goods and services to an online procurement site (www.compraschile.cl), in order to bring transparency to another long-time hotbed of bribery, fraud, and graft. Another benefit is increased efficiency. Chilean officials estimate that e-procurement is saving taxpayers 7 to 20 percent compared to the old paper-based system.[18]

Customs is another area rife with bribery and the looting of public coffers in many parts of the world. Simply clearing cargo to leave a dock in the Philippines once required ten documents, ninety steps, and more than forty signatures, each a potential opportunity for delay—and bribery. Not surprisingly, citizens regularly fingered the Philippines Customs Bureau as the most corrupt government office in the country.[19] By web-enabling its customs process, the Philippines not only has reduced fraud but cut the time it takes to release cargo anywhere from 50 to 90 percent. Similarly, in South Korea, the Seoul municipal government's anticorruption website (OPEN) has subjected over twenty once-hidden administrative procedures to public scrutiny. Users can now study a searchable index of building permit applications. OPEN requires public officials to update a given applicant's processing info at each stage of the review; citizens can check on the progress and if they notice any irregularities, they can register an online complaint.

This electronic anticorruption campaign is making a big difference. Over 84 percent of Seoul residents believe that OPEN has led to greater transparency. When a Mr. Seo, seeking to speed his application for a printing business, "stuck a cash envelope into the official's notebook, persistently rejecting his effort to give the envelope back," he ended up receiving not a permit but a visit from the Center for Clean Hands, the government's anti-bribery office.[20] The official who turned him in avoided becoming part of South Korea's bribery-prosecutions boom.

Making it easier for citizens and government whistle-blowers to report on abuses is another crucial corruption-busting tool. Nagarajan Vittal, a mild-mannered, retired civil servant who was appointed in 1988 by India's prime minister to run a tiny government department known as the Central Vigilance Commission, became known as India's "corruption buster." When Vittal took office, the commission had spent thirty-four years churning out reports on corruption that were routinely ignored while Indian corruption went from bad to worse. In one corruption perception survey, Berlin-based Transparency International ranked India sixty-sixth out of eighty-five countries. "Corruption is a low-risk, high-profit business in India," says Vittal. "I want to raise the risk."[21]

Vittal hit upon a novel way to increase the risk: public shame. He posted the names of eighty-eight senior government and police officials charged with acts of corruption on the commission's website. You would have thought the Central Vigilance Commission had posted compromising pictures of India's prime minister with another woman from the interest the site engendered—for a time, it was the hottest site in India. Citizens flocked to libraries and Internet cafes to view it; newspapers editorialized about it. Several organizations polled Indians about their reactions to it. Over 90 percent of those surveyed by the *Hindustan Times* welcomed the action; 83 percent of those polled by the *Economic Times* believed it would have a deterrent effect on corruption.[22]

Such publicity had a dramatic effect in government circles as well; some state and local governments even put the list on their own websites. More significantly, several days after Vittal posted his list of corrupt officials, federal investigators raided the home of a senior Delhi police official and found half a million dollars worth of cash and jewelry. "The vicious cycle of corruption can be broken by public transparency," says Vittal. "I want people to be empowered to fight corruption."[23]

Not surprisingly the political establishment fought back hard against Vittal and his anticorruption activities. India's parliament passed a bill that curtailed the powers of the Central Vigilance Commission to fight corruption. The image of the crime fighter is gone from the commission's website. As for Vittal, he has finally retired for good—at least from government, but he continues on with his anticorruption crusade as a private citizen, publicly criticizing any and all government attempts to rollback the gains made.

Soon Mr. Vittal and other corruption fighters may have an even more powerful technological weapon to add to their anticorruption arsenal. A company called eNeuralNet has created a software program that uses artificial intelligence to assist citizens, governments, and watchdog groups in identifying corruption. The software can sift through years' worth of council meetings, legislative votes, and procurement awards to ferret out possible patterns of impropriety. "We can take data chaos and turn it into knowledge," explains Murray Craig, the software's inventor. "We can turn disparate government records into a database that shows which politicians might not be so honest."

Greater transparency and reduced corruption offers many advantages to both developed and developing countries: easier tax collection,[24] greater foreign investment and aid money. More money becomes available to be better spent on schools, hospitals, and police; and a well-informed citizenry is better able to exercise more effective control over their political representatives. In the Information Age, governments that aren't transparent aren't credible, and thus will lose investment and aid to those countries where public information and decision making are more open. With the cheap flows of information made possible by the Internet, governments that try to resist transparency will likely be fighting a losing battle in any case. Strict control of information in a society is no longer a realistic possibility.[25]

Outside Pressure

But even in the face of such realities, it usually takes intense, prolonged pressure from outside groups for governments to let the e-sunshine in. "To talk about how the Internet is being used or not used in anticorruption in Latin America, one has to understand the local realities," says Linda Hemby, codirector of Probidad, an anticorruption organization based in El Salvador. "One of them is that there is very little political will in government and civil society to end corruption. Both have benefited from it and the latter still doesn't understand the devastating impact of corruption on our people."

Watchdog groups like Probidad and Hong Kong's Independent Commission against Corruption do their best to keep the pressure on governments that continue to insist on secrecy. Tiny, two-person Probidad maintains an online clearinghouse of information about corruption; runs a five hundred-member listserv for journalists; monitors fifty Latin American newspapers for stories about corruption; promotes laws it considers worthwhile; and pressures Central American governments to publish more info online. "You're not transparent because you've got awareness materials online," says Hemby. "You're transparent if you're putting your budget online."

Another effective Latin American anticorruption watchdog is Argentina's Poder Ciudadano, a chapter of Transparency International. The organization maintains public databases listing the backgrounds of prominent politicians and major government contractors, making it much easier to track cronyism. Poder Ciudadano has demonstrated the power of using the web to expose institutional performance, publishing a "Big Mac" survey showing a school lunch in Buenos Aires cost the equivalent of $5 compared to $.80 in rural districts. Soon after the overpricing was exposed, lunch costs in Buenos Aires fell by half.[26]

Here at home, campaign-finance watchdog sites have flourished on the web, making life easier for reporters and ordinary citizens who don't want to scan reams of documents from the Federal Election Commission. OpenSecrets, Public Campaign, and Follow the Money are just three of the many sites that track campaign donations, answering questions like: Who raked in the most cash? Which groups (tobacco, oil, labor unions, and the like) funded which candidates? Which corporations gave the most money? Follow the Money even focuses on soft-money contributions to state political parties, which are often overlooked as federal-level candidates hog the spotlight.

Meanwhile, a group called the Environmental Working Group (EWG) put a huge database of all farm subsidy payments on the web, allowing Net surfers to see how much taxpayer subsidies are going to "struggling farmers" like ABC's Sam Donaldson (who received $97,000 in farm subsidies to keep his sheep farm afloat) or Portland Trailblazers star Scottie Pippen (who received over $131,000 not to grow crops on his Arkansas farm). After the lists went up on the web, local newspapers in farming communities began to publish the names of area farmers, noting how much federal aid each received. Radio shows read the lists on the air. Angry farmers, hearing how much money went to the big farms that bought out their smaller competitors, taped the lists to their truck dashboards. "It was like being outed," said Keith R. Bolin, a grain and hog farmer from Sheffield, who received $130,343 in farm subsidy payments from the federal government over five years. "But to be honest with you, I don't mind. It was a wake-up call, making us look like we're not all that different from the welfare mothers in Chicago."[27]

Another Washington, D.C.-based watchdog group, this one called the Center for Democracy and Technology, has shamed Congress and dozens of federal agencies into posting reports and information online by publishing a constantly updated "Ten Most Wanted List" of important documents not currently on the web. The list targeted items ranging from Congressional Research Service reports and hearing transcripts to the State Department's daily briefing book to Supreme Court decisions. One-third of the items on the top ten list are now on the web. "Shame and sunlight are two of the most important ingredients of effective oversight of government," says Ari Schwartz, a senior analyst at the Center. "The goal of the top ten list is to not only bring sunlight but to give citizens a chance to turn their living room conversation about what should be online into effecting change."

As performance budgeting and accountability systems become more sophisticated, the public should be able to use the Net to quickly see how much of their property taxes went into local youth programs and whether or not the programs had any impact on youth crime rates. Instead of having to rely on the occasional investigative report, citizens should be able to log onto legislative or third-party sites like www.michiganvotes.org to get a true picture of legislators' overall voting records, comparing key votes to campaign contributions from affected parties. Transparency will encourage better performance and greater accountability. The case for transparency is airtight, right?

THE TERRORIST'S RIGHT TO KNOW?

Wrong. Just when it seemed that nothing could derail the decades-long worldwide movement toward increased government openness, along came 9/11, and with it new apprehension: While we were opening our government records to civic-minded viewers, were we opening them to terrorists as well? Could our own best instincts help terrorists obtain sensitive data that could be used to attack airports, water treatment plants, dams, nuclear reactors, and other critical infrastructure? Scores of state and federal agencies answered with a resounding "Yes," pulling millions of pages' worth of potentially sensitive information off their websites in the hours, days, and weeks after 9/11.

"It must have been some kind of freak accident," thought Avi Duvdevani, the acting chief information officer for the city of New York, when the first plane hit the World Trade Center. Then the second plane struck the second tower. Duvdevani, who grew up living with mortar explosions and car bombs in his native Israel, knew immediately it was an act of terrorism, war, or both. His thoughts soon turned to the abundance of logistics information on NYC.gov, New York City's award-winning government website. In case more attacks were coming he didn't want the terrorists to have access to all the traffic, logistics, and Geographic Information Systems (GIS) data on the site so he quickly redesigned it, temporarily removing all this information.

Meanwhile, the National Imagery and Mapping Agency stopped selling large-scale digital maps. The Federal Energy Regulatory Commission (FERC) removed all documents detailing energy facility specifications. The

Centers for Disease Control yanked a report on chemical terrorism. Other expunged government data ranged from information on pipeline mapping and water supplies to airport data and EPA risk management reports. Some federal agencies didn't even bother trying to sort through which information could be potentially dangerous in the wrong hands: the Nuclear Regulatory Commission and the Department of Energy's National Transportation Program simply shut down their sites altogether.[28] (Even after all this, fifteen months after 9/11, the FBI sent out an alert warning that al Qaeda terrorists may have been using the web to find information about potential targets such as power plants and chemical facilities.)

And many states and cities followed the Feds' lead. California removed information on dams and aqueducts from its site; New Jersey expunged chemical information; Florida curtailed access to crop duster information and driver's license data. Much of this data can still be obtained by going to public reading rooms, but it's much harder to obtain. Utah, along with other states, stopped posting its Toxic Release Inventory, which lets citizens identify where toxic substances are stored throughout the state. "We've said this looks like information that is probably a little too convenient," said an official from the Utah Department of Environmental Quality. "We're not saying we won't give it to you, we're saying we're not going to put it where it's easily accessible."[29]

Perhaps nothing made it clearer that times had changed than when the Government Printing Office (GPO) ordered all libraries in the United States to destroy a CD-ROM guide to America's reservoirs and dams—the first time in memory, according to the GPO, that an order was given to destroy government documents due to security concerns. "I hate to do it," says Christine Gladosh, a government information librarian at Cal State Los Angeles: "Libraries don't like to censor information. Freedom of information is a professional tenet."[30]

The GPO's order was the last straw for the freedom of information community. "The trend of destroying information creates this almost unheard-of image of a sort of Ray Bradbury, *Fahrenheit 451*–like world of book burnings," says Gary Bass, the executive director of OMB Watch. "What are they going to do, go around to every library in America and break the CDs?"

OMB Watch is a small, left-of-center public interest group that has spent decades pressuring federal agencies to open up access to information. Located in the basement offices of a Victorian row house in Washington, D.C.'s Dupont circle, its offices have all the trappings of a nonprofit that's long on passion but short on funds: walls covered with scuff marks and picture holes; a bathroom door that refuses to close; shelves lined with twenty-year-old mothballed reports and stacks of files caked in dust; and carpets so heavily stained it's impossible to discern their original hue.

But most people who work with OMB Watch never need to visit its aesthetically-challenged offices. OMB Watch's website became the de facto clearinghouse for information on what was taken off government websites post-9/11; the site identified at least fifteen federal agencies, and scores of state ones, that removed potentially sensitive data. Gary Bass, the executive director of OMB Watch, is about as doctrinaire as they come about the "public's right to know." But even he admits that some of the information removed from government sites likely posed too great a security threat in a time of war. "It may have been appropriate to take some information off the web," he acknowledged. "Information that is uniquely available to one source and provides significant detail, such as maps or floor plans to potential targets, shouldn't be on the web—or if it is, it should only be available to emergency workers." What Bass objected to at the time was what he perceived as the arbitrary way in which many agencies went about pulling information offline. The decisions about what should stay and what should go, he argued, should have been based on a set of publicly available and vetted criteria. "In general," says Bass, "the emphasis should continue to be on the right to know."

These are, of course, very tricky questions, and everyone comes up with his own answers. The Federation of American Scientists, a group that has long been committed to open government, pulled down two hundred pages containing detailed information on nuclear storage facilities. "Everyone's groping toward a new equilibrium," says Steven Aftergood, director of the federation's government secrecy project. "There are obviously competing pressures that cannot easily be reconciled. The critics of disclosure are saying that we're exposing our vulnerabilities to terrorists. The proponents of disclosure say that it's only by identifying our vulnerabilities that we have any hope of correcting them. I suspect that both things are true."[31]

The Federal Aviation Administration (FAA) and Boston's Logan Airport took diametrically opposing paths to releasing information about airport security breaches and enforcement actions post-9/11. The FAA removed information from its website. "We took it off," says spokeswoman Laura Brown, "because of a determination that it was what's called SSI, security sensitive information, and it shouldn't have been on our site in the first place."[32] Logan airport did precisely the opposite, posting information on previous security breaches at the airport on its website in the hope that making the information public could help prevent similar incidents from occurring in the future.

Trying to be too secretive may be a hopeless task anyway. Despite the FAA's efforts, for instance, information on security breaches lives on; the Investigative Reporters and Editors (IRE) organization has made data from the FAA site available via CD-ROM. "Given the track record of the

FAA in keeping our airports secure," says Brant Houston, executive director of IRE, "we think journalists should continue our role as watchdogs."[33]

Indeed, once something has been posted online, it's almost impossible to scrape it entirely off the web. Days after 9/11, the federal Agency for Toxic Substances and Disease Registry yanked a sensitive report called "Industrial Chemicals and Terrorism" from its website, but the report lived on all over the web; a quick search turned up copies at sites ranging from the Oklahoma City National Memorial Institute for the Prevention of Terrorism to a UC Santa Cruz graduate student's homepage to the databases of the Internet Archive, which has stored over 10 billion web pages in order to preserve web history. "You can't simply turn off information that's been online," says OMB Watch's Bass. "The Internet is a leaky faucet—it will dribble long after you've turned it off."

In retrospect, it's clear that the post-9/11 government information clampdown did not constitute the dawn of an era of stricter limits on access to public information. Some highly sensitive data—mostly about potential terrorist targets like chemical plants and nuclear energy facilities—is harder to obtain, but that's a good thing. All in all, even open-government zealots like Bass are optimistic that governments will continue to become more transparent over time. "I don't think 9/11 had much impact overall on public information flow," says Bass.

And that's a good thing too.

TIPS FOR PRACTITIONERS

- Design the website from the public's point of view. It defeats the whole purpose of transparency if it is unintelligible or unnavigable.
- Don't just put the budget online. Make it searchable and let the user decide what information she wants to see, and in what form.
- Put both good and bad stats online. As long as they are leveled with, the public will accept that not everything is perfect.
- Use the increased transparency of performance information to drive internal improvements in government.
- Develop a well-thought out set of criteria for determining what information should go online and what shouldn't for security reasons. The burden of proof should be on those who want to restrict access.
- Reduce corruption by putting corruption-prone activities such as customs and procurement online and searchable.

7

The Electronic Advocate:
Citizenry Online

In *Bowling Alone: America's Declining Social Capital*, one of the most influential public policy books in recent years, sociologist Robert Putnam argues that civic engagement in America is in precipitous decline. The signs, he insists, are all around us: voter turnout is down by 25 percent; participation in town halls, public meetings, and school board meetings has plummeted by a third; cynicism toward political institutions and parties is rising; and political loyalties are waning. "By almost any measure, Americans' direct engagement in politics and government has fallen steadily and sharply over the last generation," writes Putnam, "despite the fact that average levels of education—the best individual-level predictor of political participation—have risen sharply throughout this period."[1] And this declining civic engagement isn't unique to the United States; more Europeans vote in the Big Brother TV shows than in European Union elections.

Searching for something—anything—to reverse this slide into political apathy, politicians, pundits, and academics have cast about for a savior, and many think they've found it in the Internet. By handing the reins of government over to voters and instituting a one-mouse-one-vote direct democracy, say e-topians, the Net will awaken a sleeping citizenry and ease the crisis facing democracies everywhere. When the technopopulists first came on the scene during the 1990s dotcom hysteria, they provoked shock and backlash from pundits who saw themselves as guardians of the constitutional order. Cokie and Steve Roberts blasted the Internet democrats in a column so harsh many people thought it was an email-forward joke.[2]

SAVIOR OR VILLAIN?

So which is it? Is the Internet savior or villain?

Unsurprisingly, it's neither. The Internet *is* slowly reviving our public life, by promising to give once-marginalized citizens a voice in government without junking our constitutional system. But the Internet won't bring us InstaDemocracy—thank goodness.

Let's begin at the beginning: with the diagnoses. Are Americans apathetic? In many cases, yes. But is this really because we want to vote on a thousand referenda a month? Not likely. So what's the real problem? It's impossible to untangle all the reasons for the decline in civic participation, but it's hard to deny that many citizens feel removed from any sense of political relevance or power. Their votes are hopelessly diluted in a sea of others. The rules that govern their lives are made by bureaucrats they'll never meet, vote for, or even see on TV.

It's precisely this sense of alienation and powerlessness that the Internet has the power to address. By reducing the barriers to civic engagement and widening the opportunities for political debate, the Internet can enhance civic participation in a myriad of ways, from e-advocacy and online consultation forums to electronic town hall meetings, political information sites, and other new electronic capabilities. "E-democracy" allows citizens to participate in public life, contact public servants, and shape public opinion more easily and more effectively than ever before. It provides the means for more people to have an impact on the decisions that affect them. If these opportunities are seized, the political and social consequences will be immense.

Unsurprisingly, skeptics seeing threats have followed quick on the heels of optimists seeing boons. Too much Internet-driven direct democracy, some argue, could undermine deliberative, representative government. Others, longing for the Greek agora, are wary of the Net and other emerging information technologies because they believe face-to-face political interactions and debates are critical to a healthy democracy. Agoraphile University of Chicago law professor Cass Sunstein argues that the Net is bad for democracy because it lets people wall themselves off from divergent opinions. In his book *Republic.com*, Sunstein argues that when people personalize and filter their web experiences they deny themselves the "shared experiences" and the exposure to alternative viewpoints that are hallmarks of a healthy democracy. "[T]he Internet," he writes, "creates a large risk of group polarization, simply because it makes it so easy for like-minded people to speak with one another and ultimately to move toward a more extreme point in the same direction indicated by their pre-deliberation judgments."[3] He goes on to offer a number of possible solutions to this purported problem, including publicly subsidized websites and "must carry" rules, modeled on television regulations, that would force the most popular sites to offer exposure to more "substantive public questions" and opposing viewpoints.

You could drive a Mack truck through the holes in such prescriptions. Is the *New York Times* partisan? Who gets to decide? How many opposing viewpoints would the Democratic Leadership Council's website have to link to in order to satisfy the government content police? Who decides if the Heritage Foundation's website—or MTV's—is guilty of "failure to attend to public issues"?

But even disregarding Sunstein's scattershot solutions, there's a more fundamental problem with his line of argument: The problem he seeks to fix doesn't exist. Is the Internet really causing people to have fewer unanticipated encounters and less exposure to alternative viewpoints? The most popular sites—huge portals like AOL, MSN, and Yahoo—have long provided the "public sidewalks" Sunstein calls for, and they've done so without government pressure. Even the popular right-of-center *Drudge Report* provides links to opinion writers ranging from Rush Limbaugh on the right to Molly Ivins on the left. Then there's the freewheeling world of "weblogs": news, information, and opinion sites that maintain constantly updated links to interesting information and analysis on other sites. A distinct "blogger" community has emerged where bloggers of all political leanings will read and link to others' blogs just because they're blogs.

The online world's hyperlinked nature makes us more, not less, likely to encounter the unexpected and unfiltered when we substitute the web for TV or radio. To learn this, Sunstein could surf the Net himself—or he could just drive north. In Minnesota, a few hundred miles from Sunstein's Chicago office, a network of online deliberative-democracy sites thrives without public regulation or subsidy.

MAKING EVERY CITIZEN FEEL LIKE AN INSIDER

As R. T. Rybak pulled closer in his upstart bid to unseat Minneapolis mayor Sharon Sayles Benton in 2001, the whispering campaign grew louder and louder: Why was it, Rybak's opponents kept wondering, that the man who wanted to be mayor didn't think enough of the city's public schools to send his children there? Rybak knew he had to respond. His campaign manager suggested holding a press conference or issuing a press release—the traditional vehicles a political candidate uses to defuse a damaging story. Rybak did neither. Instead he defused this potentially explosive issue by posting his explanation to an online discussion group, "Minneapolis-Issues." The forum, which boasts some seven hundred participants ranging from city councilmen to ordinary (albeit unusually passionate) citizens, was one the world's most successful early e-democracy experiments.

Debates on the site cover issues ranging from stolen shopping carts to funding for a new stadium for the Minnesota Twins. And the forum is populated not by people with too much time on their hands yelling at each other—the cliché about online communities—but by regular folks and people with real power and influence in city affairs. "You can talk right to the powers-that-be," says list member David Christenson. "I find myself in the position of debating a candidate for governor. I get to step back and say, 'Hmm, I had the ear of this fellow for a few minutes.'"[4]

That's exactly what worries some of Mayor Rybak's political strategists. They aren't so crazy about him participating in the forum now that he's mayor, he says, "because it's such a wild forum. But I happen to like mixing it up with folks, and I don't mind getting challenged."[5] Rybak began participating in Minneapolis-Issues after he became frustrated with the direction in which then-mayor Sayles Benton was taking the city and wanted to learn what other city opinion leaders were thinking. "I found out that I wasn't alone," said the long-time community activist. "It was one of the places where I could air out my ideas and get support or criticism."[6] So when his own political crisis hit, Rybak knew just where to turn—and, like hundreds of other postings over the years on Minneapolis-Issues, the candidate's *mea culpa* was picked up the next day by the local news media.

Minneapolis-Issues is only one of several thriving online political forums in the state. Across the river, St. Paul's Issues Forum also has the ears of top local politicos. "[The list] is a sort of magnification of reality," says former St. Paul city councilmember David Thune. "In terms of government and politics, it's zero steps removed. It's a direct one-on-one communication. Every individual not only has a voice but also an ear on the other end to hear what they think."[7]

Most of the local political and civic leaders in Winona, Minnesota (population 25,000), including the mayor, police chief, city planning director, city council members, college president, school board president, and state senator and representative, participate in an online democracy forum whose email discussions cover everything from tree trimming to the war on terrorism. When Winona's mayor was considering proposing a tax increase to resurface city streets, he went on the forum and was surprised to learn that his constituents were more concerned about unmarked intersections on the streets than about resurfacing them. When one frustrated resident posted a complaint about parking restrictions during snow season, the chief of police came online and explained the tag-and-tow policy and the streets commissioner posted an email clarifying how the snowplow process worked. With a better understanding of the reasons behind the restrictions, the frustrated resident was soothed. "When people know that policymakers and decision makers are listening to them," says Steve Kranz, who runs the Winona Democracy forum, "it helps make them feel like insiders in the community, which usually makes them more active citizens."

Gauging the Public Mood

But the forums aren't just valuable for citizens; they also help elected officials gauge the public mood and test-drive new ideas. "[The forums] play a very important role in educating public officials about what the public is thinking," explains Mayor Rybak.[8] When the Park Board decided to let Dairy Queen run the city's money-losing concession stands at two local lakes, opponents from the Minneapolis forum mobilized. Within hours, Park Board members were deluged with emails and phone calls, leading them to shelve the proposal. Minneapolis Issues Forum participant and City Councilmember Barb Johnson was furious: "They've [list members] got public officials twisted around their little fingers," she charged. That's an overstatement—but it testifies to the power of the issues forum.

The issues debated in the various forums can be wildly divergent, but a common element is the diversity of viewpoints. "Most online discussion groups are all about raves and rants," says one participant. "These forums are spaces where people cherish the exposure to different opinions. They're the online equivalent of talking politics at the local coffee shop or shooting the breeze with council members after a city council meeting."

Minnesota's various online political forums all fall under the umbrella of "Minnesota e-Democracy," a nonprofit organization whose mission is to use electronic networks to improve citizen participation. "The most democratizing aspect of the Internet is the ability for people to organize and communicate in groups," says Steven Clift, the visionary, thirty-something former Minnesota state employee who founded Minnesota e-Democracy. Ask Clift why Minnesota's online discussion forums have been so successful and you get a surprising answer: While other forums require users to log onto a web page, Clift points out, the Minnesota forums' communication tool of choice is the simpler email. "Email is the most personal space controlled by users on their computer," says Clift. "With websites we're visiting someone else's property; with email we're letting people into our homes."

He believes e-democracy forums could fill a void in communities nationwide. "What's missing from our democracy," he says, "is an engaging and participatory governance system that involves citizens and helps elected officials and governments better represent the needs and desires of the people. Democracy needs an online, interactive public commons."

But Clift isn't buying Sunstein's argument that government needs to step in and force the market to provide that commons. "You won't get this from top-down government prescription," he says. "Nothing can replace the willingness of citizens to make it happen."

ONLINE CONSULTATIONS

Inspired in part by the success of projects like Minnesota e-Democracy, more formal ways of involving citizens in policymaking processes have gained ground worldwide. Many cities and states now broadcast their legislative sessions online, letting citizens watch their representatives in action, view drafts of bills, and even post comments before votes are cast. What's more, the Internet's 24/7 availability lets citizens do all this on their own schedules. "The notion that the only way to have an impact on your government is to be at a certain place at a certain time is nuts," says Clift. "People are busy; they don't have time to leave work and go to a city council meeting at 3:00 P.M."

Will citizens really use e-democracy forums to influence policy debates? They already are. When the Central Bucks School District in Pennsylvania was studying how to structure its redistricting plan, it asked for comments from parents—and received over five hundred emails on the plan. When Roswell, Georgia mayor Jere Wood asked subscribers to his weekly electronic newsletter whether city council members should get a raise, fifty of them fired back emails offering their opinions. "I'm a liaison between the public and city government," says Wood, "and you've got to communicate with [your constituents] to do that job—and part of that is feedback."[9]

At the federal level, the Environmental Protection Agency (EPA) brought together over a thousand people from across the country in July 2001 for a two-week online consultation to discuss public participation in EPA decisions. The discussion combined broad participation with the kind of intense interaction that's typically only possible in small-group settings. Over one hundred messages were posted each day, many of them by a core group of sixty or so of the most active participants. The agency turned a static public comment process into a more dynamic discussion that involved scores more people than the traditional, paper-based process. At the end of the dialogue, 87 percent of participants said the EPA should conduct more of them in the future.[10]

And the movement is even stronger overseas. When the Scots were granted self-governance in 1997 after three hundred years of English rule, they immediately began embedding e-democracy tools into their new public institutions. They were the first country to accept electronic petitions; the first, launched in July 2000 by Napier University's International Teledemocracy Centre, called on the Scottish Parliament and Executive Branch to support actions to bridge the digital divide between those with access to the Internet and those without it. In February 2004, the electronic petitions system began allowing people to debate the petitions online. Some have attracted debate from as far away as Australia, Barbados, New Zealand, and the United States.

A few miles to the south, Great Britain also uses formal online consultation processes to involve citizens in policymaking. Robin Cook, the former leader of Great Britain's House of Commons, launched these consultations to try to bring Britain's Parliament—which he scathingly described as "antique, ludicrous, Dickensian and as ritualized as eighteenth-century dueling"—into the twenty-first century. (Such language may help account for why he has been dubbed "Radical Robin" by the British press.)[11] "Democracy is richer than the right to vote every four years," explains Cook. "Democracy must also offer the right to be heard in between elections and the opportunity to shape the policies pursued by those who are elected. The Internet offers us a tool for participation without precedent in democratic history."[12]

While the Internet has enabled the physically disabled to do everything from shop to renew library books from their armchairs, online consultation holds the potential to involve and empower this often-silent sector of society in truly life-changing ways. As the net liberates them from the difficulties of transportation and provides a forum for communication, their voices can share in public debate on a level playing field.

In the United Kingdom's first online consultation, domestic violence survivors used the Net to provide hundreds of pieces of direct evidence to a parliamentary committee, a process that offered survivors a degree of confidentiality that wouldn't have been possible if they'd had to testify in person. Unsurprisingly, fully 94 percent of the nearly two hundred women who participated in the month-long consultation called it a worthwhile exercise, valuing both the interaction with other women with similar experiences and the chance to provide official evidence in the policy process.

Legislators were similarly enthusiastic. "The most useful purpose was to grasp our attention—which is very important," says Member of Parliament (MP) Linda Gilroy. "New technology is the best way, because it grasps the breadth and the depth of the messages. If you meet with a group . . . for five to ten minutes you don't always have sufficient time to listen to all the problems. This was a unique experience, because you were able to listen to a dialogue for an extensive period of time."[13]

The only real criticisms came from a few participants who felt the MPs didn't give enough feedback—a complaint that illustrates the importance of informing people beforehand exactly how their contributions will be used by decision makers.[14] "In order to attract people to . . . online consultations, governments must prove that there is a relationship between the citizen's engagement and policy outcome," says former UK cabinet minister Graham Stringer. "Democracy is not just about symbolic or cosmetic consulting—but actually using the people's voices in decision making."[15]

Connecting E-Government and E-Democracy

And the more the better, say some e-democracy theorists and practitioners, who talk of creating a "civic commons in cyberspace" that would elicit and coordinate citizens' comments and reactions to problems facing public institutions.[16] "The challenge," write e-democracy experts Stephen Coleman and John Gotz,

> is to create a link between e-government and e-democracy—to transcend the one-way model of service delivery and exploit for democratic purposes the feedback paths that are inherent to digital media. So instead of citizens simply being able to pay their taxes online (hardly a joy for most people), they would be able to enter into a public debate about how their taxes are spent.[17]

In fits and starts, this concept is becoming reality. Estonia's "Today I Decide" public website averages over 150,000 hits per month as citizens comment on draft laws and even submit their own ideas for new ones, after which the public discusses them for two weeks, then votes online; proposals that receive over 51 percent are considered by the appropriate departments and sometimes even enacted into law. Officials in Denton, Texas, use online surveys—complete with before-and-after pictures of street improvements, housing and commercial development—to help develop zoning regulations. The city of Tacoma, Washington, posted descriptions of fourteen potential construction projects on its website and asked city residents to indicate which ones they'd be willing to fund.

Local governments in Sweden have pioneered using the Internet to give citizens a greater say in policy decisions. The city of Kalix, Sweden, created an "online town hall" to provide residents with an opportunity to help city planners redesign the city center. Close to 15 percent of the town's population took part in the dialogue; nearly three-fourths of them said it was a positive experience. Meanwhile, in the nearby city of Bollnas, citizens no longer have to schlep down to City Hall and wait hours for their turn just to speak for 60 seconds at the weekly city council meeting. Bollnas residents can email questions directly to city council members during the webcasted city council meetings and then sit back and watch their emails being read aloud and discussed.[18]

Opening Up the Policy Debate

Online consultations can provide a powerful counterweight to the special interests that typically dominate policy debates. For example, when a Swedish political debate concerning whether or not to build a new airport in Stockholm became quite heated, the Swedish Civil Aviation Authority decided to launch a website called "New Airport." The goal: to give concerned citizens a chance to make their voices heard in deciding whether and where a new airport would be built. The site featured an "opinion grid" where political parties, neighborhood groups, local governments, and others could contribute their opinions, a bank of information, interviews with citizens, and a moderated discussion group where people could debate what others were saying.[19] In addition, site visitors could click on detailed descriptions of all the airport alternatives, complete with pictures, maps, and Quick-Time movies. The website was shut down less than one year after it was launched after overwhelming citizen input against the airport convinced the government to drop the project.

One of the more novel attempts to date to engage citizens in the lawmaking process in America was the "e-Government Project," an interactive experiment sponsored by Senators Joseph Lieberman (D-CT) and then-senator Fred Thompson (R-TN) in 2000 that let citizens help fashion a congressional e-government bill. This marked the first time ever that anyone with Internet access could participate in shaping an important piece of national legislation. The website was filled with short descriptions of key e-government issues, descriptions of possible legislation, and electronic forms for sending in suggestions and comments. "This is an opportunity for people to contribute their ideas and opinions before we begin drafting e-government legislation," said Lieberman at the site's debut. "We are extending an unprecedented invitation to any interested citizen to participate openly and interactively in the process of writing legislation." Lieberman later drove a landmark e-government bill through Congress incorporating a number of suggestions gleaned from the site.

The conclusion is obvious: Citizens should be able to comment on all legislation before it's voted on, view the suggestions from their fellow citizens and, using web tools such as Crit, comment directly on the text of the bills. Such an approach would begin moving us from what Swedish e-democracy activist Miklas Nordstrom calls the "DAD" principle of government—Decide, Announce, and Defend—to the "Three D Principle"—Dialogue, Discussion, and Decision. "In an open society with increased transparency people will increasingly expect to be asked what they think on issues," explains Nordstrom. "But if we ask, we also have to listen."

PUSH AND PULL E-DEMOCRACY

If digital government and digital democracy are to transform government service delivery and decision making, e-democracy tools must be integrated into government portals, websites, and electronic services. Every public site, says e-democracy guru Clift, should have "democracy buttons" that, among other things, send people email notification when their pet issues come up in the legislature. "Government decision-making bodies," he says, "should have personalized 'My Democracy' sections that allow any citizen to search in advanced ways (pull) and receive automatic notification (push) of meeting notices and proposals of interest."[20]

The state of Virginia, home of Thomas Jefferson, James Madison, and Patrick Henry, is trying to forge something close to this ideal. Log onto Virginia's legislative website, click on subjects you're interested in, and you'll be notified by email anytime there's movement on any bills dealing with those subjects. You can receive an email copy of any bill introduced by one of your representatives, along with notification of any changes that take place during the legislative process. You can get advance word of any meetings or hearings held on issues you care about. One can't help but think that the founding fathers would have approved.

Once bills are passed, bureaucrats must prepare regulations and guidelines to implement them. For citizens, interest groups, and other affected parties, influencing these rules and regulations during official "comment" periods is one of the least sexy but most effective ways to influence government behavior. It's also typically been the sole province of lobbyists and other insiders who have a large financial or policy stake in a rulemaking outcome. The inconvenient nature of the process has limited true citizen participation.

Digital democracy promises to give outsiders far more access to the process. Virginia's Regulatory Town Hall has made the extraordinarily complex regulatory process understandable to the average citizen. At www.townhall.state.va.us you can learn the daily changing status of any regulation, receive email notifications of any regulation changes, find out when comment periods are open, read minutes of public meetings, and comment on regulatory changes in dozens of different areas.[21] The architect of this remarkable site is the state's deputy director of planning and budget, a curly-haired economics professor named Dr. Bill Shobe. "Previously, you had to hire a lawyer if you wanted to track the regulations through the process," says Shobe, whose office shelves are lined with rows and rows of dusty economics texts. "We've created a one-stop shop for public access to regulations."

And they did it on a shoestring budget. Shobe did most of the programming himself, using how-to programming books, and off-the-shelf Cold

Fusion software. Some of his colleagues wanted to charge for the service. Shobe nixed this idea. "Charging people for something that you're forcing them to do would be like charging protection money," he says.

Virginia isn't the only government that's moving rule-making online. Alaska, for instance, provides comprehensive online lists of all proposed rule changes and meeting notices, organized by category, department, and location and publication date. As in Virginia, Alaskans can sign up to get rule change notifications in their areas of interest. And Washington State's Department of Ecology lets users view and respond to other citizens' comments about rules, thereby enhancing public dialogue. "Allowing any individual to see all the other comments up there increases transparency," says a rule writer at the Department of Ecology.

The Bush administration has gone ever further and begun to consolidate all the federal government's dozens of rule-making websites—which cost taxpayers about $18 million a year to maintain—into one site (www.regulation.gov). Right now people can go to comment on any of the four thousand new rules a year churned out by the 173 federal agencies that implement laws passed by Congress on regulation.gov. By 2006, it will provide a centralized docket for all federal rules and show regulatory proposals, final rules, comments, supporting documents such as cost-benefit analyses and many other aspects of the regulatory process about each and every federal rule. The website is expected to save taxpayers $70 million over five years by creating one central portal for e-rulemaking instead of each agency operating its own.[22]

The biggest concern public officials have with e-rulemaking is not that it won't work, but that works all too well, deluging them with an unmanageable number of citizen comments. According to a survey conducted by the Pew Internet and American Life Project, 42 million Americans viewed federal regulations online in 2001, with a whopping 23 million of them commenting on proposed rules, regulations, and policies.[23] When the U.S. Department of Agriculture piloted electronic rulemaking for proposed rules on organic produce, they received 275,000 public comments—hundreds of times the amount they typically received through snail mail. And federal law required them to assess each one, even though about 160,000 were cut-and-paste form letters sponsored by interest groups. Prior to allowing people to comment on new rules online, the U.S. Department of Transportation (DOT) got about three thousand comments a year. After adopting e-rulemaking, this number soared to close to 63,000 public comments. Now officials worry that the widespread adoption of e-rulemaking could overwhelm government agencies—and many have been slow to adopt e-rulemaking as a result.

What's the answer to the "deluge" problem? New procedures and new technology for citizen online commenting will also be needed to make widespread electronic rule-making viable and cost-effective. Artificial intelligence and natural language processing can identify cut-and-paste form letters and filter emails into appropriate categories. In other words, unsurprisingly, adapting to the new era will mean using more technology, not less.

INSTADEMOCRACY?

When the Federal Trade Commission sought public comments via the web about a proposed merger of Staples and Office Depot in 1999, Jamie Love of the Consumer Project on Technology encouraged members of his email list to comment on the proposal. "The Internet is the best thing in my lifetime for grassroots organizing," Love told then-ABC news pundit Cokie Roberts, arguing that the Net can help citizens cut through the special interest groups that typically dominate Beltway debates. This optimistic, seemingly benign comment deeply disturbed the Beltway's former pundit queen, who, along with her husband Steve, proceeded to pen a syndicated column titled "Internet Could Become a Threat to Representative Government." The column blasted Love's notion of opening up policy decisions to regular folks. Wrote the couple:

> According to Love, it's like an electronic town meeting. That analogy makes our blood run cold. . . . Let's just all get together, via computer, and let the politicians know what we want, so then they will do it! No more pandering to the big contributors, no more deals between members, just the voice of the people will be heard. We hear that and shudder.[24]

Opening up government to more citizen input via the Net, Steve and Cokie argued, would lead us down a slippery slope: First you let citizens and interest groups email federal officials, the next thing you know American government has been transformed into a kind of mass-rule of instant Internet plebiscites. "Representative government is under attack," they wrote. "Congress could eventually find its very existence threatened, thanks to the Internet."

Before you wonder if aliens had invaded the minds of this normally pragmatic couple, remember that they wrote their now-infamous column smack in the middle of the dotcom boom, when any number of serious observers were predicting that the Net would mean The End of Democracy as We Know It®. "The Internet," wrote the provocative Clinton administration political advisor Dick Morris in his book *Vote.com*:

> offers a potential for direct democracy so profound that it may well transform not only our system of politics but our very form of government. . . .

Bypassing national representatives and speaking directly to one another, the people of the world will use the Internet to form a political unit for the future.

Morris was and is by no means alone in advancing this kind of populist, utopian view. Technopopulists have provided the Roberts duo and other worrywarts no shortage of ammunition with which to defend their arguments against e-democracy. "Soon voters might initiate, circulate and vote on electronic ballot initiatives addressing the 'hot ticket' issues of the day," said Tracey Westen, founder of the Democracy Online Network. "Legislators and legislative bodies will respond with modifications, corrections and follow-up actions." Voters would become de facto legislators, thereby reducing their elected representatives to low-level technocrats. Westen, a respected voice in the e-democracy movement, has even developed a detailed process—"Direct Democracy in Three Easy Steps"—to get us from here to there. Step One: Electronic circulation and qualification of ballot initiatives. Step Two: Electronic voting on these initiatives. Step Three: Accelerated electronic voting on initiatives shortly after ballot qualification. "Once citizens have the power electronically to qualify and vote measures into law," asks Westen, "why would they delay exercising that power until a distant-seeming election? Why not act immediately?"

Why indeed? Why shouldn't democracy be conducted on Internet Time? Cyberspace can offer reams of information instantly; why should we have to wait years—or decades—for our representatives, many of them thoroughly beholden to interest groups, to pass a bill? Well, one answer was offered by James Madison in *Federalist* 63, two hundred years before anyone began surfing the Net:

> [T]here are times when the people, stimulated by some irregular passion . . . may call for measures which they themselves will afterwards be the most ready to lament and condemn. In these critical moments, how salutary will be the interference of some temperate and respectable body of citizens in order . . . to suspend the blow meditated by the people against themselves, until reason, justice, and truth can regain their authority.

Politicians, Madison explains, should be representatives in the fullest sense: conscious of the popular will, but armed with more information, knowledge, and wisdom than the electorate. The ideal republic would choose its representatives because they held the courage of their convictions, and would be able to go against the polls when necessary. "The challenge we have, particularly in democratic societies, is that the speed with which technology allows you to move is juxtaposed against our democratic values of deliberation and debate," says Robert O'Neill, president of the International City/County Management Association. "Right after 9/11, if you took a vote of the people, perhaps you could have rounded up all people of Muslim faith and put them in jail. The Internet allows you to better inform the debate and engage citizens with a different medium, but it shouldn't be a substitute for the deliberative process."

The technopopulists must also answer another question: Do people even *want* that much more direct democracy? The e-topians' logic—that because technology lets us vote faster and more easily, we *should* vote more often—is fundamentally flawed. Whether to vote more often is fundamentally a political, not a technological, issue; and there is nothing in polling data or in recent elections to suggest that the busy public is clamoring to abrogate the role of their representatives and participate in binding weekly votes on the "issues of the day." Do we really want to vote on the farm bill reauthorization? Or a new bankruptcy law? Whether you love or hate California's initiative and referendum process, it's a good bet that Californians probably couldn't handle much more direct democracy. Kim Alexander, founder of Calvoter.org, wrote a song to help voters distinguish between the scores of California initiatives on the ballot during a recent election year: "Oh, there once was a proposition, its number was One-A, the first of twenty measures to decide by Election Day. . . ."[25]

WEOs

There is a middle ground: crafting an online space in which WEOs (Wired Elected Officials) can use digital tools to enhance their ability to represent the rest of us.[26] The solution is not to use public engagement to supplant the decision making of elected representatives (as the technopopulists argue) or to reject online public engagement altogether (as the Net-skeptics would prefer), but to use the Net to help elected representatives strengthen their democratic mandate and develop more informed, publicly supported policy proposals. As Stephen Coleman and John Gotz point out, instead of reducing their relevance, e-democracy tools could help elected representatives "enhance their legitimacy as political mediators of the public voice."[27]

Unfortunately, many representatives and legislative bodies still fall short in deploying new electronic tools. Their web pages are still in the "brochureware" stage: pictures of the legislator, her biography, a listing of her committees, contact information, press releases, issue positions (maybe). All very nice, but all very 1995—and not at all what her increasingly wired constituents want to see. According to focus groups conducted by the Congress Online Project, a majority of citizens want to see rich content, constituent feedback, and voting records (along with explanations for those votes) on their representatives' sites.[28] "I don't want a website where they send his wife's favorite recipe for bean dip or something like that," said one participant from Phoenix. "I want to see their voting record on everything . . . that's going to tell me where they're ultimately going." Currently, only 37 percent of House members and 14 percent of Senators provide access to their voting records.[29]

One fine example of where e-democracy could go is the website of Jan Hamming, a hip young alderman of the city of Tilburg in the Netherlands. Hamming was the first Dutch politician to have a website. His site is nothing short of a virtual constituent office. Visitors can view his schedule (updated daily), send him email (he personally answers over fifty a day), log into his weekly chat room discussions, view his positions on issues, file a complaint about city services, and check out his links to other sites (including the "hippie party site").

What might compel more legislators to get a little hipper themselves? In Hamming's case, his strong web presence lets him interact with constituency groups who previously had little contact with politics and wouldn't be caught dead at a city council meeting. "My contacts, especially with youth, low-income and ethnic groups, are improving through the virtual contacts," says Hamming. "These groups visit the Internet because it is fast, approachable and everybody is equal. Knowledge is more accessible and transferable." These very advantages, however, tend to scare off politicians who prefer more scripted settings. "The advantages— having no rules—sometimes frighten politicians," says Hamming. "The Internet is said to interfere with people's portfolios, it's too open and too quick and means extra work."[30]

The observation fits many members of the U.S. Congress to a tee. So it was an encouraging sign when, in the weeks after the anthrax scare halted mail delivery to Congressional offices, many legislators urged constituents to contact them electronically. "Contact me by email rather than postal mail," urged Rep. John Linder in an online plea. "This may create the paperless democracy some of us have been anticipating," said Pam Fielding, who operates e-advocates, an electronic lobbying firm.[31]

It didn't happen—at least not back then. When the *New York Times* tested the digital responsiveness of Congress several months after the anthrax scare by sending email messages to sixty-five Senate offices to see if, when, and how they responded, the results were dismal. Apart from some automated responses, only seven Senate offices even bothered to reply within two weeks—despite the fact that the message identified the email as coming from a reporter from the *New York Times*.[32]

The dismal results were a manifestation of what was dubbed the "congressional email standoff." A massive email overload (at least 120 million email messages per year coming into Congress, and rising) was wreaking havoc on congressional offices. Facing upwards of 60,000 emails a month—mostly spammed form letters generated by companies and grassroots lobbying groups—many offices didn't even responding to email. It wasn't only American politicians who were experiencing email overload. Japanese prime minister Junichiro Koizumi, whose weekly email magazine has over 2 million subscribers, receives about 3 million email messages each day!

The perverse result is that email has become just about the least effective way to make your voice heard by elected officials. To their credit, some legislators are trying to overcome the email deluge, not by restricting email, but by using new electronic tools, such as artificial intelligence and filtering software, to manage the increased flow of information and dramatically reduce the staff work needed to keep up with the daily inbox. Many Senate offices have installed in their offices a web-based service called EchoMail that employs artificial intelligence to filter, sort, and respond to email. By identifying the tone and meaning of a message, EchoMail can tell the difference between an information request, a complaint, casework, or an opinion, and process the message accordingly.[33] It can also determine whether the email was sent from a constituent or someone outside the legislator's jurisdiction.

Other legislators are trying to shift constituent communications away from email altogether and to web-based forms. The forms reduce the need to sort messages by hand, and slash the amount of political spam reaching congressional offices by using zip code authentication to determine if the visitors are or are not residents of the district. Some e-democracy activists have been highly critical of the web forms—Clift calls them "Digital Berlin Walls"—believing that they will discourage many constituents from making their voices heard because they're far less convenient than email. Some of the more creative political offices have tried to address this by customizing the online forms to meet the particular needs of each online user. Michigan Senator Carl Levin's website has a full-service online constituent services center where the dynamically generated web form will change depending on what the constituent wants to do whether it is request a tour, obtain help with her social security, voice her opinion on an issue, or nominate someone for West Point.

Some WEOs have offered more opportunities for Netizens to "sound off" on their websites or see how the legislative process works from the inside. Tampa, Florida, city council member Bob Buckhorn encourages his constituents to "vote" on particular issues currently being considered by the council on his site and to assess his performance in different areas such as ethics. "It gives me the pulse of the community," says Buckhorn.[34] Taking a cue from successful private companies, other legislators are working to answer their constituents' questions before they're asked.[35] Former senator Don Nickles (R-OK) had a feature on his office website named "You Called It" that listed the top five issues constituents contacted him about in the past week and his position on each issue. Senator Patrick Leahy (D-VT) lets Vermonters feel like they're right there on the Senate floor with him via his "More from the Floor" website feature which provides a blow-by-blow summary of the Senate debate each day it's in session in a breezy, easy-to-read style.

For citizens who want even greater participation, weekly online chats or electronic town hall meetings allow citizens to interact more frequently with their representatives. Former congressman Tom Campbell, a Stanford Law professor held *daily* electronic town hall meetings in the 1990s, answering every constituent question himself. "Anyone could send me a question and the questions and answers were archived and searchable," Campbell recalls. "I remember when I voted against ratifying the ABM treaty, I received lots of email from constituents who strongly disagreed with me. But they were never nasty or mean-spirited. People seemed to just appreciate the fact they could voice their concerns directly to me without having to travel to Washington." The biggest problem he encountered, in fact, was that many of his own constituents refused to believe it was actually the Congressman himself responding to their email!

Former Oklahoma representative Brad Carson, long considered one of Congress's more tech-savvy members, also held town hall meetings on his site. During one week in November his rural constituents quizzed him on everything from whether he's disillusioned with Congress given all he's seen in his first year ("Definitely not") to why the Roland Post Office doesn't provide longer hours and more courteous service ("I'm looking into it"). Unlike most of his colleagues, Carson actually responds to email with email instead of postal mail. "There's an institutional bias [in Congress] against adopting new technology," he says. By shifting from mail to email, Carson's staff was one of the only ones in Congress able to continue to answer constituent postal mail during the anthrax crisis. "We had it scanned in and emailed to us," said his Chief of Staff. "If an email address is available, we respond to postal mail with email."[36]

WEOs like Hamming and Carson represent tomorrow's creative, flexible lawmakers: tech-savvy politicians who use a variety of electronic means to help their constituents become better citizens and themselves be better representatives. In time, politicians who fail to embrace e-democracy tools are likely to see their bills defeated by sophisticated online issue advocacy campaigns—or see themselves pushed out of office altogether by tech-savvy newcomers. We'll explore just how that might happen in the next chapter.

TIPS FOR PRACTITIONERS

- Develop a comprehensive approach to e-democracy, incorporating "e-democracy buttons" into as many government websites and e-government services as possible.
- Provide citizens the ability to comment online on all laws before they are voted on and all rules before they are finalized. For online consultations, use a facilitator to guide citizens through the process and keep the event moving.
- Develop personalized email notification systems that allow constituents to sign up to get emails from government based on their interests or where they live. They can be notified of public meetings, online consultations, local zoning changes, or when their pet issues come up in the legislature.
- Transform your website into a virtual constituent services office.
- Reach more citizens by partnering with trusted media organizations such as newspapers, television stations, and Internet portals to provide additional channels for citizens who want to make their voices heard. In the United Kingdom, the British Broadcasting System's (BBC) iCan website, in partnership with the government, helps Brits who want to get involved by providing tools and guidance for everything from contacting their local representatives to creating and running an issues campaign.

8

Campaigns and Elections on the Web

When former wrestling star Jesse Ventura toppled both Republican and Democratic opponents to win the 1998 Minnesota governor's race, the Internet got almost as much credit as the governor's "maverick celebrity" persona. Ventura began his campaign with no major party (and no major-party war chest), no endorsements, and no public recognition of his ideas. For several months, he didn't even have an office.[1]

But Ventura did have a webmaster: Phil Madsen, a former auto mechanic, wilderness camp guide, sales manager, and church youth director who, when the campaign began, had never even built a website. No problem. Madsen bought a copy of Microsoft FrontPage 98 and turned www.jesseventura.org into a miniature campaign headquarters, where supporters could do everything from join the JesseNet email list to purchase a Jesse action figure. The Jesse dolls made a mint for the Ventura campaign, over a third of whose contributions were collected online.[2] Ventura even added a second line of dolls with outsized nodding heads to finance his reelection campaign. These dolls, the "bobbleheads," sold out.

Ventura's website helped his campaign in strictly political terms as well. The campaign published scads of policy positions on the site, and the media responded by moving off the wrestling theme and taking the candidate more seriously. One newspaper even called him "Jesse 'The Wonk' Ventura." When he made controversial remarks (which he did quite often) or was misquoted (such as when it was widely reported that he favored legalizing prostitution), JesseNet subscribers instantly received emailed clarifications, unfiltered by reporters.[3] JesseNet, says Madsen, effectively replaced the major political parties that his boss disdained, creating "a statewide force of truth-telling missionaries" bent on spreading the gospel of Jesse.[4]

The Ventura campaign also used the Internet to recruit, coordinate, and motivate volunteers. "In the old days, we used to call people on the telephone one at a time to raise volunteers," says Madsen. "Now we can raise them by the dozens with a single email message." JesseNet also replaced more traditional advance teams, mobilizing volunteers whenever Ventura thundered into town. With few computers in the campaign office, the campaign even used JesseNet to let volunteers do online data entry from the comfort of their homes.

The Ventura campaign marked a milestone for e-campaigning. Until his election, the Internet had never been used in a sophisticated way by a major political campaign. Candidates would put up the obligatory website and use email to connect with staff and key volunteers, but most communications were still done by traditional media like phone, mail, and television. Ventura changed that by demonstrating just how valuable the Net could be to a political campaign. He showed how a candidate who catches fire can make up for a lack of traditional party infrastructure by using the Internet to market himself directly to voters, raise money, organize volunteers, and get voters to the polls—four of every campaign's most important tasks. There were too many other factors—notably, the candidate's beefy persona—to give the Internet all the credit for his startling victory. But without the Net, says Madsen, "we couldn't have won the election."[5]

THE NEW CAMPAIGN HUB

Online campaigning has made huge strides since Ventura's shocking net-fueled election. In fact, by today's standards, Ventura's then trailblazing foray into Internet campaigning might now even seem a bit primitive, that is until you stop to consider two important facts: Ventura was the first major candidate to do this; and, unlike Howard Dean and John McCain—two more recent Internet campaigning pioneers—Jesse actually won his race.

Thanks at least in part to Ventura's success, candidates for offices at all levels of government have begun to exploit the potential of a medium which can, according to PoliticsOnline.com president Phil Noble, deliver "everything a campaign is already doing, but faster, smarter and cheaper."[6] "Everything except kissing babies," he amends. "There are no cyber-lips yet." Instead of simply posting their brochures online, tech-savvy candidates are making the Net the hub of their campaign.

Some of the most promising developments have come in the most surprising of places. Internet campaigning played a huge role in South Korea's 2002 and 2004 presidential elections. Winning candidate Roh Moo-hyun's website, complete with pop-up video and animation was one of the five hundred most visited websites in the world in 2002 (the White House site was far behind at No. 1,991), attracting more than half a million visitors a day. Roh's supporters, many of them young people who had never previously been active in politics, even created an online fan club for Roh whose membership swelled to 70,000. "The young generation used not to be interested in politics, but the Internet has brought them into the heart of this election," said Huh Un-na, a top official of the ruling Millennium Democratic Party. "The Internet is as powerful as television in reaching young people in Korea."[7] To ensure that the enthusiasm for his candidacy translated into actual votes, on Election Day Roh sent text messages out to more than 800,000 supporters reminding them to go to the polls.

In 2004, on a website called "epol" South Koreans could select the district they live in via an animated map, see which candidates they'll be voting on and chat with other voters in their district about the election. In one click, they could also see whether the candidate had violated any election laws, or had had any other run-ins with the law, and also read up on all his issue positions. The National Election Commission even had a web-ad, complete with James Bond-style music, encouraging voters to send in pictures of any election violations via their mobile camera phones.[8]

As more and more candidates embrace email, the Internet, and other information technologies, many changes coming to government in general are guiding political campaigns as well. Just as citizen expectations are rising with regard to the ease and speed of government services, so are voter expectations. "Netizens" expect to not only scan candidate websites but to have a variety of options while there. Voter contact is becoming more personalized and more targeted. The ability to turn scads of voter information into useful knowledge about which voters to target and how to win them over can mean the difference between winning and losing a campaign. Campaign spending is more transparent than ever before thanks to the Net. Want to know the names of the well-heeled Bush Rangers, each one of whom raised a whopping $200,000 for President Bush in 2004? They're listed right there on www.georgewbush.com. Even volunteering is going high-tech. Many campaigns are outfitting volunteers with PDAs to share voter information when they hit the precincts.

THE NEW CAMPAIGN ATM MACHINE

Jesse Ventura was the hop. John McCain was the skip. And Howard
Dean is the quantum leap.

—Michael Cornfield, George Washington University's Institute for
Politics, Democracy and the Internet

Ventura's breakthrough campaign helped to inspire a presidential bid
that, although it did not ultimately win the White House, nonetheless
marked Internet campaigning's big-time debut. After all, Ventura was
several different kinds of anomaly—how many politicians can get away
with posing as Rodin's "Thinker" in an ad during the last days of the campaign? Sen. John McCain's massive Internet fund-raising push during the
2000 presidential primary proved that "normal" (or at least seminormal)
candidates could use the new medium as well.

Max Fose, McCain's webmaster, likes to joke that his B.A. in Criminal
Justice made him a natural for work in politics.[9] Fose fits the role of Weird-
Web-Guy perfectly, with his spiky hair and sweaters, sitting in the back of
McCain headquarters in a cramped little room lit by a flickering neon
bulb and a green scented candle.[10] Fose knew McCain was fighting an uphill battle against both public expectations and presidential son George W.
Bush's vast network of party support. His own online role, he felt, would
be crucial to overcoming the obstacles in McCain's path. "If this is David
vs. Goliath," he said, "then the Internet is our slingshot."[11]

He began by placing McCain banner ads on popular sites like the *New
York Times*, the *Wall Street Journal*, *Los Angeles Times*, and *Slate* magazine,
and it worked; about 3 percent of viewers who saw the ads "clicked
through" to McCain's campaign site—a much higher percentage than is
garnered by most direct-mail campaigns.[12] Like Ventura, McCain used the
Internet to gather volunteers and cash, to exercise damage control, and to
present the candidate's views. On just one Saturday during the California
primary campaign, the site sent out twenty-two emails to different groups
of supporters.[13] In New York, the campaign had forty-nine different people across the state, each representing a different geographical area, updating their part of the campaign site daily.

But it was McCain's upset victory in the New Hampshire primary that
most strikingly illustrated the Internet's potential political power. McCain
showed future dark-horse candidates how to capitalize on early wins by
converting his political momentum almost immediately into dollars,
which in turn, he used to build more momentum. Previously, candidates
would have to wait weeks for donations in the wake of a New Hampshire
win, by which time their comet may have already burnt out. McCain, by
contrast, raked in $20,000 via his website in the first hour after he won the

primary; $300,000 by the next morning; and $2 million by the end of the week.[14] "The Internet transforms the action-reaction dynamic of defining events," write Michael Cornfield and Jonah Sieger of George Washington University. "If an organization is prepared for a surge of traffic to arrive at some point during the campaign, it can put it to work, not only to re-define public perceptions, but to raise money, recruit volunteers, and oth-erwise multiply the impact of an event."[15] All in all, the Arizona Senator raised nearly one-third of all his campaign funds, $6.4 million, online—something that had never been done before.[16]

The Quantum Leap

It was audacious. It was inspired. It was vintage Howard Dean. In four days, Vice President Cheney was slated to raise $300,000 for the Bush-Cheney reelection committee at an event for 150 well-to-do GOP donors in South Carolina. Alongside a picture of him biting into a turkey sand-wich on his website, Dean issued a challenge to his supporters: over the next four days help me raise more money than the vice president will re-ceive in South Carolina. There was one catch. Instead of throwing $2,000-a-plate fund-raisers, Dean wanted to beat Cheney without spending a dime—by raising all the money online.

It was no contest.

Dean raised $508,640 over the Internet in four days—almost 70 percent more than Cheney's haul. Fully 9,621 supporters answered the Vermont governor's call. The average donation: about $50 a piece. The best part of the story is that the idea didn't come from Dean or his campaign manager, or some highly paid campaign consultant. In fact it didn't come from any-one on the campaign at all. It came from a blogger on his website.

The Cheney Challenge was but one example of Dean's Internet fund-raising prowess. By the summer of 2003, he had shocked the political world. In just six months Dean had gone from long-shot candidate with no money in his campaign kitty to the Dem with the most money, the most supporters and the best polling numbers. His silver bullet? The In-ternet. Dean garnered tens of millions of dollars worth of donations and hundreds of thousands of supporters from the Net. Most of the money came from small donors that Dean could go back to several times without hitting up against the $2,000 federal spending limit. His Internet fund-raising was so strong that this governor from one of the least populated states in the nation decided to opt out of public financing altogether.

In the second quarter of 2003, more than 73,000 people contributed to Dean's campaign, a full 50,000 more than to John Kerry. In the fourth quarter, Dean broke the record for campaign fund-raising in a single quar-ter, bringing in $15.9 million, far outdistancing Bill Clinton, who had taken in $10.5 million as a sitting president. By the time he withdrew from the race, 670,000 donors had given the Vermont governor more than $45 million.

Leveling the Money Playing Field

Dean and McCain both benefited greatly from the "clean" image of Internet money: no chicken-or-fish dinners with wealthy donors, no photos of the candidate in compromising proximity to honey-tongued lobbyists. The Internet, it turns out, is highly conducive to new, small-dollar donors. Thirty-one percent of McCain's Internet contributions came from people who'd never given to a political campaign before, and 71 percent came from people who had either not given money before or had given only once before.[17] Not to be outdone, Dean raised more money from $25 and $75 donations than any Democratic campaign in history. As Internet fund-raising becomes more common, the percentage of small-dollar, first-time donors is likely to rise even more.

Ironically, McCain, and to some extent Dean, were both known for an issue—campaign finance reform—which many observers believe will be rendered less pressing by online fund-raising (and maybe even made obsolete), as increased contributions by small online donors balance out the lobbyists' moneybags. According to Fose, when these small donors give online, they give significantly more than they do by mail or by phone because it is more of an impulse buy. Internet contributions can be rapidly tallied and published online, thus enhancing campaign transparency.

E-campaigners also may need less money to run. After all, email is free, and as former Louisiana legislator Ron Faucheux says, "The biggest cost item in political campaigns is *postage*."

NET ROOTS

We didn't know what we were doing half the time. We were doing things that were being tried for the first time in this country's political history.

—Joe Trippi, Howard Dean's former campaign manager

Fund-raising, of course, was only one facet of online campaigning that the Dean campaign mastered like no campaign had before. By running the first presidential campaign organized primarily through the web, Dean demonstrated how an underdog candidate with a compelling message can exploit the speed and decentralized nature of the Internet to go from relative obscurity to a front-runner for the presidency in a very short period of time. Dean was the first presidential campaign to have a blog, the first (at least in America) to experiment with wireless and text messaging, and the first to use a popular gathering spot called Meetup.com, which coordinates local gatherings for people with similar interests, to bring volunteers together from all over the country to coordinate events and discuss campaign issues.

The Meetup meetings started off as unsanctioned events spontaneously put together by supporters and morphed into monthly meetings with Dean and his senior campaign staff attending. Each month, tens of thousands of volunteers got together at restaurants, cafes, and student unions in more than one thousand cities and towns across the country to discuss the Dean campaign and listen to the candidate. By the time he dropped out of the race, more than 200,000 people had registered at Meetup.com for Howard Dean, making it the most popular Meetup group on the web—right ahead of witches, pagans, and Elvis enthusiasts. Dean used Meetup and other web-based tools such as DeanLink, a Friendstar-like program that helped supporters recruit their friends and family to join the campaign, to create hundreds of networks of loosely organized volunteers who in turn were linked to each other and to the national campaign. "When you don't have money for mailings and fund-raisers and you're outside the power structure, the Net is just a wonderful tool to get things rolling," said Mark Naccarato, cochairman of the Dean campaign in Nashville, Tennessee, "The Internet is just a very efficient way to connect people . . . what it changes is the ability to organize quickly and efficiently."[18]

By the beginning of 2004, Dean had signed up nearly 900,000 people online to assist his campaign in one way or another. These supporters, who the campaign team called the "Net roots," were the heart and the soul of the Dean campaign. They helped him walk away with MoveOn.org's highly publicized Internet-based Democratic presidential primary, winning 44 percent of the vote—not to mention millions of dollars worth of free publicity and $3 million in campaign donations that came in the week following the vote.

The really novel part about the Dean campaign was not that it managed to recruit a lot of supporters—other campaigns had done that before—but that it moved beyond the one-way conversation national campaigns traditionally had with their supporters to a genuine dialogue. The Dean campaign vested a tremendous amount of trust and authority in the Net roots. A handful of the most innovative ideas from the campaign, such as the Cheney Challenge, came from bloggers on Dean's website. When Dean was deciding whether or not to opt out of public financing—and thereby the campaign spending limits—he spelled out the pros and cons on his weblog and then left the decision up to his supporters via a national online

PINPOINT TARGETING

Today, through polls, focus groups, voting records, geographical sorts and the like, campaigns go to great lengths to target their voter appeals. Such targeting, however, requires costly polling, targeted television and radio buys, and dozens of mailings—much too expensive for many challenger campaigns. The Net lets candidates and issue groups target and customize their pitches on a mass scale at a fraction of the cost of mail, TV, or radio. Explains Harvard professor David King: "With the Internet, we hear the creaky beginnings of a new political machine . . . the Internet can help political organizers communicate with finely drawn slices of the electorate . . . the political Internet will narrowcast, focusing on individual interests and exploring block by block the virtual precincts of local issues."[a]

Just as government innovators are using customer relationship management tools and personalization to enable citizens to have unique experiences with governments online, savvy campaign managers can create even more personalized online experiences for voters. By investing time and resources in acquiring, sorting, and merging electronic lists of voters' email addresses and online browsing patterns they can tailor candidate websites and emails to the interests of specific voters the same way Amazon personalizes your online bookstore.

We are also likely to see campaigns adopt radical new marketing and promotional strategies like the kind of word-of-mouth, "viral" marketing campaigns that stirred advanced interest in movies such as *Lord of the Rings* and *The Blair Witch Project*. The best viral marketers understand that the website is only one of many ways to get the word out about your product (or in the case of Net politics, your candidate or issue). Truly wired campaigns will link with other sites, get the candidate listed with search engines, send out creative and humorous emails that supporters will forward to their friends and create relationships with well-placed bloggers.[b]

a. David King, "Catching Voters in the Web" in *governance.com: Democracy in the Information Age,* ed. Elaine Ciulla Kamarck and Joseph S. Nye Jr. (Washington, D.C.: Brookings Institution Press, 2002), 109.
b. Cornfield and Sieger, "The Net and the Nomination."

vote. "We're actually trying to get people to participate in democracy again," explained Dean's tech-savvy campaign manager Joe Trippi at the time. "And we're using the Internet to get the message out faster and earlier and asking supporters to help spread the word."[19]

Dean, of course, ultimately lost the Democratic primary in what surely will go down as one of the fastest and steepest crashes in recent presidential history. Countless political wags likened the Dean flameout to the dot-com crash. The meltdown, we were told, demonstrated that the Internet model of political organization was a failure—or at least that it failed Dean. "Dean offered the Democratic Party a different model of organizing, a distinctive approach to political mobilization," wrote David Broder, the Beltway's dean of political journalism. "Its conspicuous failure in its first road tests . . . brings into question the whole notion that Internet-based populism is the wave of the future."[20]

The Internet didn't fail Dean. Dean failed Dean. Once subjected to the "front-runner's glare," he made a bevy of mistakes: a gaffe a day for weeks on end (from Osama to Saddam to Confederate flags), the refusal to talk at all about his family (thereby making it hard for voters to get to know him as a person), spending millions of dollars on television commercials outside of Iowa months before a single primary was held (who could forget the $100,000 in Texas), and, of course, "the scream" (enough said). Smelling blood, his primary opponents, as well as the media, were happy to pile on and the rest was history. "This [wasn't] a dot-com crash," argues Trippi. "It's a dot-com miracle being shot down is what it is . . . the dot-com was supposed to make money, and the Howard Dean campaign put more money together than any Democrat in history so where did it mess up there? It's the broadcast politics of the party, it's the scream speech run over and over again, and yes to be honest about it, the governor admits it's himself."[21]

To be sure Trippi has a vested interest in this account, but he is nonetheless correct. The Internet-based model Trippi pioneered helped bring Dean to the dance, but when it came time to dance with the homecoming queen, the underdog turned frontrunner just couldn't get his feet right.

CATALYZING AND MOBILIZING

Political candidates may be the most visible people using the Internet to effect political change, but they're hardly the most innovative. Issue advocacy has flourished online for years. When the FDIC, for instance, proposed a new "Know Your Customer" regulation that required banks to develop customer profiles, determine where they get their money, monitor their transactions and report any "unusual activity," the agency knew it would be controversial. What they didn't know was that they would wind up on the losing end of one of the first major examples of cyberdemocracy in action.

"The purpose of this website is to drive an email spike into the heart of Know Your Customer," said Libertarian Party National Director Steve Dasbach, announcing the launch of a site wholly devoted to killing the initiative. "DefendYourPrivacy.com educates, agitates, and activates people—all with a click of a mouse." Less than a week after the site's launch, over 37,000 people had signed an electronic petition opposing the regulation, and more than eight thousand protesting emails a day reached the FDIC. (The total eventually reached 250,000.) "The FDIC was just stunned," recalls Libertarian Party press secretary George Getz. "They didn't know what hit them. They had to comment on it publicly—they were getting all sorts of calls from print reporters."

The Internet, says Getz, helped persuade people that the anti-Know Your Customer coalition wasn't just making wild assertions. "Anyone could go [online] and read that regulation in all of its nefariousness," he notes. "Before the Internet, if you told someone, 'There's this terrible federal regulation! It's been published in the *Federal Register*!', what's a guy in Des Moines going to do? Get on a plane and track down the *Federal Register*?"

In the end, the negative response to the initiative was so immense, and the quality of the emails from the Libertarians so high, that the FDIC simply backed down. "We never dreamed we'd be able to kill it when we set up the site," says Dasbach. "It was the longest of long shots. The Internet is what modern-day patriots use to curb the excesses of government that's gone too far. It's the musket of the twenty-first century."[22]

And this is only the beginning. The Net's near future will include vastly increased computing power, broadband in most homes, and a stunning increase in the power of software to help us organize our activities, allowing citizens to aggregate their political efforts and view political activity in fundamentally new ways. The Internet is likely to accelerate the process of interest group formation, and let even groups far outside the political mainstream organize and advocate more quickly and effectively than they could have before.

Some groups are already reaching across national borders. In 1997, online advocacy won its first Nobel Peace Prize. You typically picture Peace Prize winners as daring, visionary heads of state, or heroic dissidents locked behind bars by nasty dictatorships. You don't picture the Vermont farmhouse at the end of a dirt road where Jody Williams organized the International Campaign to Ban Land Mines. Williams, hired by the Vietnam Veterans Association, had no staff and no office—nothing but a computer. When the campaign began in 1991, one participant guessed that it would take thirty years to have any effect.[23] Instead, six years later, reporters were struggling to follow directions like, "It's the farmhouse past the beaver pond," so they could quiz Williams on how it felt to win a Nobel Prize by getting more than eighty-nine countries to sign an agreement banning land mines.

Williams began by using faxes, since she lacked both the time to trundle thousands of letters down to the post office and the money to mail them. "Then email came along in 1994," she says, "and we reduced our fax bills by thousands of dollars."[24] When Williams couldn't win an ally over email, she'd fly out for personal persuasion, but the bulk of her contacts were over the Internet.[25] She managed to get everyone from Sen. Patrick Leahy to Britain's Princess Diana to sign on to the antiland mine campaign. Even countries that didn't sign the treaty—like the United States—agreed to help clear minefields.[26]

It's a telling anecdote about an emerging era in which international organizing is so easy that even the most local issues will no longer be truly local—as when members of an online R.E.M. fan club learned that the city of Athens, Georgia, was about to demolish the train trestles featured on the cover of the group's early masterpiece, *Murmur*. The resulting "Save the Trestles" campaign eventually gathered support from around the world. The trestle-lovers were able to convince Athens-Clarke County to keep the trestles and solicit funds for their restoration.

To be sure, most successful e-advocacy campaigns haven't shown much staying power. They tend to be issue-specific, emerging to promote (or defeat) a certain bill or cause, then fading away once the issue has been decided. One e-advocacy campaign that's been able to buck this trend is MoveOn.org, originally formed to defeat the effort to impeach President Bill Clinton. The group recruited thousands of volunteers who delivered petitions to their representatives on October 29, 1998.[27] One minute after the House of Representatives voted for impeachment, MoveOn launched "We Will Remember," an online pledge drive dedicated to defeating members of Congress in swing districts who'd voted to impeach. At the end of the pledge drive's first day, MoveOn had received over $5 million in online pledges for candidates opposing the impeachers.[28]

And in 2001, long after Clinton had left office, MoveOn.org was still going strong, having transformed itself into a supple, member-driven organization focused on a small number of issues. In March, the group gathered 30,000 messages supporting the McCain-Feingold campaign finance reform and delivered them to Senator Mitch McConnell, who had commented that Americans cared as much about campaign finance as they cared about static cling. MoveOn.org member John Hlinko cheekily attached socks and boxer shorts to his clothes, claiming to be a "static cling victim," and delivered sheets of "Bounce" fabric softener and paper copies of the emails to Senator Mitch McConnell's office.[29]

By 2004, just a few years removed from being a tiny two-person operation, MoveOn.org had managed to leverage its Internet savvy to become a major force in American liberal politics, raising and spending tens of millions of dollars to defeat President George W. Bush and training thousands of other liberal activists in the art of using the Net to wage political warfare. One of the first things John Kerry did when he won the

Democratic Party nomination was to hire one of the MoveOn.org founders to run his website operations.

But perhaps the most potent (albeit almost unnoticed) use of the Internet for political organization so far may have been the work of the anti-globalization protesters at the 1999 World Trade Organization (WTO) meeting in Seattle. The sheer numbers of the Seattle protests came as a shock to the major media, which hadn't been paying much attention as online activists planned their events. The WTO riots showed the darker side of online organizing as intermittently destructive protest groups took advantage of the Internet's flexible, decentralized nature to form, strike, and then melt back into the shadows. Organizers hid behind online aliases, making it difficult, even impossible, to hold anyone accountable for the violence. Al Qaeda uses the Net in much the same way, as a tool to help.

For better or worse, the meteoric growth of text messaging as a communications tool—especially in Europe and Asia—will make this kind of political mobilization even easier. In Hungary, where over 50 percent of the population has cellular phones, the extremely close 2002 parliamentary election campaign saw the emergence of cell phone text messaging as a force in political campaigns.[30] Text messaging was used to mobilize supporters for campaign events, communicate the "message of the day" to supporters and the media, and to get people to the polls. It was also employed in a more nefarious way: to spread unsubstantiated rumors about the opposition (such as, "The Prime Minister beats his wife"). All in all, cell phone text messages soared a remarkable 20 to 30 percent between the two rounds of the election, with analysts attributing the large increase mostly to political activity.

BYTE THE BALLOT

The question is not whether the Internet should be used for elections, but when. Internet voting is the future of voting in the United States.

—Michael Alvarez and Thad E. Hall, authors of *Point, Click & Vote.*

Once the campaigning is over, it's time to vote. Probably no area of e-government has received more attention and more debate in recent years than electronic voting. After the endless recounts and legal wars of the 2000 presidential election, many Americans were ready to embrace any voting system that meant never again hearing the words "pregnant chad." A wave of post-Florida expert analysis predicted the rise of the era of e-voting—with punch cards and chads giving way to the PIN codes of digital signatures that could enable online, or at least, electronic ballot box-style, voting. Citizens, we were told, would be able to research candidates and issues and someday even vote from the comfort of their homes. Internet voting was cast as a cost-cutting, mistake-cutting, and participation-enhancing cure for our ailing election system.

Electronic voting, it was hoped, would solve many of the problems of our troubled election system. Just how sick was our election system? So sick that, as far as the year 2000 voting problems went, Florida wasn't even the worst state; Illinois, South Carolina, and Georgia all had higher rates of spoiled or uncounted ballots. In Chicago, almost one out of every ten ballots for president didn't even register a vote. In New York City, there were reports of improperly printed ballots and broken lever machines.[31] A CalTech/MIT report concluded that "between four and six million presidential votes were lost in the 2000 election." Adding up error rates in all aspects of the election process—voter registration, election set-up, ballot design, actual voting, ballot tabulation—would probably triple or quadruple this number.

As for vote fraud—take a deep breath before you read this.[32] A Miami election in 1998 was thrown out when it was learned that "vote brokers" had signed hundreds of fake ballots; that same year, former Democratic Congresswoman Austin Murphy was convicted of absentee ballot fraud. In 1999, *60 Minutes* found California ballots bearing the names of imaginary people and pets. The year 2000 brought vote fraud scandals in St. Louis and Philadelphia. By the time Florida came along, almost no one disputed anymore that our voting and voter registration system was broken.

One reform that emerged after the Florida fiasco was the introduction of ATM-like electronic voting machines at voting places across the country. By the 2004 presidential election, about 50 percent of all voters were voting on electronic touch-screen machines—up from just a few thousand voters in 2000. As would be expected, with the introduction of a new technology on such a massive scale the switchover encountered some technical glitches in scattered locations throughout the nation, though not serious enough to derail the momentum for electronic voting, given its advantages over punch card ballots.

Electronic voting mechanisms, for example, can prevent "overvotes" (a voter inadvertently choosing two candidates instead of one) and "undervotes" (in which a vote fails to be recorded because the voter marks his ballot incorrectly). If, for example, a voter leaves a section of the ballot unmarked, a prompt could appear: "You have not yet voted for President. Would you like to continue, or go back and vote?" After the ballot has been marked, a prompt could say, "You have chosen William Smith for President. To continue voting, click here. To change your vote, click here." Simple changes like this would have prevented much of the Florida turmoil, but face challenges themselves, since voters who still use paper ballots are at a disadvantage compared to those who have access to the new e-ballots.

These electronic voting systems, while in many ways an improvement over punch card ballots, are really nothing more than self-contained electronic ballot boxes. The results are tabulated on individual digital cards. The machines are not tied together, nor connected in any way to the Internet. Electronic ballot boxes are an important step toward modernizing our voting systems but they are not transformative. To participate in an election, people still need to trudge down to the polling place on a certain day—or in some states fill in a mail-in ballot. The differences from the previous system are important but don't represent a paradigm shift.

Internet voting, on the other hand, is a different story. It would mean no more worrying about lost or late military ballots; no more excuses that you didn't vote because you were on a business trip. It would mean that you could vote from the comfort of your home or even by text message while fishing on the lake. It would mean that younger voters who grew up on the web could vote using a more comfortable medium for them than punch cards, thereby holding the potential for increased voter turnout. "I suspect that for anybody under forty, polling day is the only point in the year when they actually see a pencil stub," says Robin Cook, the former leader of the British House of Commons, "and that's probably why it's tied to a piece of string, because it's so rare and they might pocket it as a souvenir."[33] Lastly, Internet voting would make voting much easier for the blind and the disabled, both of whom are heavily disadvantaged by the current election system. Internet voting can present ballots through voice commands for blind voters wearing headphones, and voters who cannot use their arms can use a "sip-and-puff" wand to signal their choices.

While the benefits of Internet voting are easy to see, the real question is whether it's even possible. At first, several pilot Internet voting projects seemed to lend credence to the idea. Amid all the butterfly ballots and missing votes, the first valid "Internet votes" in a U.S. general presidential election were cast in 2000. Eighty-five members of the U.S. military voted from computers in their homes, offices, or U.S. embassies abroad. "The military voters loved it, it was wonderful for them," says Marti Taylor, an elections official from South Carolina who was involved in the experiment. "We had no problems at all. It worked like clockwork."[34]

A handful of other high-profile Internet voting experiments were undertaken in the United States, Great Britain, and Switzerland. In an effort to boost sagging voter turnout, the Arizona state party hosted the nation's first binding election conducted partly over the Internet during the 2000 Democratic primary. Four years earlier, only 12,800 of 843,000 registered Arizona Democrats had voted in the presidential primary. The Dems figured they couldn't possibly do any worse—and they might do a lot better—by letting people vote in their pajamas.

They weren't disappointed. "Arizona's Demos Throng to Globe's First e-Election" screamed the headline in a local paper, as countless news outlets reported turnout increased more than 600 percent from the previous primary, cutting across all ethnic and sociological groups, from wired undergraduates who held dorm-room voting parties to tech-savvy seniors who turned their homes into polling places for their blue-haired friends. Clearly, Internet voting was the future, and the future was here.

Or was it?

Once you looked under the hood, some serious problems were apparent in the pilot. A Compaq Computer Corporation techie named David Jefferson served as Chairman of California's Internet Voting Task Force, which came up with a set of guidelines for reaching the online-voting future. The Arizona Democrats, he says, were a prime example of "how *not* to run an online election," and their experiment left a string of unresolved questions in its wake:

- Why did the server go down for an hour on the first day of voting?
- Would a determined hacker have been able to get voters' information?
- Did vote fraud occur?
- Did Election.com employees, who had access to voters' PIN numbers and other identification, use their opportunity to "read" people's votes?
- What would something like "The Love Bug" have done to the primary (which had very little protection against computer viruses)?

Nobody knows. In fact, Election.com officials and the Arizona Dems didn't even try to defend themselves against Jefferson's critique, choosing instead to chalk up any problems to growing pains. "Whenever you introduce a new technology and huge changes to a process, there is a learning curve and processes that need to be worked through," says Julia Glidden, a former senior executive at Election.com (which is now part of Accenture). "The important thing is to move forward and fix the problems." And as for the turnout numbers, an evaluation by election researchers Michael Alvarez and Thad Hall found that the turnout was actually fairly low when compared against other statewide Democratic primaries in the 1990s.[35] Internet voting was also allowed in the 2004 Michigan Democratic Primary; while turnout increased slightly, it didn't boost voter participation nearly to the extent anticipated.

More extensive Internet voting trials have taken place in the United Kingdom. In a handful of voting wards across the country during the 2002 and 2003 local elections, voters received a card in the mail with their password and a PIN number that they could use to vote from home, special kiosks, or even from their cell phones, via text messaging.[36] A major goal of the efforts was to increase voter turnout, which had been declining for years. The results were mixed at best. In wards in Liverpool and Sheffield, where people were allowed a week to vote online, turnout jumped appreciably in the 2002 elections. In Liverpool, turnout jumped 10 percentage points, with 41 percent of all votes being cast digitally. "I voted for council from the front seat of my lorry," one truck driver said. "It would have taken me an hour to get to the polling station and wait in the queue. But with my mobile [phone] it took twenty seconds. I got a message right back that said, 'Thanx 4 Ur vote.'"[37] Another advantage was that votes were counted much faster than before. In several other jurisdictions, however, there was no increase in turnout.

With this limited success also came security and authentication problems that mirrored some of those experienced in Arizona. There were myriad anecdotal reports of passwords and PINs being sent to people who had moved or died. One Church ward voter from Allerton, England, said: "We have had three cards through the door with secret PIN numbers but they are for people who have not lived here in years."[38]

Authentication is one of the more bedeviling issues relating to Internet voting. In many states, of course, voter authentication today is based essentially on the honor system. Unlike getting a passport or a driver's license, registering to vote doesn't require a personal appearance, a laxness that has been tolerated because it would take so much effort to commit vote fraud on a large scale. The current registration system involves paper forms with live signatures, and real people inspecting the forms, meaning any attempt to commit *massive* fraud successfully by registering a *large* number of ineligible or nonexistent voters would be risky and complicated. Online voting, however, would make major vote fraud much, much easier (at least until every adult American has a verifiable digital signature). How do you know, for example, that it's not a family member using the voter's computer? How do you know the voter hasn't sold her password to someone trying to steal the election? E-voting, critics contend, could open the door to election fraud on a mass scale.

Then there's the matter of security. Online voting poses more security problems than online commercial transactions because votes must be kept secret—there's no way to check, for example, that a given vote was recorded correctly. Moreover, various types of malicious software could change the votes; reveal them to outsiders; or even prevent them from being recorded at all in a given precinct. And as security measures increase, the convenience to the voter drops, a nasty pattern that could someday leave online voting fairly secure—but less "convenient" than programming your VCR. Preventing virus contamination, for instance, could mean rebooting your computer to load a clean, county-provided operating system which would freeze any other programs, preventing both hacking and "spoofing" (setting up mock-voting sites, directing voters to send their personal information to www.californiavote.com rather than www.californiavote.gov, for example). Employees may not be able to vote from the office if linked computers prove too difficult to secure. And a vote, once cast, must disappear completely from the voter's computer. No ghostly votes can be left flickering in hard drives, caches, cookies, or anywhere else—even in encrypted form. There must be no way for someone to extract a vote from the computer after the voter has left.

Even intermediate stages of Internet voting—for example, putting Internet-connected voting machines into traditional polling places—pose an array of problems. Some hurdles are purely logistical, such as that polling places like school auditoriums or neighbors' garages aren't usually connected to the Net. But others involve big questions like ballot encryption, recount and audit procedures, and "denial of service" attacks. That's why none of the electronic touch-screen machines used in the 2004 elections were connected to the Internet.

With the 2004 Madrid bombings making clear that influencing elections is now a prime objective of terrorists, wide-scale Internet voting would almost surely be subject to massive cyberterrorist attacks. Until there is almost absolute confidence in the security of the systems, the risks of sabotage would seem to argue strongly against Internet voting. This, at least, was the verdict of a handful of high-profile reports on Internet voting commissioned from the likes of CalTech/MIT, the National Science Foundation, the State of California, and the Pentagon. "The bottom line is we could have our president selected by [hackers in] Iran," argues Barbara Simons, a member of the panel of security experts the Department of Defense asked to examine Internet voting for military personnel. "We basically feel they are trying to solve an impossible problem."[39] Simons, the past president of the Association of Computing Machinery, believes it may never be safe to vote on the Internet. A project to allow more than 100,000 overseas military personnel to vote online during the 2004 primary elections was cancelled at the last minute as a result of the panel's findings.

Not everyone agrees with these grim assessments. MIT computer scientist Ted Selker was involved in both the Pentagon panel and MIT/CalTech's exhaustive Internet voting study. "Their conclusions are wrong," he says angrily when asked about the reports. "They don't understand that the future of technology is different than the past." Security is what's scaring everyone, says Selker, but he insists that a completely secure remote Internet voting system is possible—and not in several decades but in the next few years. The key is built-in redundancy. Every stage of the system would have multiple software programs that would have to agree in order for a vote to count, thus preventing some rogue programmer from sabotaging the system by inserting a hidden code into any portion of the product. "No one person ever does any one stage of the system," Selker explains. "All of it is tested carefully against others. You would need to have massive collusion across organizations to tamper with the design." This structure would also provide a nearly insurmountable anti-hacker firewall. "For multiple, redundant, simultaneous voting systems that have never been seen by anyone before to all be hacked separately," he insists, "is crazy."

Selker is also utterly sanguine about authentication. "We can use several different redundant metrics to evaluate whether the person is who they say they are: location, biometrics, password," he says confidently. "I can even tell you who's at the computer by the way they move the mouse. I can distinguish whether it's you or a family member."

To be sure, it's hard to imagine that a country with no national ID card is going to be checking DNA samples or mouse-click patterns from a state-run biometric database anytime soon. Selker tends to gloss over deeply ingrained societal and political obstacles to the introduction of a new technology, even as he acknowledges that some kinks need to be worked out before Internet voting is as easy as buying this book on Amazon.

But he may be right that many of his computer science colleagues, who tend to judge Internet voting against a perfect ideal rather than the current entirely imperfect system, are unduly pessimistic about the long-term prospects of Internet voting. In time, perhaps, the problems can and will be fixed. "Get the punks in the MIT Media Lab to try some things," he says. "Don't just dismiss this out of hand without trying some experiments."

More experiments will surely continue, particularly in Europe where there seems to be far more enthusiasm for Internet voting than in America. Estonia, for example, is planning to allow voters to vote over the Internet from their home in the country's 2005 local elections. Switzerland piloted Internet voting in Geneva in 2003 and even hired a team of hackers to try and break into the system over a three-week period. They failed.[40]

Even in the United States, it's possible to sketch a timeline for the progression of Internet voting. Despite dropping plans for Internet voting in 2004, the likeliest first candidate in America still might be the military, whose secure worldwide communications capability and extremely high voting rate—75 percent in the 2000 election—makes it the perfect constituency for electronic voting. It's also a motivated constituency; fresh from watching thousands of overseas military ballots being tossed in the trash can. Another motivated constituency is the blind and disabled. Because of its relatively small size, allowing this population to vote online shouldn't carry with it too great a risk.

The next logical step could be online voting for absentee voters. Traditional absentee voting has many of the problems that face Internet voting, including potential for coercion, difficulty of maintaining the secrecy of the ballot, and questions about voter identity. In fact, when it comes to absentee voters, Internet voting may even be made safer than mail-in voting. Security software, for example, could protect online voters against coercion or vote-selling through the use of "duress alarms" that would let a voter signal that he was being coerced.[41] It's also faster than traditional mail-in voting: no waiting for days as those last ballots trickle in from overseas. Belgium, France, Switzerland, and several other countries are all seriously exploring Internet voting for absentee voters.

The next phase of Internet voting will let you submit a request for an Internet ballot, just as you'd request an absentee ballot. When the request is approved, you'd receive information (such as a password) by which you would prove your identity online.[42] Then you'd simply head over to the local mall, pick up some new towels at the Election Day White Sale, and use the local voting kiosk at your leisure, even outside normal voting hours—an advantage in convenience that would eventually be matched by public cost savings, since far fewer poll-watchers would be needed.

The final step will be to allow voting from any connected computer, at any time, for all voters from their home or office or neighbor's house. This won't happen at the national level until all the risks I've already discussed are severely minimized and digital signatures—or some other universally accepted form of authentication—are as ubiquitous as driver's licenses. (Estonia and Spain both already issue identification cards with digital signatures embedded in them; other European countries are not far behind.) However, there is no reason that carefully designed and controlled pilot projects for local elections can't be conducted during this period. The key point is that the transition to ubiquitous Internet voting—assuming it happens at all—should be incremental and based on a careful analysis of risks and benefits.

TIPS FOR PRACTITIONERS

- Create more personalized online experiences for voters by tailoring candidate websites and emails to the interests of specific voters the same way Amazon personalizes your online bookstore.
- Understand that the website is only one of many ways to get the word out about your campaign. Taking a cue from "viral marketing" campaigns, link with other sites, get the candidate listed with search engines, send out creative and humorous emails that supporters will forward to their friends and create relationships with well-placed bloggers.
- Use email and the Net to move from one-way communications with supporters and volunteers to a genuine two-way dialogue.
- Test Internet voting in small-scale, carefully controlled experiments rather than dismissing it out of hand or implementing it wholesale before all the security and authentication issues are fully worked out.

IV

BREAKING THROUGH
THE BARRIERS

9

Solving the Privacy and Security Riddle

TEMPEST IN A COOKIE JAR

The third week of June 2000 was a very bad, very long week for the White House's Office of Drug Control policy. That week the Drug Czar's office faced a slew of unfavorable newspaper articles; scores of angry letters from interest groups; a rebuke from the Office of Management and Budget (OMB); and multiple verbal spankings from members of Congress.

What had caused all this consternation? Drug busts gone awry? A staffer on the take from drug kingpins? Neither. The Drug Czar's office was caught using "cookies"—small pieces of software placed on a website visitor's hard drive to track which web pages the visitor views—without his knowledge. Cookies make web surfing more convenient for users in a myriad of ways, for example, cookies can remember password information, and anyone can set the browser to turn cookies off. But privacy advocates argue that in government's hands, they give the prying eyes of the state too much monitoring ability, especially if we don't even know we're being watched.

The public firestorm forced OMB to rush out a memorandum informing federal agencies in no uncertain terms that cookies were a big no-no. Just to make sure agencies got the message, Congress added language to an appropriations bill ordering agencies to keep out of the cookie jar.

And so ended "cookie-gate"—just one of many high-profile digital privacy dramas that transpired in the first year of the millennium. The previous year had been a banner one for proponents of privacy regulation, as

Congress passed scores of digital privacy laws, covering everything from financial and medical privacy to encryption. The laws built upon a foundation of dozens of privacy laws enacted over the previous few decades, beginning with the landmark Privacy Act of 1974.

Fast-forward to October 2001. The cookies fight seems like child's play as Congress debates whether to allow government agencies to eavesdrop on email conversations, monitor Internet activity, peer into bank accounts, and mine myriad computer systems for suspicious behavior, all in the name of the post-9/11 antiterrorist "Patriot" legislation. Patriot was fiercely opposed by an unlikely coalition of conservatives, left-wingers, and civil libertarians of all stripes. Bob Barr and Phyllis Schlafly teamed up with Barney Frank and the ACLU to fight parts of the legislation. "We are very much against the government monitoring activities of law-abiding Americans, whether it's computers or video cameras or email," said Phyllis Schlafly, president of the Eagle Forum.[1]

The swift passage of Patriot demonstrated just how dramatically September 11 changed the axis of the security/privacy debate in America—and around the world. Since 9/11, Australia, Canada, France, the United Kingdom, and many other countries have enacted laws making it easier for law enforcement agencies to share information and engage in surveillance activities. What was unthinkable pre-September 11 now seems utterly reasonable: biometric technologies—i.e., technology that identifies a person by unique physical characteristics—that can pick a terrorist out of a crowded stadium, surveillance tools that can detect dangerous objects or substances in homes and cars, "smart" visas and ID cards containing computer chips and digitized fingerprints, "key-logger" snooping devices inside computers that secretly record everything a suspect types, integrated government databases of citizen information, even remote-sensing devices and satellite-based optics that enable camera operators to see in the dark and peer inside buildings, and thermal cameras that can tell if a person is lying.

Civil libertarians argue that these technologies represent grave threats to privacy, particularly in the hands of the state. "Day by day we lose more privacy as we move into the electronic era," warns Simon Davies, president of privacy.[2] Many privacy proponents seek to protect us from the state by simply prohibiting government agencies from using many of these new digital technologies. Their fear-borne rallying cries advocate simply unplugging the technology: Stop cross-government agency information sharing. Tear down the surveillance cameras. Ban government from using face-recognition intelligence, and other biometric technologies.

While such sentiments are understandable, prohibition is the wrong approach for protecting our privacy. First of all, any strategy predicated on stopping technology is unlikely to work. More importantly, do we really want an analog government in a digital world? Is it safe or sensible to ask law enforcement to effectively bring knives to a gunfight by requiring them to apprehend criminals and terrorists with the electronic equivalent of fountain pens and buggy whips? Privacy is not an absolute right that should trump everything else. It must be balanced against other goods such as security, convenience, efficiency, and access. The government snoop or the cop has power over our lives, power he might abuse. But al Qaeda's terrorists also have power that they're determined to abuse. We shouldn't let fear of either one blind us to the other. Lastly, as we will see throughout this chapter, technology is privacy-neutral. It can be used for good or evil—to dismiss it as inherently destructive of privacy is mistaken.[3]

Privacy is likely to be one of the most contentious issues in America and other industrialized countries in the years ahead. But rather than asking how to stop government from using cutting-edge technology, we need to ask what rules must be put in place to control government's use of such technologies. Rather than reflexively reverting to Luddism, we should be figuring out which of the new technologies will actually make us safer, *and which will only make us feel safer,* and then design privacy-friendly approaches for using this technology. Rather than wondering whether technology will mean the end of privacy, we should be asking how we can harness new technologies to protect privacy and empower individuals. "Government cannot protect privacy," says privacy advocate Jim Harper from Privacilla.org. "It can only foster or destroy people's ability to protect their own privacy. Privacy is maintained by people having authority and responsibility for what information about them is shared, and on what terms."

IT'S TEN O'CLOCK. DO YOU KNOW WHERE YOUR RECORDS ARE?

Americans no longer know how their personal information will be applied, who will gain access to it, and what decisions will be made with it. Individuals whose personal data are shared, processed and stored by a mysterious, incalculable bureaucracy will be more likely to act as the government wishes them to behave.

—Law professor Paul Schwartz[4]

They never meant the children's records to become public.

In November 2001, sixty-two children and teens learned that their psychological records were available on a University of Montana website.

Due to some unknown student's or employee's mistake, anyone could stumble across four hundred pages of names, dates of birth, home addresses, and descriptions like:

"She has been cruel to animals . . . often refuses to eat and will make herself vomit."
"... anger outbursts, gender identity issues [and bedwetting]."

Both of those quotes came from the records of eight-year-old children.[5]
This is the ultimate privacy nightmare: the electronic strip search. Our most intimate secrets, others' evaluations of us, all searchable on Google. This is the kind of event people fear when they hear about firms that sell guides for easy access to public records. This is the kind of thing that has led many government agencies to remove some databases from the web, the kind of thing you can only do with the Internet—there is simply no equivalent mishap in the offline world. (In a non-reassuring statement, the university's attorney said that private legal or medical data often find their way online by mistake, and it's usually removed quickly.)

Even the collection of records that are already public bothers many people, especially as the Internet makes gaining access to public data easier. In fact, when local governments started putting public records online, many people were dismayed to find out just how much was publicly available. BRB Publications started out just selling *The Motor Vehicle Book*, a guide to finding and using motor vehicle records. But then it branched out, and now offers comprehensive guides to uncovering all kinds of public information. Mark Snaky, the company president, said that his customers range from families trying to trace their genealogies to cautious boyfriends scoping out potential wives. Snaky defended his business against those who don't like the idea of people snooping through their electronic trashcans. "When the government responds to public pressure to close the doors on public records, it affects a lot of good work," he lamented. "It makes it difficult to check up on whether your son's Little League coach has a criminal record."

Many people hate the idea that all their information is collected in an easily searched depository. They especially hate the thought that governments would compile such databases, for two main reasons: You can't avoid using government, and people don't trust the government to police itself. As leading cyber-thinker John Perry Barlow has said: "Trusting government with privacy is like having a peeping Tom install window blinds."[6]

Yet as government takes on more and more tasks, it needs more and more information to act efficiently. So it asks citizens to provide discrete chunks of data, which are stored in many different locations. The IRS knows who you are, how much you make, where you live, how many kids you have, and whether you're chintzy about charitable giving. The Department of Education knows where you work and how much you make. If you're old or poor, the Department of Health and Human Services probably has detailed records on your health.

Then somebody realizes that you can connect the dots. Some of those new employees on the Social Security list are deadbeat dads. Some of those lottery winners owe back taxes. Some of those bus driver applicants may have bad driving records or, worse, a criminal record. And if we linked the databases, we'd know which ones. Pretty soon the counselor at your children's school knows you were arrested in a bar fight back in college, and your daughter isn't allowed to check out books at the county library because you forgot to pay your parking ticket.

To be sure, there are plenty of laws on the books intended to guard against these scenarios. The 1974 Federal Privacy Act, for one, bans federal agencies from assembling a dossier of personal information about individuals unless they're actively investigating the individual. Another federal law requires agencies to enter into public, information-sharing arrangements to protect citizens' privacy and to publish the agreements in the Federal Register.[7]

These and other legal protections have slowed down government data sharing—but not much. And there is continuous pressure from law enforcement and other government agencies to relax or remove these restrictions—pressures that increased dramatically after 9/11. While it's tempting to pin the blame for this pressure on power-hungry bureaucrats, most of the time they're just reacting to demands from us citizens. As was discussed in chapter 2, we hate the fact that every time we contact a different government agency, we have to waste time supplying the same information we've already given out to countless other government agencies—why can't bureaucrats get their act together and share the information, we wonder? Moreover, we want our government to stop fraud in welfare and Medicaid, catch criminals, make sure child molesters aren't hired to teach our kids, go after deadbeat dads, and keep terrorists out of the country.

Accomplishing all this requires extensive data sharing among government agencies. As long as we continue to ask governments to do such things, the collection, sharing, mining, and analyzing of citizens' personal information will increase—and will probably do so exponentially. Any privacy strategy that relies simply on stopping or reversing this development is almost certainly doomed to failure. "You're not going to turn back the information-sharing trend," says Solveig Singleton, a privacy expert

at the libertarian Competitive Enterprise Institute. "If you have a government that's doing what voters think it should be doing, it's difficult to object when they ask for information to accomplish the mission."

This doesn't mean governments should be given free rein to collect any
information about us they want and share it with whomever they choose.
From the internment of Japanese-Americans during World War II—made
possible by Census Bureau data—to J. Edgar Hoover's FBI, history demonstrates that governments with too much information can be downright
dangerous. One of the worst offenders in modern times, of course, was
President Richard Nixon, who infamously used IRS information to harass
his political enemies. When selecting his IRS Commissioner in 1971, Nixon
vowed that the person he would select would be "a ruthless son of a
bitch," who "will do what he's told," show him "every income tax return
I want to see" and "will go after our enemies and not go after our friends."[8]

COMMONSENSE PRINCIPLES FOR PROTECTING OUR PRIVACY

A root problem with government collection and sharing of personal information is that we citizens feel powerless. Most of us have no idea who
gets to see our personal data, what information the government has about
us, or how to get it fixed if it's wrong. And unlike with a private company,
we can't just choose not to use government services. Instead of being the
masters of our government, we're the clueless children and the state is the
tight-lipped parent. This inverts the whole master/servant relationship
articulated by the Founding Fathers. What is needed are ways in which
we as free individuals can protect our privacy against the state without
impairing law enforcement's ability to catch criminals and terrorists. Although privacy and security will sometimes conflict, we should constantly seek to reduce or dissolve this conflict. These five commonsense
principles can help ordinary citizens restrain our government.

What They Don't Know Can't Hurt You

Under the logic that government can't misuse information it doesn't have,
the first protection against government abuse is to insist that the state collect only as much information as is absolutely necessary to do its job. Government shouldn't be able to collect information about us without justifi-
cation. The best way of institutionalizing this very simple principle is to
require government agencies to conduct a privacy impact assessment
each and every time before collecting any new information from citizens.
The assessment would involve evaluating whether the project has conducted privacy training, gathering information on the project's privacy

protection procedures, and identifying and resolving privacy risks.[9] The government of Ontario, Canada, requires such an assessment before approving any new IT projects.

Similarly, in the United States, every federal agency is now required to conduct privacy impact assessments before developing large IT systems or initiating any new electronic collections of personal information from citizens or businesses. The Internal Revenue Service's privacy assessments are considered among the best in the country; the IRS assesses the privacy impact at every stage of the project's development. Similarly, at the United States Postal Service (USPS), privacy officers have the authority to request a privacy assessment at any time during the project's life cycle.[10]

Because the assessments have only been required for a few years, it's still too early to thoroughly evaluate how well they've worked. In the regulatory arena, however, such an approach has been somewhat effective in balancing proposed regulations against economic consequences.[11] And early indications are that privacy impact assessments are helping to ensure that information needs are balanced against privacy concerns.[12]

Put More Control into the Hands of Citizens

In 1999, Ireland created a new agency called "Reach" and charged it with making citizens' dealings with the government easier, less frustrating, and more personalized. Achieving these goals requires the agency to have a consolidated view of citizen data.[13] What makes this different from other government attempts to aggregate citizen data is that the individual citizen, instead of the government, gets to decide what information is shared with other agencies. Each citizen is able to enter his personal data into a "personal data vault." Then he can choose whether or not to release the data when applying for a specific program or service. For example, a citizen may choose to allow all government agencies access to her data vault to retrieve address change information, but deny them access to her health information.

The government of Ontario, Canada, also uses sophisticated technology to ensure that no information is shared without the citizen's explicit permission. When a citizen of the province wants to notify government agencies of a change in address, for example, she is faced with a screen on the website where she can indicate to which agencies she wants the notice sent.

Build Privacy-Friendly Websites and Databases

There is no reason your foot doctor should have your complete psychiatric profile. And there's no reason why a government agency with a database containing marriage certificates needs to know what type of car the newlyweds drive. When personal information is collected by government, it should be done in privacy-friendly ways, such as by limiting the number of data fields in the database, or leaving the owner's name off the record when property tax files are posted online. If you want to purchase a house, for example, as part of the home loan approval process you're probably going to be asked to sign an IRS form giving the mortgage company access to your tax records. Previously, in the paper world, by signing this form you were handing over to mortgage companies access to over two hundred pieces of information about you. Moreover, the IRS put no restrictions on the ability of mortgage companies to sell the information. When the IRS put this form online, however, it limited access to the twenty-six data elements actually necessary for mortgage review and restricted the right of mortgage companies to release the information.[14]

Another privacy-enhancing tool is data disassociation, which encrypts and delinks the data held about an individual from the individual's identity. The idea is to make the data traceable but not identifiable. For health records, for example, this would enable government to collect aggregate statistics on diseases but wouldn't enable someone to gain access to and publish a list of everyone with AIDS. This principle of separating the data itself from the actual identity of particular individuals unless there is a high degree of suspicion that the person poses a threat could be applied to many other areas, including data-mining systems (generalizations about patterns of behavior would still be possible) and even potentially certain types of airline profiling systems.[15]

As a simple matter of fairness, we citizens should also be guaranteed access to our records and allowed to amend information if we can prove it's wrong. The Health Insurance Portability and Accountability Act (HIPAA), the medical privacy law that went into effect in 1999, gives people the right to do these things related to their health records. Savvy policymakers understand that building privacy into government computer systems is really a form of self-protection, helping avoid politically treacherous problems down the road.

Privacy protections should also be embedded into government websites and portals. Thanks to recent technological advances governments can automate privacy compliance enforcement. The Department of Veterans Affairs uses a web-based privacy compliance system to collect and report on privacy violations. The USPS has technology that monitors its websites looking for privacy violations. Coming soon: smart technologies that embed privacy rules directly into software used to create online content.[16]

Who's Been Looking in My Records?

We also need to increase the odds that anyone who misuses access to government databases will get caught and then suffer stiff penalties. Building auditing capabilities into government databases, for example, can provide an "electronic paper trail" of when, by whom, and for what purpose our personal information is viewed. Just as video cameras installed over cash registers deter employees from stealing from their employer, electronic auditing capabilities—like the software used at the IRS that records each time an employee opens an individual tax return—can deter employee snooping. By making it very risky for rogue employees and governments to abuse privacy, these abuses can be curtailed.

Throw the Book at 'Em

In the mid-1990s, more than five hundred IRS employees were caught poking through celebrities' tax files. In the end, only a handful of the offenders were fired, sending the message that there weren't real consequences for snooping through citizens' personal information. This has since changed—at least at the IRS, where stiff penalties now meet any employee caught snooping through tax returns. Public employees and officials who engage in unauthorized snooping and information disclosure should at least lose their jobs and face stiff civil penalties. In Florida, a legislative proposal to create a web-based database to track who is prescribing and using prescription drugs that was defeated on privacy grounds did, however, include a provision making it a third-degree felony to illegally tap into the database.

DIGITAL-AGE IDENTITY

In the late 1990s, the Social Security Administration proved that no good deed goes unpunished. All the agency was trying to do was to make it easier for us citizens to view our Social Security statement. Rather than make us mail or phone in requests for statements detailing our lifetime earnings and expected Social Security benefits upon retirement, the Social Security Administration decided to let us view this information online. At the time, it seemed like a no-brainer. They couldn't have been more mistaken. It didn't take long after the front-page headline "Your Social Security Records Are Online" appeared in *USA Today* for the angry letters, phone calls, and emails to start coming in by the thousands. Three days after the *USA Today* story hit the newsstands, the information was taken off the website.

The Social Security case showed how just the word "online" can raise fears. In fact, the way the new system was set up, gaining access to your Social Security statements on the web required even more proof of identity than requesting the information by mail or phone. In order to view their records online, individuals were required to present all the information they had needed before—name, date of birth, and Social Security number—plus place of birth and mother's maiden name.

So why were Americans so bent out of shape? Identity fraud. People feared that criminals would hack into the system and use the Social Security numbers to order credit cards, create phony driver's licenses, and plunder bank accounts. Identity theft soared in the 1990s as the Internet gained in popularity, rising sixteen-fold between 1992 and 1997.[17] It remains one of the fastest growing (and most profitable) crimes, with identity theft complaints to the Federal Trade Commission increasing sevenfold between 2000 and 2003, from 31,117 to 214,905.[18] Although some reports suggest that identity fraud is still a fairly low-level problem, poll after poll shows it's the biggest concern citizens have with connecting government databases to the Internet.[19]

The big-time identity thieves often get started in the offline world. They use credit card skimmers at cash registers, they steal mail and comb through it for credit card applications and other documents that contain personal information, they "dumpster dive," rifling through trash bins for discarded papers. The Internet didn't create identity theft. But, in some cases, it made crime pay more. "The Internet acts as a force multiplier," according to Martha Stansell-Gamm, the Justice Department's chief of computer crime and intellectual property.[20]

The web also helps fraudsters simply by making so much information so easy to find. One privacy advocate made this point more forcefully than he intended, when he posted the names and Social Security numbers of more than 4,500 U.S. military officers on his website. He was trying to show how easy it was to get personal information from the Congressional Record, but visitors with less benevolent motives used the information to make more than one hundred phony credit cards. They stole about $300,000 worth of goods before they were caught.[21]

Identity is vital to the functioning of a free market economy. Being able to prove you are who you say you are and to own something based on your identity are basic foundations of property rights. Widespread identity fraud costs the economy billions of dollars, makes it more difficult to control our borders, and ultimately destroys trust in business and personal relationships.

The problem is that the methods governments use to authenticate us are broken—or in the online world, entirely underdeveloped. Driver's licenses are too easy to forge or steal. Mother's maiden names are available on public birth records. Passwords are too easy to lose, forget, or break into ("a weak link for important information," says Microsoft's Bill Gates). Social Security numbers, used by many states in their publicly available driver's license records, have become completely insecure. It's estimated that more than 100,000 noncitizens obtained fraudulent Social Security numbers in 2000.[22] "I doubt there is any document in America more fraudulently produced than a Social Security card," says former Rep. Bill McCollum (R-FL).

The Rise of Biometrics

How can we fix this problem and secure our identity in our increasingly digital, increasingly security-conscious world? One of the most promising developments is biometrics, the science of identifying people by their unique physical characteristics: facial patterns, retinal scans, handprints, fingerprints, and voice recognition. Instead of being identified by something I know that I might forget (a password), or something I have that I might leave at home (such as a badge), I'm identified based on something I am (and I can't leave my iris at home). Biometrics have been around forever; today's systems simply convert the biometric—fingerprints, faces, voices, handwritten signatures—into digital form and compare it against a computer database (see table 9-1).[23] The digitization means the biometric can be used for authentication in both the physical and the digital world by using scanners and smart card readers.

If current trends continue, within the next decade biometric technologies will become the main way we authenticate and safeguard our identity. Already, digitized fingerprints, retinal scans, face and voice recognition, and other forms of biometrics are being used to help with everything from keeping track of prisoners and parolees to controlling access to borders, buildings, and facilities:

- When West Virginians apply for a driver's license, the state digitally stores the photographs so that when they renew their licenses, or try to replace lost or stolen ones, the system captures their photo and automatically compares it with their previous photo. The goal: verifying identity and preventing fraud.
- In New York City, 35,000 low-risk probationers can scan their hands at kiosks located throughout the city to prove they're still in the city, leaving probation officers free to focus on higher-risk probationers.[24]
- At Amsterdam's Schiphol airport, registered travelers who prefer not to wait in long lines can instead pass customs by swiping their smart card through a scanner and then staring for a second into a lens using the airport's iris-scanning system.

Table 9.1. Biometric Technologies

Biometric	Acquisition Device	Sample	Feature Extracted
Iris	infrared-enabled video camera, PC camera	black-and-white iris image	furrows and striations in iris
Fingerprint	desktop peripheral, PC card, mouse, chip or reader embedded in keyboard	fingerprint image (optical, silicon, ultrasound, or touchless)	location and direction of ridge endings and bifurcations on fingerprint, minutiae
Voice	microphone, telephone	voice recording	frequency, cadence and duration of vocal pattern
Signature	signature tablet, motion-sensitive stylus	image of signature and record of related dynamics measurements	speed, stroke order, pressure, and appearance of signature
Face	video camera, PC camera, single-image camera	facial image (optical or thermal)	relative position and shape of nose, position of cheekbones
Hand	proprietary wall-mounted unit	3-D image of top and sides of hand	height and width of bones and joints in hands and fingers
Retina	proprietary desktop or wall-mountable unit	retina image	blood vessel patterns on retina

Source: Gartner Group.

- In New York, Newark (New Jersey), Toronto, Los Angeles, and several other airports, after being screened for security risks, low-risk travelers can bypass lines when crossing the border by swiping a personal identification card and placing one hand in a scanner under the INS's Inspass program, in effect since 1993.[25]
- At Montana's Canadian border, prescreened travelers just enter a personal identification number and speak a previously recorded secret password into a telephone in order to cross the border.[26]
- An information-sharing system along the U.S./Canada border will be rolled out December 2004, in order to electronically capture biographic information on travelers and facilitate border crossings.[27]
- Since September 2002, the U.S. Department of Justice has used biometric fingerprint technology to apprehend hundreds of foreigners attempting to illegally enter the United States.
- Student visas issued by the State Department now come with biometric identifiers and the multibillion dollar U.S.-Visit border control system will eventually check the identity—and record the arrival and departure—of every visitor to the United States through the use of biometric technology.

- The International Civil Aviation Organization (ICAO) plans to create an international "identity register" that would require biometrics on all passports by 2015.

Most of these uses of biometrics aren't terribly controversial. Who's going to object to making it harder for terrorists to obtain fraudulent student visas? The same cannot be said for another proposed use: smart driver's licenses and identification cards embedded with computer chips containing a biometric fingerprint. Retail stores, airports, and other entities trying to verify your identity would ask you to simply swipe the card and your finger past a scanner to make sure they match. The scanner would check your fingerprint against the fingerprint on the card, making sure it matches and checking for its "liveness," i.e., that no one has cut off your finger in an attempt to assume your identity.

Smart Licenses: First Step to a Police State?

Smart licenses, backed by the American Association of Motor Vehicle Administrators (AAMV), the Democractic Leadership Council, various other organizations, and Illinois senator Richard Durbin, are supposed to prevent people from obtaining fraudulent licenses and ID cards, make it harder for terrorists and other criminals to move freely within our borders, and bring greater uniformity and control to the issuing of state licenses. "If people continue using licenses as identification documents, we would like to make sure from a safety perspective that they are good, credible documents," says Jay Maxwell, a spokesperson for the AAMV.

Opponents don't view biometric licenses so benignly. Evoking images of Nazi Germany, concentration camp tattoos, and the former Soviet Union, they say that biometric ID cards are nothing more than a backdoor scheme to get a national ID card that would lead inexorably to a police state where government tracks our every movement. "This would essentially give the government the power to demand that we show our papers," says former Congressman Tom Campbell, currently a Stanford law professor. "It is a very dangerous thing." The digital nature of the card would enable it to be wired into huge, sophisticated government databases, a capability that worries many critics. "With a small microchip on the card, the government could storehouse every conceivable piece of data about our private lives on the card," says Stephen Moore, a fellow at the libertarian Cato Institute.

These arguments, while well-meaning and widely held, are ultimately overblown. There is little reason to believe that simply digitizing driver's licenses would suddenly turn us into a "show me your papers" society. Some of the arguments against smart cards are also based on erroneous information about the actual technological design of the cards. When the grocery store asks to see and scan your ID, they don't make a call in to Big Brother. In the same way, smart cards could be designed so that the fingerprint is stored only on the card, not in a government database. The scanner would only match your fingerprint against the biometric on the card; the state wouldn't be notified in the course of the transaction; and there would be no link into a national government database.[28] Moreover, the notion that the government would take all our private information on the cards and link it to a giant government database is incorrect. Most people probably wouldn't put any additional information on the chips. Those who did choose to put credit card and medical information on the cards would be able to encrypt the information and strictly control access to it.

The Need for Modernization

Our state-run driver's license and ID systems are primitive. Within the decade, we will likely use smart cards and wireless devices to do everything from opening car doors to unlocking houses to accessing secure websites. By the time this happens it's hard to believe that we'll still be relying purely on paper-based, easily forged driver's licenses and ID cards as our primary legal means of proving our identity.

But this doesn't mean that Congress should pass a law tomorrow mandating that every state begin immediately to issue smart licenses and ID cards to every citizen. First of all, no one knows how such a proposal might affect freedom, privacy, and citizenship. Other than Italy, the only two countries with much experience with smart ID cards, Brunei and Malaysia, are not exactly paragons of freedom.

What's more, the deeply ingrained political, cultural, and religious opposition to smart driver's licenses—let alone a digital national ID card—would be so fierce and so divisive that it would make the debate about Hillary Clinton's national health care proposal look mild in comparison. A not insignificant portion of the population might even equate such a proposal with the Biblical mark of the beast. In the extremely unlikely event that a bill was to pass Congress and be signed by the president, there would surely be massive civil disobedience to the law. Lastly, the perceived extra security provided by biometric licenses might increase the economic incentive to forge or steal them—as difficult as this might be to do—so before we force every state to adopt them, the security issues must be more fully worked out.

A better approach is one that is incremental and relies on trial-and-error, state experimentation, voluntary citizen adoption—at least for now—and encouraging a marketplace for authentication devices. The first step toward such an approach would be to encourage states and private companies to experiment with voluntary approaches for biometric

ID cards and smart licenses. Japan, Estonia, Finland, Malaysia, and other countries, as well as companies like American Express, have all introduced voluntary smart ID cards.

Why would anyone want to volunteer for a smart license or ID card? The most obvious reason is convenience. Hong Kong smart-card holders can use the cards to speed through immigration, bypassing long waits by using self-service kiosks that match the biometric data on the card with a fingerprint image read by a scanner. In the United States, the Department of Transportation is moving ahead with a proposal to institute voluntary "registered traveler" cards to passengers. Passengers would avoid long lines and basic questioning at airports in exchange for providing detailed background information establishing that they pose no security risk. One survey of 5,500 travelers found that 73 percent of them would voluntarily use a national travel card if it cut waiting times.[29] In Israel, citizens carrying a similar card can get through the check-in process in twenty seconds as opposed to the two hours needed to process someone without a card.[30] From a technology perspective, there is no reason why trusted traveler cards couldn't be merged with biometric driver's licenses—again, with the caveat that this be voluntary.

Not only should the smart cards be voluntary, but government should do what it can to encourage a thriving marketplace in authentication devices so that individuals who would like the benefits of smart identification cards but who are leery of government control would have other options. Already a company called Verified Identity Card Inc., owned by a consortium that includes attorney Stephen Brill, the founder of Brill's Content and Court TV, TransCore, the manufacturer of the E-ZPass device and ChoicePoint, the private data broker powerhouse (more on them later), is trying to create a market for such a card. The idea is that with the card— or it may even be a chip implanted in your credit card—you'd be considered a trusted identity and be able to breeze through the fast lanes at airport checkpoints, public buildings, and other security-conscious venues.[31]

The effort is being replicated in the online world where the Liberty Alliance (led by Sun Microsystems, AOL Time Warner, and MasterCard) and Microsoft are competing to produce the preferred authentication tool people will use on the web. Under its "e-identification" initiative, the federal government is looking to use Microsoft's Passport, the Liberty Alliance, or another private authentication tool as a way to verify the online identity of citizens, federal employees, and businesses.

Today, your grocery store and bank might require a state-issued driver's license or ID card to cash a check, but tomorrow there is no reason why private-sector issued smart cards that store your preferences, traits, and identities—cards that could even have your driver's license embedded within them—couldn't engender the same level of trust.

"SAY CHEESE": GUARDING PRIVACY
IN AN AGE OF SURVEILLANCE

We are at risk of turning into a Surveillance Society. The explosion of computers, cameras, sensors, wireless communication, GPS, biometrics, and other technologies in just the last ten years is feeding a surveillance monster that is growing silently in our midst.

—The American Civil Liberties Association (ACLU)[32]

What could be more public than the Super Bowl? Each sports fan is surrounded by thousands of fellow fans, and each one knows he could end up on television, holding a homemade sign, yelling his head off, or waving a big foam finger. But even at the Super Bowl, there's an expectation of privacy, a desire to keep one's identity from the crowd. During the 2002 Super Bowl in Tampa, however, cameras scanned the unknowing crowd of spectators, capturing their images and producing a digitized "faceprint" that was cross-checked (at the rate of a million images a minute) against a database of suspected terrorists and known criminals. Though no terrorists were identified, nineteen people with criminal histories—most of them ticket scalpers—were spotted in the 100,000-person crowd. No arrests were made.

Several months later, Tampa decided to mount thirty-six of these surveillance cameras (quickly dubbed "spycams" by critics) outside the throbbing discos and fancy restaurants in its busy entertainment district. The cameras were linked to a database of one thousand felons, sex offenders, and teenage runaways and operated by remote control from a nearby police command post.

The national uproar began immediately after the cameras went up. "Do we really want a society where one cannot walk down the street without Big Brother tracking our every move?" thundered then-House Majority Leader Dick Armey (R-TX). Locally, Green Party demonstrators—one of whom was dressed up as a computer monitor with the Mayor's face on it—marched on City Hall chanting "Big Bro, hell, no!" The ACLU attacked the cameras on the basis that the face-recognition technology violated people's basic constitutional rights. "Merely by walking down the street, a person is in essence put into an electronic police lineup without even knowing it," said Gregory Nojeim from the ACLU. "If this isn't Big Brother, I don't know what is."[33]

After the charge of creeping Big Brotherism failed to stop Tampa from using the cameras, the ACLU switched gears, arguing instead that the cameras should be junked because they didn't work. They claimed that a review of police logs showed that in four months the cameras hadn't nabbed a single criminal, producing only hundreds of false alarms.[34] According to the ACLU, the face-recognition system can be foiled by a fake beard, weight gain, or a bad picture of the person in the database. In two cases, the cameras even "matched" people of the opposite sex. (Lt. Bill Todd of the Ybor City police department said that those cases don't mean much, since the system is intentionally designed to be race-and-sex-neutral.)[35] "If we're going to go down the road of becoming a society under total surveillance, it's got to have some kind of payoff, some kind of benefit," said another ACLU spokesman.[36]

Eventually the ACLU got its wish. By August 2003, two years after it had started using the face-recognition software, Tampa unplugged it, citing no evidence that it had any impact—other than to get the city a ton of unwanted national publicity. In two years, the system had failed to lead to even one arrest or positive identification. "It's just proven not to have any benefit to us," said Capt. Bob Guidara. Other early forays into face-recognition technology were similarly disappointing. After 9/11, Boston, Fresno, St. Petersburg, and other cities installed face-recognition at their airports. Two years later, the interest in using face-recognition at airports had all but disappeared. "It wasn't ready for primetime," Jose Juves, spokesman for Logan airport told ABC News.[37]

Here, There, and Everywhere

Given these experiences, the widespread deployment of face-recognition technology is probably a few years away, however, the use of plain old surveillance cameras is skyrocketing. More than 11 million surveillance cameras have been installed in the United States.[38] Thousands of city governments now use surveillance cameras to do everything from nabbing red-light runners to curtailing drug dealing. Fully 90 percent of America's 19,000 police departments use them, according to the International Association of Chiefs of Police.

The most extensive public surveillance system in America is in the nation's capital. On the fifth floor of D.C.'s police headquarters sits a multi-million dollar command center where law enforcement officials from the D.C. police department, the Secret Service, the FBI, the Capitol police, and dozens of other agencies monitor surveillance cameras pointed at federal buildings and monuments from forty individual video stations and on giant video screens on the walls. In February 2004, the Department of Homeland Security (DHS) rolled out the Homeland Security Information Network (HSIN) at D.C.'s command center. DHS Secretary Tom Ridge said HSIN will allow police to "receive and share tactical information, quickly piece together the puzzle and see if an incident poses a threat."[39] Eventually the camera network will be expanded to include schools, the subway, highways, and high foot-traffic areas such as Georgetown. Stephen Gaffigan, who heads the video surveillance project for the Washington Metropolitan Police Department, says the cameras represent nothing more than a way to use modern technology to do something that the police are already doing—the electronic equivalent of putting a cop on the street corner. "We don't have enough officers to watch everything," said Gaffigan. "This allows us to monitor more places and frees up officers to do their work in the neighborhoods."[40]

To opponents, surveillance cameras and face-recognition systems represent something much more insidious: the tools to enable Big Brother to track and spy on ordinary citizens. The *Washington Times* accused the D.C. police department of trying to turn the nation's capital into a "prison yard," while the ACLU said the technology is giving government what amounts to Superman vision.

Privacy advocates from the Left and Right are correct in one respect: If the cameras' proliferation by government is left unchecked, they could gradually turn us into a paranoid, conformist, risk-averse society. But the future need not be so grim. We've been living with cameras for years now—but few of us find ourselves censoring our words and actions in the Mini Mart, or at the ATM. The 9/11 attack demonstrated just how many of our movements are already caught on surveillance cameras. Two of the hijackers of American Airlines Flight 11 turned up on videotape all over Portland the day before the attacks—withdrawing money from an ATM, getting gas, shopping at Wal-Mart. A chilling image shows the two terrorists exiting the security clearance line at the Portland, Maine, airport at 5:45 A.M., September 11.

Living with Spycams *and* Maintaining Privacy

While many people may find the cameras invasive, any woman who's had to walk through a deserted parking garage to her car, or anyone who's lost a loved one to a red-light runner, knows why many people might welcome cameras. Although the technology is still at an early stage, computer-linked surveillance cameras can identify crimes as they occur, reduce false arrests and convictions, and provide much better evidence than notoriously unreliable witness testimony. Linked to biometric databases, the cameras could eventually help prevent fraud, keep terrorists out of airports and pedophiles out of schools, or even find a lost child. In Great Britain, the country's National Crime Squad has created a database of close to three million pictures seized in raids of child pornography rings. By matching these images against those of missing children, British law enforcement authorities hope to find the children—or at least generate clues that would help them to do so.[41]

Moreover, the cameras don't necessarily violate anyone's privacy, because they're located in public places where people's faces are visible to everyone. The Fourth Amendment doesn't guarantee privacy in public places.

The cameras aren't likely to just go away, and neither is biometrics. We can live with them—and even with digitally connected, face-recognition surveillance systems—if we act now to safeguard privacy against potential governmental abuses.

Let Machines Do the Watching

The international poster child for the new surveillance society is Great Britain, where more than 4.3 million closed circuit surveillance cameras (CCTV) watch the Brits day and night as they stroll in public parks, shop for shoes, board the subway, drive on the highway, watch their favorite rugby team, and enter public buildings.[42] There are speed cameras and red-light cameras, cameras in day care centers and high schools, on the backs of buses, and in hospitals. Over three-fourths of British localities use video cameras to patrol public places, and the number keeps going up. Experts predict that the number of CCTV cameras will skyrocket to 25 million by 2007.[43] Far from minding having a camera staring at them nearly everywhere they go, most Brits welcome them, believing the cameras make them safer. (Most research, however, suggests that the cameras don't have nearly the impact on crime rates as most Brits believe they do.)[44]

Some observers, however, have reported bored officers in Britain using surveillance cams to ogle attractive women, which points to a very basic objection to cameras: the creepiness of feeling you're always being watched. Many women may like the feeling of extra security the cameras provide, but others wonder whether the invisible person controlling the camera is a leering man who's zooming in on her body parts.

Reducing human involvement and maximizing that of machines can help prevent this problem, as well as easing the fear that the cameras might target certain groups like gay couples, political protestors, or swarthy-looking men. Cameras equipped with face-recognition technology could do the bulk of the "watching," alerting humans only when they find a positive face match that needs verification. With behavioral-recognition technology, the cameras could also be programmed to set off an alert when they detect suspicious movements such as fighting, weapon use, or going from vehicle to vehicle at a parking garage (often a sign that a car thief is scoping out targets). "The more information is sorted by machine and rejected as irrelevant, the less it winds up in the hands of a government agent," explains Shane Ham from the Progressive Policy Institute.

Researchers at Kingston University in London, for example, have developed software that can enable "robot cameras" to flag suspicious behavior patterns and notify police that a crime may be imminent or in progress. Because the cameras' risk-detectors are automated, the potential for human abuse is limited—unlike real cops, for example, the robot cams can't seek out members of unpopular ethnicities or political parties. They also aren't likely to be programmed to look for casually permitted law-breaking or nonconformity—such as jaywalking or snuggling a woman not your wife. "The better we can make this technology, the less human surveillance there has to be and the less of a threat to people's anonymity," explains Yale law professor Robert Slaughter, the author of *The Right of Privacy*.[45]

Today, the technology isn't accurate enough to do any of these things reliably. Face-recognition systems have been tricked by everything from wigs to fake mustaches. "The laboratory results suggest that this type of system has no chance in hell of working," says Jim Wayman, director of the San Jose State University's Biometric Test Center, referring to face-recognition technology. "To these systems . . . one out of every fifty people looks like Carlos the Jackal [an infamous terrorist] and the real Carlos has only a 50 percent chance of looking like himself."[46]

Today, Wayman is right. But the Feds are pouring millions of dollars into research to perfect biometrics, and few experts are willing to bet against face-recognition technologies in the long run. "There is little reason to doubt that as technology improves, it will eventually be able to identify faces in a crowd as effectively as it currently identifies a face scanned under controlled circumstances," says John Woodward, an ex-CIA man who writes about biometrics for the RAND Corporation. The accuracy rate will have to be extremely high—well over 99 percent—to avoid flagging hundreds of innocent people each day in busy places like airports and downtown entertainment districts.[47]

Watch the Watchers

At London's Charing Cross subway station, the security guards operating the cameras sit in a glass-walled control room in the middle of the subway station. The guards themselves are under a kind of surveillance from the constant parade of travelers, many of whom stop for a minute or two to watch the guards watching.

This points to another powerful antidote to the problem of abuse of the surveillance cameras—what author David Brin terms "watching the watchers." Because governments don't have a monopoly on surveillance technologies, the technologies can also be used to hold government accountable. The same surveillance camera that might videotape a mugging would also videotape possible police misconduct in an arrest. We saw the first stirrings of this potential in the Los Angeles Rodney King incident, in which a bystander filmed local policemen beating King after an arrest.

Many police departments install cameras on squad cars to knock down false police brutality charges, but the cameras also record real uses of excessive force. Public defender Don Landis Jr. represented one arrestee whose case was dismissed after the videotape of his arrest proved that the arresting officer had lied. Landis noted, "The cameras bring accountability." Video cameras are also used by over two thousand police agencies to videotape interrogations. In Charlottesville, Virginia, a detective was charged with assault after an interrogation camera caught him beating a suspect. "[Videotaping] assures an accurate account of what happened during the interview," says a county attorney from Minneapolis, Minnesota, a jurisdiction that tapes all police interrogations. "It is an inducement to follow the rules, because they want to convict the bad guy."[48]

Prevent Function Creep

Spycam boosters say face-recognition cameras will only be used to identify criminals and terrorists and won't store any images of regular folk. The technology just checks your face against a database of known criminals and if there's no match, your image is discarded. All well and good, but tomorrow—when one presumes the technology will be greatly improved—what's to stop them from using face-recognition cams to track down deadbeat dads or ferret out the identities of protesters at a political rally?

To prevent such abuses, surveillance technology must be strictly limited. Preventing terrorists from entering a nuclear plant is reasonable. Catching jaywalkers is not. Strict limits should also be placed on who goes in the databases. Photos of violent criminals and terrorists are acceptable. Photos of smokers are not. The debate about where to draw these lines will not be easy, but it's a better solution to the privacy/security problem than simply refusing to draw any lines at all.

Inform the Public

During the 1989 Tiananmen Square demonstrations, student protesters were identified with surveillance cameras that purportedly had been installed to monitor traffic, but in reality were being used to secretly keep tabs on how many times Chinese met with foreigners. To prevent such a thing from happening, surveillance technology should be used openly, and as much information as possible must be given to the public regarding where it's in use, the reasons for its use, and what safeguards exist to prevent abuses. In addition, governments could appoint independent, citizen watchdog groups to monitor the use of the technologies. Lastly, there should also be sanctions—legally, and in the court of public opinion—for politicians, cops, or anyone else who breaks these rules.

In the end, of course, all of our liberties depend upon a vigilant culture that will revile anyone in power who misuses a video database to draw up anything like an "electronic enemies list." If we don't care about police or government abuses, we'll get them no matter what technology we use; if we do watch the watchers, no camera will protect an abuser from the press and the populace.

"EVERY BREATH YOU TAKE . . ."

In order to make flying safer after 9/11, federal aviation authorities decided to establish a sophisticated computer network that would pull together every passenger's travel history, living arrangements, wealth and credit information. Artificial intelligence technologies would sift through all the information and assign a threat index score for every passenger—acceptable, unknown, or unacceptable. The goal: verify that a passenger is who he claims he is and has no terrorist ties. "This is not fantasy stuff," said Joseph Del Balzo, a former acting administrator of the Federal Aviation Administration and now a security consultant. "This technology, based on transaction analysis, gives us a pretty good idea of what's going on in a person's mind."[49] Critics charged that the system, the Computer Assisted Passenger Prescreening System (known as CAPPS II), would be the largest, most intrusive monitoring and surveillance system ever created by government. In addition to vociferous opposition from privacy advocates, CAPPS II also faced technical hurdles and opposition from industry groups.[50] "[T]his approach is unacceptable to corporate America, which will undoubtedly bear the brunt and expense of the charges and ultimately the costs of lost business and productivity," argued Nancy Holtzman, executive director of the Association of Corporate Travel Executives who claimed CAPPS II would cost the travel industry up to $2 billion.[51] Due to these and other concerns, CAPPS II was eventually killed, despite the government having spent about $100 million to develop the technology.

CAPPS II represented only the most prominent example of a trend that threatens to make all the other privacy issues discussed earlier in this chapter seem trivial in comparison: convergence. This refers to the integration of information from databases, email, cameras, cell phones, biometrics, radio identification tags on cars, and public and private sources. The combination of cheaper and more widespread computational power with ubiquitous surveillance technologies will eventually allow surveillance databases to depict where an individual is at any particular time, say many computer experts.[52] Already, we can track the movements of anyone who carries a cell phone.[53] Combine this with other strands of information—subway card, E-ZPass and face-recognition cameras, which library books we checked out, which TV shows we ordered from pay-per-view—and it would enable government to not only track our movements, but compile, in effect, a complete map of our everyday activities. The state would know where we've been, whom we've been with, what we were wearing and what we were doing.[54] "It's like the song by Sting where 'every move you make, every step you take' is recorded," remarked MIT professor of sociology Gary Marx.[55]

Today, practical and legal barriers stand in the way of such an Orwellian future. First, the police need a court order to access nearly all this information. Second, the databases are mostly incompatible, limiting the ability to exchange and integrate the information. Lastly, because the systems aren't linked together, the information needs to be pieced together manually—an extraordinarily time-consuming process—making it impractical to do except in cases when law enforcement is trying to nab serious criminals. All this is about to change as many of these practical and legal barriers come tumbling down. XML, the computer coding breakthrough discussed in a previous chapter, is allowing far-flung, incompatible databases to "talk to each other," while scores of government agencies, including the FBI, the IRS, and the Drug Enforcement Administration, purchase information about us from private data brokers that have information on more than 200 million consumers in their databases.[56]

The result of all this data integration will inevitably be what investigative journalist Adam Penenberg calls the "surveillance web." "Surveillance is here," says Penenberg, the author of *Spooked: Espionage in Corporate America*. "As the line between the public and private sector blurs, the data will flow like never before."[57] The consequences of the surveillance web are potentially very scary.

Say I was put on a "watch list" by government authorities. Wherever I went my faceprint would be matched against information in the "watch list" database, allowing a government agent to track my movements and activities. If this information were then combined with other personal data that the government and commercial databases held about me—tax returns, police complaints, lawsuits I've been involved in, articles I've written, credit card purchases, websites I visited, phone numbers I called—a complete digital dossier on me and my associates could easily be compiled. With all the information and images digitized and residing in huge searchable databases, the state could also compile profiles of my activities from months—or even years—earlier.

"Think of all these factoids residing not in some static database but in a dynamic environment in which strands of information can be pulled together from a huge variety of sources based on a user's request," writes Penenberg. "It's not Microsoft Outlook, it's Google."[58] Yale computer scientist David Gelernter has created a technology called "lifestreams" that electronically captures your whole life—every email message, digital photo, document, fax, and voice mail message—all in one place and makes any item easily searchable and retrievable. But what if someone seizes access to your electronic life story? "The thief will have stolen not only your past and present but also a reliable guide to your future," says Gelernter.[59]

Atlanta-based ChoicePoint Inc., one of the country's largest data brokers, probably already has your life story and, for the right price, will happily sell it to the highest bidder. ChoicePoint's database, containing 19 billion records, puts anything that the government has to shame. The company's principle business is connecting the dots—about you and me. It's exceptionally good at taking the abundant data it has on us regular folk—credit card applications, car registrations, property tax bills, marriage records, social security numbers—and piecing it together to paint a picture of us for its customers.[60] ChoicePoint will tell your insurance company whether they should sell you a homeowner's insurance policy. They'll help the IRS hunt for any hidden assets you might have. If you've been identified by the FBI as a "person of interest" ChoicePoint will run your name through its database and tell the bureau everything it knows about you.

But ChoicePoint isn't the only company in this lucrative business. Applied Systems Intelligence out of Roswell, Georgia, is working on a software program called Karnac that would scan everything from gun registrations to phone records to website cookies in order to pull together information about an individual based on a user's request.

This is the ultimate Big Brother fear: government with the ability to easily watch and track our movements by using its own information and that held by private companies. The lines between public and private disappear. The boundary that protects people from the eyes of the outside world is erased. Every individual feels like he's subjected to the same scrutiny as celebrities and politicians—but without the fame, money, and power. Inadvertent disclosure of information (through hacking or a mistake) destroys an individual's life. We're unable to escape our past . . . any of it . . . ever. Every mistake, every youthful indiscretion follows us around forever. The result: a society of paranoid and risk-averse people—or alternately we just stop caring about other people's past transgressions. Either way, it would be a very different society than we now live in—and not one most of us would see as an improvement.[61]

Many of the privacy proposals outlined earlier—watching the watchers, limiting who goes in the face-recognition databases, limiting how long the information is kept, giving people the right to review the information government collects about them and so on—can offer some protection. And while it may be true that in a Google world, there may be no way to prevent government from having considerably more information about us in the future than it does now, it won't be able to do anything with the information as long as solid legal protections are in place. As Cato Institute scholar Roger Pilon notes, technology does not suddenly render a search a nonsearch, meaning we will continue to have to rely on the Constitution and other legal protections to protect us from government abuse.

IS PRIVACY DEAD?

> This privacy you're concerned about is largely an illusion. All you have to give up is your illusions, not any of your privacy. Right now, you can go onto the Internet and get a credit report about your neighbor and find out where your neighbor works, how much they earn and if they had a late mortgage payment and tons of other information.
>
> —Oracle CEO and founder Larry Ellison[62]

Is Ellison right? Is privacy dead? A quaint relic of an era that has passed? "History provides a modest degree of comfort that that is not the case," explains Ohio State University law professor Peter Swire, the privacy czar in the Clinton White House. He points out that when the polygraph machine was developed in the 1950s, everyone thought that polygraph tests would be a part of everyday life. It didn't happen. In the 1960s, the consolidation of government databases was inevitable. Forty years later, it still hasn't happened.

In the late 1960s, privacy guru Alan Westin wrote a book called "Privacy and Freedom" that was absolutely apocalyptic in its outlook on the future of privacy. Westin's book reflected the feeling at the time that the steady march of technology would eventually cause us to lose most of our privacy. Again, it didn't happen. Despite phenomenal technological advances, we have at least as much—if not more—freedom and privacy as we had then.

If history tells us anything, it's that far more important than the current state of technology in determining the level of privacy protections is the culture of our society and structure of our government. Repressive regimes will, no doubt, continue to use digital surveillance technologies to control their citizens and quench dissent. But they are fighting a constant battle against enterprising, tech-savvy individuals in their countries who find ways around government snooping and surveillance. In the immortal words of Electronic Frontier Foundation founder John Gilmore, "The Internet treats censorship like damage, and routes around it."

In open societies like America, where the idea of being free to do what we want is an ingrained part of our culture and where massive government spying on citizens is reviled, citizens will rise up and defeat any politician who fails to respect the long-standing boundary that protects people from the state. And as long as the public is concerned about privacy, we can be sure that there will always be plenty of politicians who will champion the issue and remain vigilant for signs of government abuse—if only because there will be a political payoff for doing so.[63] In fact, as George Washington University law professor Jeffrey Rosen argues in *The Naked Crowd*, his compelling book on privacy and security, Congress—and to a lesser extent state legislatures—offer probably the best hope for creating the necessary systems of oversight to protect liberty in our increasingly security-conscious world.[64] As mentioned earlier in the chapter, Congress has passed a series of privacy laws over the course of the last three decades and, for better or worse, has shown little reluctance to step in and kill initiatives deemed too privacy-invasive, as the team leading the Pentagon's Total Information Awareness project (described in the Introduction) learned in 2003.

Lastly, if technology is indeed giving government more ability to "see" what all of us are up to, then it is only fair that we citizens are given a better view to "see in" to what government is doing on our behalf. As David Brin writes in his provocative book, *The Transparent Society*: "If the government says it needs new powers of sight in order to protect us, we should not spurn the requests of skilled and dedicated professionals without a hearing. On the other hand, we should make government come begging deferentially, and extract something in return each time. New kinds of supervision. New guarantees of openness. . . . New measures to keep us confident that government is still our loyal dog, and not the wolf that all too many others have become."[65] This concept, transparency, was, of course, the subject of chapter 6. It is vitally important as a safeguard to our privacy, but all the openness and all the privacy protections in the world are meaningless unless we can secure government websites and databases against hackers. This threat, and how to meet it, will be discussed in the next chapter.

TIPS FOR PRACTITIONERS

- Build privacy-friendly IT systems to guard privacy while increasing security. Prohibition is the wrong approach for protecting our privacy, and any strategy predicated on stopping technology is unlikely to work.
- Conduct a privacy impact assessment before procuring large IT systems or collecting any new information from citizens.
- Let individual citizens, instead of the government, decide what information of theirs is shared with other agencies.
- When there is a public need to combine citizen information—for example to aggregate statistics on diseases—encrypt and delink the data held about individuals from their identity.
- Begin modernizing our means of authentication by piloting voluntary approaches, and by encouraging a marketplace for authentication devices.
- Diminish the potential for surveillance camera abuse by reducing human involvement and maximizing that of machines. Researchers have developed software, for example, that can enable "robot cameras" to flag suspicious behavior patterns and notify police that a crime may be imminent or in progress.
- Prevent abuses of surveillance technology by putting strict limits on its use and punishing those who violate the limits.

10

Cyber Defense

There are but two powers in the world, the sword, and the mind. In the long run the sword is always beaten by the mind.

—Napoleon Bonaparte

Fairfax County school administrators were just trying to find a way to improve school evaluations. They wanted to find out things like which schools were failing to help children with learning disorders, and which schools were doing well at educating poor children. Previously, uncovering this information meant endless hours of drudgework in an offline system, tramping from file cabinet to file cabinet. Fairfax decided to cut the grunt work by creating a robust online database that would consolidate student information so searches could be conducted instantaneously. The reaction from parents was swift, certain, and nearly uniformly negative. The parents in this well-to-do Washington, D.C., suburban community objected fiercely to the idea of creating a database with hundreds of snippets of information about their kids—medical and dental histories, records of behavioral problems, family income, everything except the schoolyard nickname.[1]

In response, the school board assured parents that the records would only be made available to others with the parents' consent. John C. Gay, Fairfax schools' assistant superintendent for information technology (IT), explained, "A school nurse, for example, doesn't need to access a student's grade records. So we would block that out." Sounds good. But unfortunately, Gay misread the motive of the opposition. It wasn't the official data-keeping policies that bothered Fairfax parents. They were worried that an accident or a hacker invasion would spill their families' secrets. Parents cited concerns that anyone from insurance companies to pedophiles to schoolyard bullies could wrongly gain access to the data.

The fear that hackers could break into leaky government computer systems and steal or alter personal information is Americans' leading concern with digital government. According to a Hart-Teeter poll, nearly two-thirds of Americans are extremely worried about hackers breaking into government computers.[2] "If someone hacks into the department of health and social services and publishes who has AIDS in Washington State, we would experience a total loss of trust in state government," explains a top Washington State government computer security official.

Electronic government will never realize its full potential until citizens have the utmost confidence that their personal information is secure from cyber criminals who would use the information in malicious ways. Until then, many people will refrain from filing taxes online, allowing their medical information to be exchanged electronically, or conducting a host of other government transactions online.

HACK ATTACKS

Government websites and computer systems are under continual attack. Every day thousands of intruders try to enter Pentagon computer systems; thousands more try to break into the White House site. One of the biggest ongoing cyber assaults ever launched against the U.S. government received the Pentagon code name "Moonlight Maze." The attack began in 1998 and continued to drain information from unclassified Pentagon networks four years later. Nobody ever traced the infiltrators. The moonlight criminals snuck into the Energy Department's nuclear weapon and research networks, the National Aeronautics and Space Administration, university research facilities, and defense contractors. It was believed that they never obtained any top-secret classified data. But given the extent of the attack, that wasn't too reassuring. Even unclassified data includes information to make terrorists and unfriendly foreign governments drool: military logistics, emails between Pentagon officials, purchasing and personnel information.[3]

The FBI had a suspect profile, but it consisted of only one word: Russian. The Moonlight Maze trail died in Russia, and the attacks always occurred during Russian workday hours, never on Russian holidays.[4] Some experts speculated that somebody was being paid to hack the government, but his salary was coming from outside his own country. Others suggested that what the hackers were really looking for was commercial secrets, like bidding documents and contracts. But nobody really knew. As organized crime expert Frank Cilluffo put it, "Who's behind the clickety-clack of a computer? It could be a block away and made to look like it's coming from halfway around the world."[5]

Hackers are opportunistic: They take the easiest and most expedient routes to get into computer systems, and exploit the best-known flaws with weapons that are usually widely available on the Net. They range from teenagers running premade attack scripts, called "Newbies" or "Script Kiddies," to "Cyberpunks," who are out to make money or fight for a cause, to cyberterrorists (more on them later), also known as "Internet Guerrillas," who use the Internet to inflict devastating damage on their enemies. All in all, cyber attacks cost businesses alone more than $13 billion in 2003 in damage and clean up expenses.[6]

In 2001 a hacker broke into the computer systems of the Bureau of Indian Affairs at the U.S. Department of the Interior and falsified scores of Native American eligibility records. Fortunately, no harm was done. Why not? Because this particular hacker was hired by the government—a federal judge, to be precise—to investigate the department's information security.

The expert's finding? There was no security.

The judge ordered the department's Internet access shut off until it fixed the leaks, causing the entire 90,000-person agency to go without email or Internet access for months. But the Interior Department wasn't the only federal government agency found to have inadequate security protections. The same year, Rep. Steve Horn (R-CA) graded twenty-four U.S. government agencies on their security practices, and handed out a slew of F's, including to the Department of Defense, Energy, Commerce, and Treasury.[7] "E-government got a little ahead of e-security," was one cyber security analyst's sublime understatement. Three years of intensive scrutiny later, Rep. Adam Putnam (R-FL), who had taken over the chairmanship of Horn's subcommittee, handed out the grades. This time the federal government had managed only to move up from an overall score of F to D. Eight agencies, including the Department of Homeland Security, got failing grades. Federal agencies didn't do much better when the White House itself gave the report cards. Not a single one managed to complete all the steps necessary for the Office of Management and Budget to rate its information systems secure in 2004.[8]

State and local government systems have even more holes because they don't spend as much money as the feds do on security. In New Mexico, the state highway department was shut down for two days when the Love Bug computer virus attacked its system. The department estimated that up to 60,000 files in its engineering department alone were infected.

KEEPING THE BAD GUYS OUT

Security experts say that safeguarding computer systems against hackers and crackers isn't terribly different from protecting your house or business:

Close the windows, shut the doors, lock the gates, put a fence around the yard, and don't give out too many keys. The first step is to lock down the computer systems—making sure that no government computer is linked to the Net until it meets minimum-security standards and all holes in the software systems have been plugged. "When you buy a system today it comes with all the doors and windows unlocked," says cyber security expert Alan Paller, president of the SANS Institute, which trains thousands of public officials each year in cyber security. "We're saying, lock the doors first."

Nearly every piece of software produced to run computer systems comes with mistakes, called "bugs," that hackers can exploit to gain access to computer systems. Manufacturers are constantly putting out updated code called "patches" to fix these bugs, but staying up to date with them is a constant struggle for large, decentralized organizations. Computer security experts at the Lawrence Livermore National Laboratory have developed an innovative solution to the problem. Rather than relying on individual employees and system administrators to download every new security patch, they created a computer program that automatically finds and installs patches.[9] Software and hardware manufacturers must also do a much better job of eliminating the security holes *before* they ship their products off to the customers.

Once the system is locked down, access must be tightly controlled by encryption and a process called two- or three-factor authentication. Two-factor authentication simply means an individual needs to present something she has (a physical token, such as a government ID card) and something she knows (a password or PIN) to gain access to the system. It's like having a door key and a combination lock. Three-factor authentication is even more secure because it means the person also needs to present something she is (biometric data, such as iris scan or handprint) to gain access. Tightening access is critical, because many security breaches come from disgruntled employees or saboteurs inside organizations.[10]

Then there's the matter of building a wall to keep out the bad guys. Many governments are tempted to build one massive firewall to protect against hackers. Building one giant Internet firewall tends to fail for the same reason that the supposedly impregnable Maginot Line failed to protect France against the Germans during World War I: Hackers only have to breach one security layer of one company's technology to get in. No security system should be designed with only a single point of failure. A far more effective approach is to build multiple, overlapping, crosschecking layers of deterrence. With a layered defense, a hacker must breach lots of smaller firewalls run on different platforms. In front of each wall should be the virtual equivalent of a "Checkpoint Charlie" that buffers the Internet at large from the government's secure information technology, turning the bad guys away before they near the gate.

But even with the best defenses, governments shouldn't just sit back and wait to be attacked. It's important that they take a proactive approach to security by continuously searching for holes in their own defenses. Many governments hire "white knight" hackers and security organizations to do this, while others deploy specially designed software to prowl their systems for leaks. Maricopa County, Arizona, developed a software tool that constantly scans the agency's network of computer systems and servers, simulating attacks and looking for vulnerabilities that can be exploited. "You almost have to become your own hacker," explains county network manager Tom Crosby. "We know everyone else is going to try. We might as well have someone internally doing the same thing."[11]

Basic security steps like these will keep out 99.99 percent of hackers,[12] but they're probably not enough to protect systems from what many experts predict will be the future of warfare: cyberwar.

JIHAD ON THE INTERNET

> In cyber-terrorism, the goal is to cut the digital arteries of the economy and the companies that make up the economy, leaving them to bleed money and resources into the streets.
>
> —Dan Verton, author of *Black Ice: The Invisible Threat of Cyber-Terrorism*

We rely more and more on cyber-based systems to run our economy, operate our government, sustain our health care, maintain national security, and organize our society. The networked nature of these systems (many of which are now run on the Internet) helps to make economic activity and growth possible, but also poses huge security problems because of the system's interdependence and complexity. It stands to reason that the more we rely on such systems and the more interdependent they become, the more tempting a target they present to terrorists and others who would do us harm. Explains National Security Advisor Condoleezza Rice:

> Water supply, transportation, energy, banking and finance, telecommunications, public health—all of these rely upon computers and the fiber optic lines, switches and routers that connect them. Corrupt those networks and you disrupt the nation. It is a paradox of our times: The very technology that makes our economy so dynamic and our military forces so dominating also makes us more vulnerable.[13]

What could happen if our computer systems were systematically attacked by a hostile country or terrorist organization? Massive economic disruption: telephone systems downed; freight and passenger trains colliding; oil refineries exploding; cities in blackout. Knocking out the stock exchange alone, for just a few days, could bring down the global economy. PriceWaterhouseCoopers estimates that the total effect of U.S. network security failures could add up to more than $1 trillion a year—a figure equal to the entire GDP of France.[14] Clearly the protection of our critical infrastructure, 90 percent of which is owned and operated by the private sector, is an essential component of homeland security.

The vast damage a successful large-scale cyber or physical attack on computer systems could do to us economically and to our national psyche makes it a tempting target for terrorists. For this very reason, many counterterrorism experts believe that cyberspace will be the next great battleground in the war with terrorists. "[Its] a logical extension of traditional forms of terrorism, which are continuously being adapted by a thinking enemy to the realities of a modern world," writes former Marine Corps Intelligence officer Dan Verton in *Black Ice: The Invisible Threat of Cyber-Terrorism*, "cyber-terrorism exists because it is in the cyber realm that most industrialized nations are weakest."[15]

Cyber attacks also might be potentially easier for terrorists to carry out on American soil than conventional attacks. With a cyber-attack terrorists needn't smuggle bombs into the United States—or even physically enter the country, for that matter—to wreak serious damage. "Remote attacks on Internet networks are possible in complete anonymity [and the] needed equipment to conduct attacks on the Internet does not cost much [or does it] require extraordinary skill," a senior advisor to Osama Bin Laden has written warning that this line of attack is coming.[16]

Just how vulnerable are we to such attacks? Woefully. Michael Jacobs, the NSA's director of information assurance, told a homeland security conference after 9/11 that, "If we experienced a serious cyber-based attack, could we figure out who did it and recover from it? The answer is no. Is the federal government properly organized for this? The answer is no."

So far, the overwhelming majority of cyber attacks have been thwarted—but not all of them. In June 1997, the Joint Chiefs of Staff launched a test of the government's computer security. The scenario involved a military crisis on the Korean peninsula, in which the U.S. had to send troops and aircraft to South Korea as quickly as possible. Four teams from the National Security Agency played North Korean hackers. They had no special information about U.S. computer networks, they could not break U.S. law, and they could use only publicly available equipment and information. In other words, they weren't nearly as powerful as real cyber warriors would be. They had two weeks to get into U.S. computers and wreak as much havoc as they could.

If the hackers had been real, the United States might still be recovering from their devastation. They managed to simultaneously break into nine cities' power grids and their 911 systems; with a few more taps on the keyboard, those cities would have lost power and emergency communications. Then the hackers got into thirty-six of the Pentagon's computer networks. They had the ability to send the wrong supplies to troops in urgent need; they could send fake orders and fake news reports. As soon as the first fakes were exposed, they would have shattered all trust in the chain of command. Nobody would have known which orders were the right ones.

In October 1999, the government tried again, to see what it had learned since 1997. This time, the pseudohackers shut off the power to several military bases, and then brought down the local 911 systems. There had been a few improvements, but not nearly enough. Determined hackers could still disable the military without any inside knowledge or secret tools.[17]

And eventually, the real attacks will come. Al Qaeda and other terrorist organizations, as well as about twenty nations are preparing for information warfare, including some of America's longtime enemies.[18] From the Middle East to the Taiwan Strait, worms, viruses, Trojan horses, logic bombs, trap doors, denial of service (DOS) attacks, malicious code and other cyber weapons are more and more being used to wage war on longtime enemies—and cyber attacks often go hand-in-hand with physical attacks. "It is not a question of if but when," says Yonah Alexander, a senior fellow at the Potomac Institute for Policy Studies. "The entire United States is on the front line."[19] The United States is especially vulnerable to cyber attacks precisely because of its unchallenged military strength. Conventional warfare against the United States is a bad bet, but "asymmetric" war—like the 9/11 terrorist attacks—can use American technology against itself. Information warfare is a weapon of the weak.

And when the cyber attacks come, they're more likely to be against Wall Street, dams, electric power, or municipal water systems than against the Pentagon. Private critical infrastructure is easily our biggest vulnerability to cyber warfare—whether we're attacked by terrorists or other nations. "Most information warfare defense here in the United States, and around the world, has focused on defending military properties and infrastructure," explains Michael Erbschloe, the author of *Information Warfare: How to Survive Cyber Attacks*, who has worked closely with the Pentagon on information warfare. "But the dot-coms and the civilian business sector in general are incredibly vulnerable to attack. And this includes the stock market. We're ignoring the commercial side of the world." What worries national security officials the most are cyber attacks that disable or take control of physical structures that have become increasingly reliant on twenty-first-century technology and information networks. The damage that terrorists could cause to this infrastructure, which is run by computer systems and digital devices that are now connected to the Internet, is on a scale otherwise not possible except by a massive physical attack.[20]

In 1992, a young hacker gained access to the computer systems that ran all the dams in Northern California. By opening the gates to just one of the dams, he could have flooded the surrounding region, triggering catastrophic damage and killing hundreds or thousands of people.[21] Eight years later, a forty-eight-year-old computer expert broke into an Australian wastewater treatment system forty-six times, programming it to leak hundreds of thousands of gallons of putrid sludge into parks and rivers over a two-month span, turning the water black and killing marine life. During his break-ins, he had unlimited control of the entire system, from the sewage to the drinking water. "He could have done anything he liked to the drinking water . . ." said one expert.[22] Why did he do it? Apparently, he hoped to obtain a lucrative consulting contract to fix all the problems he caused.

Even more troubling are the effects that a successful cyber attack could have on the electricity grid.[23] In 2000, Chinese hackers nearly gained access to California's power grid. Two years later, in the aftermath of 9/11, cyber attacks on power and energy companies soared 77 percent, many of them severe attacks that could have disrupted power flows if they hadn't been detected immediately.[24] No one has any idea just how the grid would respond to a successful cyber attack, but we do know that the current levels of security are inadequate to repel a sophisticated assault. The Department of Energy has conducted eighteen mock attacks against regional electrical power grids. Every single one of them succeeded. The electric industry has concluded that the only way to truly secure the power grid may be to build a parallel private Internet network.[25]

What counterterrorism experts fear most are coordinated physical and cyber attacks. "The biggest issue we've got to worry about is what we call the swarming attack, where we have a physical event . . . that occurs at the same time we have a degradation or an impact on our telecommunications services," explains cyber security guru Howard Schmidt. "That's where we have that interdependency we clearly worry about the most."[26] A June 2002 exercise in the Pacific Northwest (code-named Blue Cascades) which involved scores of government organizations, utilities, and private companies demonstrated not only the havoc that could be wreaked by such attacks, but also how highly interdependent the physical cyber and cyber worlds have become. In this case, the economic infrastructure within a multistate region was crippled. Power outages caused by the attacks took down the Internet and caused major breakdowns in the communications infrastructure and in two natural gas distribution systems.[27] Transportation, emergency services, hospitals, and water services were all severely disrupted.

PLAYING DEFENSE AND . . . OFFENSE

In the future, war will be not about taking out places but taking out information systems.

—Cyber Security Expert Alan Paller

The U.S. government and industry together are spending billions of dollars to make sure that when cyber war comes, we'll win. Recognizing the vulnerability of private-sector systems, President George W. Bush created the Critical Infrastructure Protection Board in the weeks after 9/11 and charged it with looking at information security comprehensively across the public and private sector. "The President asked us to create a national strategy to defend cyber space," explained Howard Schmidt, the former chair of the Critical Infrastructure Board. "Our job is to help the private sector understand exactly what their role is in defending against cyber attacks." Planning and resources are focused on three major areas:

1. Enhancing our ability to detect cyber attacks;
2. Reducing national vulnerability to attacks; and
3. Improving our capabilities to respond to and recover from an attack.

Improving our ability to detect cyber attacks requires most of all for organizations to stop thinking of security as a purely internal issue.[28] Sharing detailed information about attacks and intrusions as soon as they occur with the government and other companies helps others to prepare their defenses. The goods news is that there is no shortage of secure public-private networks that have been established to facilitate information sharing about cyber attacks and industry vulnerabilities. Nearly every major industry sector (energy, transportation, financial services, and so on) has its own Information Sharing and Analysis Center (ISAC)—private computer networks that allow private industry and government to share information and keep in touch in case of a large cyber attack. The centers send out crisis alerts to government agencies and member firms about attacks and vulnerabilities. There is also InfraGard, an association comprised of the FBI, private companies, academic institutions, and state and local law enforcement agencies that share information about cyber security and critical infrastructure protection. And not to be forgotten is the National Cyber Security Partnership, which is comprised of various business industry groups and government and academic experts.

The bad news is that despite all these avenues for collaboration and information sharing, companies generally have been highly reluctant to share information about intrusions. Currently, the FBI receives only about one-third of the intrusion reports that it needs from private companies says FBI Director Robert Mueller.[29] The reluctance to share this information is understandable; firms fear news headlines like "Bank Loses Millions from Hacker Break-Ins" and the resulting loss of customer confidence and potential legal liability that would result. Nevertheless, more sharing is a prerequisite for reaping the benefits of many new security technologies. Columbia University researchers, for example, are developing pattern-finding software that can monitor fraud and attacks throughout an entire industry. Meanwhile Carnegie Mellon University, in conjunction with the U.S. General Service Administration, is working on a system for analyzing and reporting patterns of cyber intrusion for the Feds.[30] The only way these systems can work, however, is if each company and government agency allows access to their streams of data about previous attacks and financial transactions.

Better information sharing is also critical to reducing the vulnerability of public and private IT systems to cyber attacks. Hardening systems against cyber attacks requires having a keen understanding of previous successful intrusions and then using this knowledge to devise adequate defenses against attacks. If no one ever knows that a firewall was pierced in the first place, such learning cannot occur.

Technological advances will also be critical to reducing our vulnerability to attacks. Today, encryption technology, with its ability to assure the privacy of sensitive government and business information, is the basic foundation for protecting information systems from attack. Looking to the future, researchers are working on unbreakable codes based on quantum physics.[31] Scientists at Los Alamos National Laboratory are using single photons to send cryptographic keys over fiber-optic links and even over just plain air. The scientists are exploiting the Heisenberg uncertainty principle, which states that observing a quantum particle changes it. So if hackers look at the quantum keys, the keys become useless. Scientists are still trying to figure out how to keep outside influences like light from spoiling the keys.[32]

Such technology breakthroughs could go a long way toward making the systems more secure, however no system will ever be completely immune to a cyber attack. Just as it's easier to build a nuclear weapon to destroy a city than construct a missile defense to protect it, defending against cyber attacks will always be more challenging than launching them. "Our ability to wage information warfare is the best in the world," explains Erbschloe. "To defend, on the other hand, is a different story. It's easier to attack anytime. When we're training attackers, we create attack and defense teams, and then they have to switch places. Without a doubt, they all tell us it's very frustrating to attempt to defend."

Given this difficulty, some leading security experts are creating cyber defenses based on the principle that the bad guys will inevitably find a way in. University of California computer science professor Matt Bishop is developing systems that will be able to take a hit in attacks but recover from them by limiting the damage, containing the enemy to small areas of the computer systems, and striking back at them once they're in.[33] In a similar vein, in order to make computer systems more likely to survive a cyber attack, researchers from the Defense Advanced Research Projects Agency (DARPA) are designing a security system that is "less like a moat around a castle and more like a nice, safe sandbox."[34] With the DARPA approach, centralized security enforcement of computer systems would be replaced by a compartmentalized model in which every object has its own individual security; if its security walls are penetrated, only that object would be affected. Each computer application would be placed inside a wrapper that would monitor its actions, keeping it in a self-contained "safe" area where all its actions could be watched. Thus a single security failure would not compromise the normal operation of the system. This approach is based on the widely accepted security dictum that the best test of a security measure is not how well it works, but how well it fails.[35] "No firewall will ever work," argues security guru William Wulf, the former assistant director of the National Science Foundation, who is involved in the project. "Somebody finds a way to get through the firewall and then there is no additional defense beyond that."[36] This vision of individualized security is where computer security is headed, but it likely is still a few years away.

Ethical Issues

At a 2000 hacker convention held in sweltering Las Vegas, more than 1,500 people listened to a plea for help from the National Security Agency's Brian Snow, who was using the meeting to recruit hackers.[37] The hackers would join the U.S. military's growing cyber war machine, which is readying its response to a potential cyber attack against enemies. Such an attack would likely involve colossal distributed DOS attacks, unleashing computer viruses and Trojan Horses, and jamming enemy computer systems.

Strengthening America's offensive capability to wage cyber war raises tough questions of international law and the ethics of war. Cyber war can be *more* ethical in one way, because it can be "preventative medicine"—essentially, disarming the enemy rather than killing him. But "peace" is bought at a high civilian price. Many of the most effective attacks target civilian infrastructure, like the banking system or the port authority. Instead of blowing them apart physically, you do it electronically. For countries in fragile economic conditions, tangling cash flow or contractual arrangements for weeks (or even just days) could really set them back economically, because they don't have the cushion to absorb it like the United States and other big countries. But if you totally destroy a budding economy, the people who suffer most will be the people in the street, not those in power. For these reasons, the United States has so far rejected the practice of targeting civilians in cyber warfare. In Bosnia, the U.S. military suggested cyber attacks against the Serbs that would disable the country's financial systems, but the Justice Department questioned the legality of the action and ultimately the decision was made not to launch the attack.[38]

How do we judge proportionality in war? What is a just payback for an attack that destroys a dam and the city beneath it? Can a country legitimately respond to information attack with armed force? Many of those questions seem to have been answered after 9/11, when most nations agreed that the United States acted appropriately in responding to a deadly "asymmetric" attack with conventional warfare in Afghanistan. In the future, there is little doubt that we would respond to a devastating cyber attack with massive force. "We reserve the right to respond in any way appropriate: through covert action, through military action, any of the tools available to the president," said former White House cyberterrorism chief Richard Clarke in explaining how the United States would respond to a cyber attack.[39]

* * * * *

As we harden our defenses against cyber attacks, it's important to retain a sense of perspective. While the dangers of computer attacks and cyberterrorism are very real, and the consequences of failing to rebuff assaults are dire, at the time that this book went to press no one had died from a computer virus and no economy had been brought down by computer hacking. These kinds of scenarios may lie in our future, but they haven't yet occurred. Physical attacks are still a greater danger to our neighborhoods, our families, and our way of life than cyber attacks. Even al Qaeda, which has shown an exceptionally sophisticated ability to use the Internet to coordinate its attacks through coded messages, ultimately relied on a brute-force physical attack rather than a cyber attack. And as with our physical security, in the cyber world, we will never come to a point where we've achieved absolute security. As former White House cyber security chief Howard Schmidt explains, "Security is a journey, not a destination."

TIPS FOR PRACTITIONERS

- Make sure that no government computer is linked to the Net until it meets minimum-security standards and all holes in the software systems have been plugged.
- Rather than relying on individual employees and system administrators to download every new security patch, utilize computer programs that automatically find and install patches.
- No security system should be designed with only a single point of failure. The most effective approach for defending against attack is to build multiple, overlapping, cross-checking layers of deterrence, rather than one massive firewall.
- Don't wait for the hackers to come to you. Take a proactive approach to security by continuously searching for holes in your own defenses.
- Reduce the vulnerability of public and private IT systems to cyber attack by increasing information sharing. Hardening systems against cyber attacks requires having a keen understanding of previous successful intrusions and then using this knowledge to devise adequate defenses against attacks.
- The best test of a security measure is not how well it works, but how well it fails. Develop systems that will be able to take a hit in attacks but recover from them by limiting the damage, containing the enemy to small areas of the computer systems, and then striking back at them. In a similar vein, promising research is also underway to replace centralized security enforcement of computer systems with a compartmentalized model in which every object has its own individual security. This way if security walls are penetrated, only that object would be affected.

11

Overcoming Hidden Hurdles

If you are going to sin, sin against God, not the bureaucracy. God will forgive you but the bureaucracy won't.

—Admiral Hyman Rickover

One day in 1999, David Barram stood in his kitchen and stared down at a *Washington Times* headline, which screamed that his proposal to close down the General Service Administration's (GSA) eight warehouses was going to get a bunch of blind people fired. The one thought running through his head was, "Ushering in the future can be a lousy job."

Barram, a Clinton administration political appointee, was head of the GSA, the federal agency responsible for erecting and maintaining government buildings; purchasing and distributing billions of dollars in goods and services; maintaining the vehicle fleet; and innumerable other mundane, complex, expensive, and unsexy tasks that keep Uncle Sam functioning. By the mid-1990s it became uncomfortably clear the GSA was in trouble.

In corporate America, almost everything an agency did—from procuring supplies to selling surplus property—was being transformed by technology. But the GSA went about its business the same way it had for decades, funded solely by revenues from services it provided to other federal agencies—services that other companies could now perform far more efficiently. Barram, a Washington transplant who spent decades managing the financial operations of Silicon Valley colossi such as Apple Computer and Silicon Graphics, was painfully aware the agency had to either rise with the digital tide or get swamped by it. During his first week on the job, the former Apple executive asked for a Macintosh in his office. A few hours later, he received a dusty, five-year-old Mac 2 that was ceremoniously produced from the far corners of the building's basement.

This was precisely the sort of archaic mentality Barram was determined to banish. "Given where they were, it was impossible in the environment I came into at GSA to use technology too much," he said. His early attempts to turn the agency into a public-sector exemplar of private-sector efficiency included such relatively uncontroversial projects as GSA Advantage—a virtual marketplace that let federal employees purchase more than 100,000 different supply items online; mandatory purchase cards (in essence, government credit cards) for transactions under $2,500; and FirstGov.com, the federal government's Internet portal.

From a private-sector perspective, Barram's decision about the warehouses seemed straightforward. The advent of online procurement, just-in-time delivery methods, electronic purchase cards, and nationwide supply companies, such as Office Depot, had long since rendered obsolete the practice of warehousing huge stockpiles of goods for weeks, months, or even years at a time. (Dell Computer Corp., for example, maintains less than a week's worth of inventory at any one time.) The GSA's supply-chain system, by painful contrast, remained dominated by hamlet-sized warehouses considered state-of-the-art back when America liked Ike.

Clearly the GSA could save many millions of taxpayer dollars by moving its operations out of the warehouses and onto the web. In fact, Barram's early initiatives, like GSA Advantage and purchase cards, already partially achieved this goal.

So in July 1999, Barram announced his intention to shut down the GSA's eight monstrous warehouses and move toward a "virtual platform." Henceforth, supplies would be ordered from GSA's web page and delivered directly from vendors to agencies. "The warehouse business was a billion and a half dollar business that had declined to under $1 billion, and eventually it was going to zero," Barram said. "There was no point in trying to hold onto a declining program."

If Barram were still at Apple, the same decision would have been a no-brainer. In fact, failing to perform such cost cutting might be considered reasonable grounds for dismissing a Fortune 500 CFO. But in government, no one can cut even one dollar from any service for any reason without generating an equal and opposite (or greater) reaction from the entrenched powers whose budgets are being threatened. In this case it was the unions—the American Federation of Government Employees (AFGE) to be precise. The question of whether keeping the warehouses would be good or bad for the American people as a whole was not necessarily of primary importance to the union, whose reasoning was self-interested. Closing the warehouses meant the loss of dues-paying mem-

bers. QED. As Barram soon discovered, the union considered his announcement tantamount to declaring war.

It didn't thrill GSA's private-sector partners, either. Numerous vendors
who'd enjoyed many lucrative years moving goods into and out of GSA
warehouses faced increased competition, and thus decreased profits, if
Barram managed to move their longtime fiefdoms online. "We're going to
lose a whole lot of business," said a manager for Polaroid Corporation's
Fairfax office. "When [customers] find that the warehouses are closed,
they're probably going to take their credit cards to Wal-Mart."[1] Barram's
initiative would save the taxpayers lots of money—but it could also cost
some other people their jobs.

And some of them might be blind. "GSA Plan to Shut Warehouses
Down May Put Blind Out of Work," read the *Washington Times* headline.
For more than fifty years, GSA was the principal distributor of goods produced by the National Industries for the Blind (NIB), which argued that
1,400 blind and disabled workers might be affected by the closures. "The
domino effect could jeopardize the whole program," warned NIB president Jim Gibbons. So roughly a year before a presidential election, Barram
faced an enraged coalition of business and usually Democrat-friendly labor, and the NIB layoff PR catastrophe added fuel to the fire.

If all that didn't put him far enough behind the eight ball, AFGE took the
GSA to court, arguing that Barram's warehouse plan violated a 1993 memorandum of understanding between the union and the agency. The arbitrator agreed and ordered GSA to keep the warehouses open. At this point,
not even the most feverish cost-cutter would have blamed Barram—or as
some GSA staffers called him, "Scrooge"—for folding his tent. Live to fight
another day. You gave it your best shot, right?

Wrong. "In government, the usual practice if you do a good job is to jump
in the foxhole to avoid the bullets," Barram said. "But I was determined to
see this one through. Philosophically, we're better off as Democrats if we
don't always kowtow to the unions and other special interests." Just three
days after the arbitrator's decision, Barram issued a defiant statement saying he would go ahead with the closures, pending an appeal to the Federal
Labor Relations Authority. "Nobody at the White House ever told me not
to do this," Barram recalled. "I think they were frustrated that I couldn't
make it work with the unions, but they didn't ask me to give in."

In autumn 2001—several grueling years and one change in administration later—six federal supply warehouses were shut down. The closures
will save American taxpayers $176 million over ten years. At the end of
the day, only sixty-three warehouse employees received pink slips.[2] And
the blind workers still have their jobs.

Barram's saga is not all that unusual. As government innovators try to
use information technology (IT) to try to transform Byzantine, outmoded

systems, they'll face opposition from many fronts. Anybody who feels threatened by change is a potential opponent—from public employees who fear losing their jobs, to department heads who worry about losing control and budgetary authority. "We discovered that technology was the least of the challenges," recalled John Kost, former Michigan CIO and current vice president at Gartner Group. "The bigger problems were turf battles, organizational problems and politics."

I've seen the manifestation of these barriers countless times from the distrust among law enforcement agencies that impedes information sharing to the interest groups that have fought against virtual charter schools. Throughout the book, I've presented tips for overcoming these and other obstacles and laid out some guidelines for making everything from digital democracy to e-learning a reality. In this final chapter, I'll address some of the larger challenges that cut across the various areas of digital government and offer eight broad strategies for achieving technology-enabled transformation.

STRATEGIES FOR WINNING THE TRANSFORMATION BATTLE

> Obstacles are those frightful things you see when you take your eyes off your goal.
>
> —Henry Ford

Don't Back Down

Typically opponents of reform—interest groups, permanent bureaucracy, businesses that benefit from the status quo—try to wear down innovators through inaction, delay, and obstruction. They figure, usually rightly, that the hard-charging political appointee or the Cabinet official hired as a change agent will not stick around more than a few years. They can wait them out. Just enough delay, just enough obstruction will ensure things stay pretty much where they are.

Nine times out of ten, this strategy works, but every once in a while an individual like David Barram will come along and throw a wrench into the plan. Despite repeated obstacles thrown in his path, vigorous opposition of powerful interest groups and some really bad press, he stuck it out when others would have folded. He ended up staying a full year more at the GSA than he had planned for no other reason but to see this project through. And the GSA and the federal supply system are both better off for it. Barram's saga illustrates the importance of persistence—refusing to back down even in the face of overwhelming obstacles. "E-government transformation will be a matter of will," says former Texas CIO Carolyn Purcell. "Government leaders have to have the will to revamp their systems."

Devote Serious Attention to Privacy and Security

Privacy and security are digital government's two principal perils. A couple of high profile break-ins to government databases that result in confidential citizen information being splattered all over the web could set back for years the digital transformation of government. Privacy and security challenges loom in nearly every major policy area discussed in this book, whether it's online learning, intelligent transportation systems, or homeland security. Poorly designed or executed privacy and security policies could doom even the best technology-enabled change initiatives.

And the privacy and security issues aren't going to get any easier. The better we get at using technology to make government more seamless, personalized, and customer-centered, the greater the potential risks to privacy. The more we rely on technology to operate our government and run our economy, the more catastrophic the potential consequences of a successful cyber attack. It's almost inevitable that at some point in the not so distant future a prominent politician will lose an election as a result of a lapse in cyber security or a perceived violation of privacy. As explained in chapters 9 and 10 there are a number of policies government officials should adopt to avoid suffering this fate. While there are no guarantees, baking privacy and security into every technology-enabled change initiative is a necessary first step.

Change the Culture

When he became CIO of the Department of Commerce in 1998, Roger Baker had what he thought was a pretty simple idea: The Census Bureau should let Americans fill out their 2000 census forms online. When he broached the idea with Census, the notoriously change-resistant agency wanted no part of it, calling the use of online forms "experimental." Baker, a former high-tech executive, couldn't believe what he was hearing. "How can you look at the Internet as experimental in the year 2000?" he asked. "They really didn't want to do it," he recalls. "They spent six months trying to get around me." Fortunately, Baker's boss, then-Commerce Secretary Bill Daley, liked the idea, so eventually the Census Bureau relented and put the census questionnaire online. Story over?

Not quite. Rather than prominently displaying an icon on the agency's home page, the online forms were buried in the bowels of the website. Anyone wanting to fill out his census form in cyberspace had to have the detective skills of Philip Marlowe to find it. Baker attributes the opposition to simple fear of the unknown. "They didn't know if people would answer questions differently online, so their first instinct was to kill the idea," he explained.

Not every government agency is so adamantly antichange. But many are. Employees don't want to rock the boat. Managers are unwilling to take risks. Hard-charging department heads are too often captured by the bureaucracy. Change often threatens deeply held values and habits—and bureaucracies are very good at resisting changes they want to resist.

Success requires changing people's attitudes, belief systems, and ways of doing business—helping move them from what they know to something new and strange. Inevitably, some people will be unable to adapt. Others will be unwilling, hoping the change will fail because failure is in their interest. Overcoming such opposition requires a cadre of people who are maniacal about transforming government. "A governor or mayor can give a lot of speeches about the importance of technology, but if you don't staff it up with the right person, then you don't get very far," said former Michigan governor John Engler.

Where do you find such people? Sometimes, you need to bring them in from the outside to shake up the organization (hence the large number of IT executives recruited to serve as public-sector CIOs). Sometimes outsourcing the function is the only way to accomplish the needed transformation. "Before I came into government, I was not a big fan of outsourcing," says former Georgia CIO Larry Singer, now with Sun Microsystems. "But sometimes it's necessary to bring about major business and cultural changes."

More often than not, the revolutionaries already exist in government— they just need to be identified, trained, and empowered. That's the goal of Washington State's Digital Government Applications Academy, a place where employees from different agencies work together on building e-government services. In addition to the technical goal, Washington State officials seek to change state agency culture by creating a corps of digital government professionals to unleash on the agencies. "One of the main points of the academy was to create a set of insurgents to send out to agencies to fight for a different way of doing business," said former Washington CIO Steve Kolodney who founded the academy. "To achieve change in government, you have to figure out ways to intrude into these long-standing organizations."

Intrude would be a mild way of describing what William Bratton did to the culture of the NYPD when Rudy Giuliani named him his first police commissioner. When Bratton took over the department, the NYPD culture was completely dysfunctional: Bureaus didn't talk to each other; beat cops didn't talk to detectives; and years of negative publicity and fear of corruption had paralyzed many officers. Surveys of NYPD beat cops revealed the activities they believed were most valued by their supervisors were "holding down overtime," "staying out of trouble," and "treating bosses with deference." "Reducing crime, disorder and, fear"—Bratton's top priority—was considered by officers to be the activity least valued by their superiors.[3] Bratton knew he had to thoroughly transform the culture of the organization if he hoped to bring about the massive crime reductions he had promised the mayor.

His most famous strategy for doing this, Compstat, gave Bratton and his lieutenants the information they needed to make decisions on resource deployment, while helping to focus precinct commanders on results. But Compstat was only one part of Bratton's multipronged culture war strategy. In addition, he purged the department of the old guard, devolved power to precinct commanders, won over rank-and-file officers by backing them up in confrontations with the public (unless there was clear evidence of wrongdoing), created real consequences for poor performers, and established audacious goals, such as reducing crime by 40 percent. "You need to set the tone, and you need to set stretch goals that would inspire people," explained Bratton.[4]

Smash the Silos

The year 2000 brought one of Florida's worst droughts in years. Craig Fugate, director of Florida's Emergency Management Agency, asked his staff to find available federal assistance for drought victims. Florida officials discovered there was no central place to find this information and were forced to navigate their way through a convoluted maze of more than one thousand federal disaster response grant programs in 250 different federal agencies.

"We made dozens of calls and went to hundreds of websites," Fugate recalled, adding that he estimated the process occupied hundreds of hours of staff time. "To obtain this kind of information, you have to become an expert on how every agency is organized." It took Fugate and his staff more than a year to finish researching the grants, by which time the drought assistance was no longer needed. It had started raining again in Florida.

At the time Fugate's experience was pretty standard fare when it came to dealing with the federal government. Cities, counties, states, and even average citizens faced similar tribulations daily. The root of the problem: Stovepipes dominated the federal government. While nearly all governments experience some problems getting agencies to cooperate with each other, nowhere was the problem worse than in the federal government.

Take e-government for example. It has been used elsewhere to connect stovepipes and present a unified face to the public, but as Fugate's experience demonstrated, the feds had used e-government mostly as a way to replicate in cyberspace the information silos and duplication existing in brick-and-mortar government. The result: endless islands of automation. (Exhibit A: the Department of Health and Human Services' two thousand websites and three thousand different servers.)

This is the grim situation Mark Forman confronted when President George W. Bush appointed him as the fed's technology and e-government czar. Hardly anyone in the know in Washington expected Forman to do much about this state of affairs. Jaded Beltway insiders said he'd never get turf-obsessed federal agencies to cooperate with each other. They warned him Congress would never let him get away with shifting IT money from individual agencies to cross-agency projects. They snickered when he said he hoped to change the culture of federal agencies in eighteen to twenty-four months.[5] They told the press that a non-Senate confirmed, OMB associate deputy wouldn't have the power or authority to knock bureaucratic heads together. "eGov will not achieve the transformation everyone dreams of because of the inertia," said a former federal CIO in what was a typical comment at the time. "Mark has a bigger job than anyone could possibly do. I'm not sure the president can hit this with a big enough hammer to make it move."[6]

It was hard to argue with the gloom-and-doomers—history, after all, was on their side. The permanent Washington bureaucracy already chewed up and spit out countless wild-eyed reformers who tried much less ambitious things than what Forman had in mind. There was just one problem this time: Forman wasn't listening. "They had such a constrained vision of what was possible to accomplish," Forman recalled. "I just didn't believe we needed to be years and years behind private industry, so I just told the agencies that we're going to do this—and we did it."

His third day on the job, Forman said the feds might have been spending too much on IT due to the existence of hundreds of duplicative and overlapping federal IT projects. The statement shocked federal contractors, who assumed this former tech executive would usher in an era of unfettered IT budgets. A few days later, he told federal managers that many federal digital government efforts were just spinning their wheels. "If twenty agencies are improving their service to a citizen by moving it online, but not working together, it still means the citizen has to walk through twenty doors," Forman noted. "It just digitizes the confusion." All in all, Forman estimated the duplication in the federal government was costing taxpayers at least $9 billion in IT costs alone.

Simplify and Unify

As the person most responsible for making good on Bush's campaign promise to make the federal government citizen-centered, Forman's goal was to reach a point where citizens could walk through just one door to conduct most interactions with the feds. To get to this point, he and his staff developed a plan to eliminate redundant systems, consolidate e-government projects, convince agencies to look beyond their traditional silos, and focus attention and money toward cross-agency and cross-governmental projects. This ambitious approach, dubbed "simplify and unify," while it did not reach every single one of its ninety-one original objectives, did against all odds meet many of them, resulting in major improvements in how the federal government delivers online services in areas ranging from tax filing to grants management. As such, it offers several lessons for how to break up stovepipes:

Create Champions

One of the first manifestations of "simplify and unify" came days after 9/11, when the Office of Management and Budget (OMB) announced that more than three hundred federal e-government projects would be consolidated into just twenty-five "Quicksilver" initiatives. Forman created champions for each one by designating the agency with the most "skin in the game" (usually the one with the most resources invested) as the lead agency responsible for the day-to-day work of each project. For example, the e-grants project—which involved consolidating eight hundred different federal grant applications into one online process—was managed by the Department of Health and Human Services (HHS) because it doled out more grant money than anyone else. Dozens of federal agencies had their own grant processes and were asked to not only cooperate with HHS, but to give up some control over budget, policy, and resources. This lead agency model provided each of the lead agencies with several powerful incentives to shepherd the project to completion: more recognition, more turf, and more money.

Establish Consequences

Even with these incentives, Forman, and Karen Evans who succeeded him in 2003 when he left the administration to run a Silicon Valley start-up, still had their share of problems with the lead agencies. A handful of project managers were replaced and several projects were taken from lead agencies that weren't getting the job done. Such problems were trivial, however, in comparison to the resistance OMB faced from many of the "partner" agencies, all of which would lose a certain degree of control and funding under OMB's plan. Several agencies tried to block the GovBenefits initiative, for example, which aimed to consolidate information on all federal benefits programs on one website, by rebuffing efforts to get them to share information about their benefit programs.[7] "No one wants to give up something they are already working on," explains an official from the Social Security Administration. "Other agencies don't want to cooperate with our project and we don't want to cooperate with theirs."[8]

One strategy that helped agencies play together was the scorecard. Each agency was graded on their progress in meeting the president's management goals. Those that refused to play ball received failing grades—represented by red dots. The grades were made public, and Bush even referred to them in meetings with his Cabinet secretaries. "The Cabinet secretaries don't want to be red," said one senior OMB official. "They'll do what they have to do to get out of the red."

Another weapon Forman had in their arsenal was also the OMB's most powerful weapon: money. An obscure provision in a little-known congressional law called the Clinger-Cohen Act—a law that Forman himself helped draft when he was a Senate staffer—gave him the authority to transfer IT funds from one agency to another. The fear of antagonizing powerful, turf-conscious congressional appropriators kept anyone from previously using the authority, but Forman was undeterred. "If it frees up money that can be used for other things, the Hill will be happy," Forman said. "If it looks like we're trying to impinge on their power of the purse, they'll be upset."

In the summer of 2002, Forman made good on his threats. He sent out a batch of Clinger-Cohen letters to noncompliant agencies stating in no uncertain terms he was shutting down their IT projects. "You need a head on the pike so other people sit up and take notice," he said matter-of-factly.

He got their attention. The group of powerful deputy Cabinet secretaries who collectively form the President's Management Council had a fit. "The deputy secretaries all ganged up on me and said, 'You can't do this,'" Forman said.

The final pièce de résistance came later when the OMB froze billions of dollars in IT modernization and infrastructure funding for agencies slated to become part of the new Department of Homeland Security. Forman justified the action by citing estimates that consolidation would save several hundred million dollars. The action surprised the federal IT community, coming as it did months before Congress even passed legislation to create the department—let alone agreed on which agencies would be included. But the goal of OMB's preemptive strike was unmistakable: To the extent possible, the new Department of Homeland Security would be stovepipe-free.

To be sure, the federal government's ambitious cross-agency Quicksilver projects took longer to realize than originally planned, faced more trials and tribulations than anyone could have anticipated and, in some cases, looked like they were close to collapsing at different points on the journey from inception to deployment. But at the end of the day, by Election Day November 2004, most of the projects were fully deployed, saving more than $100 million in redundant spending and vastly improving customer service. The moral is clear: busting up silos and smashing stovepipes is an arduous, frustrating, and extremely challenging undertaking, but with strong leadership and the right strategies, structures, and incentives, it can be accomplished.

Use Creative Funding Mechanisms

One of the most formidable obstacles many public-sector leaders face is finding money to pay for digital government and modernization. Confronted with either maintaining school budgets or investing money in digital government, legislators choose schools every time. The funding challenge is particularly acute for local governments, which have fewer IT dollars to disperse even before the state aid cutbacks of recent years.

One of the most promising ways to overcome the funding barrier is to squeeze some savings out of current IT spending and reinvest it back into digital government. Every ex-CIO will say there's plenty of duplicative, redundant, and wasteful IT spending hidden in individual agencies. Consolidating IT operations and spending—not unlike Forman's "simplify and unify" strategy—could bring considerable savings. One former CIO says most states could run their IT shops on half of what they're spending now. "What's buried in the base [of the IT budget] is very important," says Singer, the former Georgia CIO. "If the CIO's office can partner with the budget agency to peel the onion and show the inefficiencies, then these funds become funds of opportunity."

Sounds reasonable, except for one little problem: Most governments don't have a clue about how much they spend on IT. "When I became governor, I asked two basic questions," says Virginia governor Mark Warner, a tech-savvy Democrat. "First, how much do we spend on information technology? And second, how many people work in technology?"[9] Instead of a spreadsheet, Warner got blank stares. "They told me it's somewhere between $800 million and $1.2 billion," recalls the governor, who was incredulous that they couldn't get any closer than a $400 million spread.

Warner wasted no time charging his handpicked CIO George Newstrom, a Republican plucked from Electronic Data System's Asia operations, with getting answers to his simple questions. It took Newstrom's team nine months, but the wait was worth it. The inventory of IT spending uncovered enormous amounts of duplication in what Newstrom calls the "factory of technology"—mainframes, servers, storage, networks, and service and call centers. "We had every email system known to mankind—and none of them talked to each other," Warner said, his voice dripping with disdain.

The inventory results gave Warner and Newstrom sufficient ammunition to propose one of the most far-reaching IT consolidation plans ever attempted by a government entity. Virginia is consolidating nearly all state IT operations, spending and staff into a newly created office of IT. Cost savings: a whopping $100 million over three years. A chunk of this savings will come from consolidating the dozens of state data centers now scattered all over Richmond. Several other states have already realized multimillion dollar savings from consolidating data centers.[10] The most ambitious effort to date was in Pennsylvania, which saved $140 million over five years by consolidating eighteen data centers into one.[11]

Another approach for digging savings from IT budgets is to "retire" clunky mainframe systems—a euphemism for sending IT systems to the computer graveyard. The Transportation Security Administration, for example, retired more than seven hundred of the Federal Aviation Administration's legacy mainframe systems as part of its effort to web-enable all processes and information flows around a common enterprise-wide platform.

Similarly, the Department of Education's Federal Student Aid Office (FSA) saved $46 million from retiring five redundant mainframe computers, enough to pay for a chunk of FSA's modernization and e-government efforts. Best of all, it didn't cost the agency a dime, because the contractor fronted all project costs in return for a percentage of future savings.

For smaller cities and counties with small IT budgets, the most promising funding approaches are either piggybacking off the state's digital infrastructure, or sharing costs with other local governmental entities. All sixty-seven Florida county clerk offices joined together in 2002 to create a centralized portal where citizens could go to find, search, and purchase marriage licenses, birth certificates, and other official records online. The cost of building and operating the portal would have been too high for any single county clerk's office. However, by linking together, they saved millions of dollars, as well as provided better customer service by allowing citizens to go to one place to view official records from any Florida county.

Partner Up

As technological advances increasingly blur the lines between the public and private sectors and the boundaries between them become more permeable, stronger and deeper collaboration between governments and private firms is essential to fulfilling many policy goals. Protecting the nation's critical infrastructure from cyber attacks, for example, depends on partnerships between private companies, the feds, and the local law enforcement community. Wiring the nation's roads involves partnerships between state transportation agencies, the U.S. Department of Transportation, telematics providers, technology companies, and road builders. Boosting adoption of e-government services among citizens and businesses requires channel partnerships between government and those private companies and nonprofits that can achieve a greater reach into the marketplace. And keeping the country safe from terrorists depends just as much on the security efforts of the private sector as the Department of Homeland Security. The list could go on and on.

One consequence of the increasing reliance on partnerships is that policymakers will need to develop new governance structures and management practices. Today's hierarchical structures are ill suited to a more horizontal, networked government. Those interested in delving deeper into this topic can learn more by reading *Governing by Network: The New Shape of Government* (Brookings Press), a book I coauthored in 2004 on the transition from hierarchical to networked government.

Ease the Transition for Employees

No aspect of government reform provokes a fiercer reaction than threatening the jobs of public employees. Connecticut governor John Rowland found this out the hard way in the mid-1990s when he proposed consolidating and outsourcing all state IT operations. Despite the governor's promise that all displaced public employees would be given jobs with the private sector for at least two years, his plan engendered intense opposition from the state public employees' union. After years of battling both the union and its legislative allies, Rowland finally dropped his signature government-reform initiative—what would have been the largest state outsourcing deal in history—four years after its introduction.

To date, very few public employees anywhere have lost their jobs as a result of digitization. Even the few layoffs resulting from the GSA warehouse shutdown were anomalies. Thanks to continuing fiscal pressures, this is likely to change. Digitization will result in the elimination of some positions. Policymakers are increasing reliance on technology not only to provide better services to citizens, but also to fulfill the old promise that tech innovations can cut costs. As more citizens take care of government needs on the web, fewer government clerks will need to process requests, fewer human resource professionals will fill out personnel forms, and fewer data processors will transfer information from paper to computer. These and countless other tasks will be done by machines, or by citizens themselves via self-service web transactions. The Texas Health and Human Services Commission has calculated that $389 million could be saved by shifting Medicaid applications from face-to-face interviews to call centers and the web, which would mean cutting state employee workloads in half, shuttering more than 200 field offices and trimming close to 4,500 state jobs.[12]

Another government job likely to be affected by automation is the issuance of licenses and permits. Around 17,000 different government entities in the United States issue 100 million-odd building permits each year. The annual cost of administering these permits is around $16 billion—or $160 per permit.[13] With electronic permitting, a good chunk of these costs go away. Because most of the costs are in staff time, eventually fewer employees will be needed to hand out building permits.

Public employee unions are clearly worried about the potential impact of technology on government jobs. The Social Security Administration (SSA) maintains over 1,300 field offices, an average of two and one-half for each Congressional district. Fearing job losses, the union representing SSA is categorically opposed to closing any of them and considers e-government the biggest potential threat to the existence of the offices. "Congress should be alerted to watch closely and recognize that Internet claims taking could result in more centralized workloads, and the closing and consolidation of community-based offices in every congressional district," Witold Skwierczynski, president of the union representing Social Security employees, told a congressional committee several years ago.[14]

Although the potential loss of public-sector jobs will surely complicate any attempts by budget offices to extract hard cost savings from information technology, it shouldn't be viewed as a deal-killer. There are ways to cut workloads and jobs without massive layoffs. "It's the same as any other business," said Harvard professor and former Indianapolis mayor Stephen Goldsmith. "Some people will retire. Some will be retrained. Some will be employed in the private sector. Some will actually be moved to more meaningful work. Instead of determining whether people are eligible for a service, their job would be to actually help them."

Many agencies already are struggling with increased demand. Automating some of their workload or shifting it to a self-service model will come as a godsend, helping them meet new demand without piling more work onto existing employees. "By [2010] we're going to be looking at workloads that are 22 percent to 28 percent higher than they are now," says John Erwin, a member of the SSA's Internet projects team. "How do you get 28 percent more work with the same staff? You have to find a way to offload that work, and get the public to help themselves."[15]

Moreover, governments will need to cut fewer jobs than it may at first appear because the governmental workforce is graying. More than 70 percent of senior federal civil servants (Senior Executive Service) are now eligible for retirement; by 2007 more than half of them are likely to leave government service according to the General Accounting Office (GAO).[16]

At the state and local level, 42 percent of all government workers are between forty-five and sixty-four years old. Many other countries are also facing an exodus due to the retirement of Baby Boomers. In Canada, 80 percent of public-sector executives and executive feeder groups will be eligible for retirement by the decade's end.[17]

The graying workforces allow policymakers to reshape their workforces to meet Information Age realities without huge layoffs by using attrition. Careful workforce planning will allow them to ascertain their future human capital gaps, match this up against the jobs most likely to be eliminated due to technology and then redeploy and retrain workers accordingly.

Engage the Political Leadership

Nothing is more important in the transformation from Industrial Age to Information Age government than the unwavering support of a strong chief executive. It's not enough for chief executives to simply delegate the transformation effort to others. They must be personally engaged. This sends a signal to the rest of the organization that technology modernization is a top priority, a lesson learned the hard way at the Federal Bureau of Investigation (FBI).

By all accounts, Louis Freeh, the FBI director throughout most of the 1990s, is a passionate, charismatic, hard-charging individual. A former FBI agent himself, Freeh was more respected by G-men in the field than any director in decades. This, along with his political skills, helped Freeh become the most powerful FBI director since J. Edgar Hoover. When he left the bureau in May 2001, Freeh was widely praised by Democrats and Republicans alike. President George W. Bush asked the Clinton appointee to stay on, while allies on Capitol Hill, such as Senate Judiciary Chairman Patrick Leahy (D-VT), praised Freeh's legacy as "an updated attitude appropriate to twenty-first-century law enforcement."[18]

Freeh didn't have long to bask in the bipartisan adoration, however. In the aftermath of 9/11, his reputation was badly tarnished—as was that of the agency he once led. Countless daily news articles, investigative reports, congressional testimony, and the 2004 9/11 commission all focused attention on the failings of the FBI. The reports made our nation's most elite law enforcement agency sound like the worst kind of slow-moving, turf-defending, information-hoarding, dinosaur bureaucracy—the Department of Motor Vehicles, with guns. Forget about real-time information sharing with the CIA or the INS. FBI agents didn't even have the ability to quickly pass information along to each other. More than a year *after* 9/11, many G-men were still working on archaic 486-generation desktop PCs attached to green-and-black screen monitors; connecting to the Internet through 56K dial-up modems;

and hunting for information through thirty-five or more unconnected databases that couldn't communicate with each other.[19] In the unlikely event that
an agent went through all the hassles of individually searching the dozens
of separate databases, she probably still wouldn't have found the information she needed: Over half the FBI's records were still in paper form. A query
about Mohammed Atta might have turned up paper records in Los Angeles,
New York, and Virginia.[20] Writer Shane Harris wittily described the prehis-
toric state of the FBI's computer systems in a piece in *Government Executive*
magazine:

> If you own a personal computer, or use one in your office, you can get a sense
> of what's it's been like for FBI agents over the past decade. First, disconnect
> the computer from the Internet. This will keep you from accessing the web
> and receiving emails. Now, throw the computer away. It's far more modern
> than anything FBI personnel have used for years. Throw out the mouse, too.
> Replace everything with a machine that was manufactured in the 1980s, rec-
> ognizable by its black background and flashing green cursor, and by the de-
> lay of a second or so before typed characters appear on the screen.[21]

How did an organization that was considered the premier law enforcement agency in the world become such a technology backwater? Much of
the blame lies with the technophobia of Louis Freeh himself. Ronald
Kessler, the author of *The Bureau: The Secret History of the FBI,* explains:
"Repeatedly Freeh was told by people in the bureau that they needed to
upgrade [the technology]. [He] made it clear that he wasn't interested in
technology. . . . Freeh's aversion to technology—he did not himself use
email—led to the fact that the FBI until recently had computers that no
one would take even as donations to churches. With these machines . . .
the FBI was supposed to keep track of terrorists."[22] According to Kessler,
one of Freeh's first actions as FBI director was to order the bureau to get
rid of the computer on his desk.

A leader sets the tone for the organization, and in this case Freeh never
devoted adequate resources or managerial attention to modernizing the
bureau's information systems. "Frequently the bureau would take money
from the technical sides and apply it to needs elsewhere—cases that
arose," said former FBI agent I. C. Smith. "It was a cash cow."[23] The result
of Freeh's exceedingly weak technology leadership was an agency that, at
times, was about as technologically sophisticated as a junior high school
classroom.

It would be hard to find a greater contrast to Freeh's technophobia than
Florida governor Jeb Bush. Sitting atop Bush's L-shaped desk in his small
office—outside the "official" one he uses only for meetings—is an IBM
think pad, a sleek, 19-inch flat-screen LCD display and a Cieva digital picture frame that he uses to exchange digital photos with his famous par-

ents and other friends and relatives. The governor uses technology extensively in his daily life—and has for years. He has to be the only governor in the country who regularly gives out his private email account, meaning anyone listening to him on a radio call-in show has about the same electronic access to him as his famous brother and father.

In many other states, governors might like digital government, but their direct involvement doesn't go much beyond making sure their picture and name are displayed prominently on the state homepage. Not so in Florida. Bush is without question the main driver and cheerleader for the state's digital government program. A top aide admitted sheepishly that because the governor knows more about technology than all but two or three of his senior staff, he occasionally has to tutor *them* on technology subjects.

A governor, mayor, or agency head does not need to know how to write XML code in order to demonstrate leadership and vision on technology issues. However, she does need a vision for how technology can transform government, and she must be able to communicate that vision—and it doesn't hurt if she's actually used a computer a few times herself. "You need to understand things in a hands-on way if you're going to be a leader of an organization," said Angus King, the tech-savvy former governor of Maine who went as far as to personally review the technology specifications in state IT requisitions. "If you've never used it yourself you don't know what to ask nor are you able to understand the capacity and needs."[24]

Effective leaders often use simple but powerful slogans and symbols to encapsulate their vision and demonstrate their commitment to a cause. During his two terms in office, former Pennsylvania governor Tom Ridge was one of the nation's most aggressive governors in moving services online. He never stopped talking about how important technology was to his state's future. Few actions he took in office symbolized this more than when he insisted that the state's website address be prominently displayed on all Pennsylvania license plates. With that simple but powerful action, Ridge signaled that in Pennsylvania, digital government would be more than just a passing fancy.

Technology-enabled transformation entails breaking old habits, learning to do business in new ways, and adopting a radically different approach to serving your customers. This, in turn, requires taking risks and embracing change. None of this comes naturally to government. In fact, nearly all the incentives in government work against all of these things. That is why strong leadership is so indispensable to achieving the kind of fundamental changes laid out in this book and why, absent such leadership, the transformation effort will inevitably fall short.[25] We've seen signs of such leadership from the likes of a diverse group of politicians from across the ideological spectrum, ranging from Mexican president Vicente Fox to former British House of Commons leader "Radical" Robin Cook.

But the leadership needed for achieving the transformation cannot come just from mayors, governors, legislators, heads of state, and other politicians. It must also come from ordinary people. We have already met many of these citizen leaders throughout this book: tech-savvy teachers like Pat Herr, the Leesburg, Virginia middle-school teacher who has used technology to change the way she teaches and the way her students learn; career civil servants like OSHA's Ed Stern, who has spent more than a decade pushing his agency to change the way it regulates business; socially minded entrepreneurs like E2C's Chris Warner, who is using the web to bring previously locked-up public information to millions of people; and Linda Hemby, the head of Probidad, the El Salvador anticorruption organization that is pressuring Central American governments to publish more info online. There is much we can learn about courage, perseverance, and change from these and other pioneers about how to transition from Industrial Age to Information Age government. But ultimately, they can't achieve this revolution alone either. Everyone reading this book also has some responsibility for making it happen. As Mahatma Gandhi once said: "You must be the change you hope to see in the world."

Epilogue

Two Futures

The stories in this book show the slow, steady trickle of technology seeping into our tired bureaucracies. If we ignore eGov, that progress will continue. But the usual budget issues, turf wars, and lassitude could make the "digital government revolution" little more than a facelift: Leviathan with email.

In the vision-impaired future, construction permits are online—but due to turf battles within government, citizens and businesses still must navigate scores of state, local, and federal agencies. The mayor might have posted a few friendly stats on a public website but the real state of the city remains hidden away. Computers are in the classrooms, but they're still mostly distractions from learning rather than conveyor belts of education. Digitization hasn't caused policymakers to confront the duplication and overlap in physical government. The redundancies have continued unabated, and the chasm between virtual government and brick-and-mortar government has widened; they now bear almost no resemblance to each other. Cost savings from information technology (IT) have disappeared into the black hole of individual agency and division budgets. In short, government has become wired—but it certainly has not been transformed.

But there's a far more promising alternative future—the future this book has sought to promote. In this world, farsighted political leaders have responded to the Information Age with vision, rather than torpor, and used technology to redesign government. Interacting with the state online is like visiting Amazon.com. Everything we want to do involving government—from checking garbage collection schedules to viewing local crime stats—is calibrated to our interests, location, and needs. We rarely fill out government forms anymore: As soon as we authenticate ourselves to government online, all the information we've previously supplied is called up from our personal digital briefcases.

Citizens, businesses, and even other governments can conduct transactions with multiple levels of government via a single contact point. For countless electronic transactions with government, we don't even need to go to a government website, as more and more private-sector companies bundle them with their own electronic products and services. Healtheon/WebMD provides online Medicare and Medicaid benefits registration; the American Automobile Association (AAA) offers real-time driver's license renewal.

E-learning has changed how teachers teach, how students learn, how schools are managed, even what schools are. It seems almost inconceivable that public education was once defined solely by which district a student happened to live in and whether or not he turned up at a government building at 9:00 A.M.

The costs of complying with government rules and regulations have plummeted, and not just because the old forms are online. Governments used web-enablement as an opportunity to radically overhaul the regulatory process, culling counterproductive regulations and slashing duplicate rules. And governments have increasingly experimented with transparency as an alternative to top-down command-and-control regulation for regulating some business practices. The result: enormous savings in time, money, and headaches for millions of businesses.

Transportation departments are no longer judged merely by the miles of pavement they lay down. Instead, ITS technologies have enabled us to track how well the transportation system is performing on a block-by-block basis in clearing accidents, travel time reliability, and the thoroughness of traveler information. Travelers use this information to plan their trips and bypass traffic jams, while legislators use it to tie funding directly to system performance. Nobody writes stories about "road rage" anymore, either; why get mad when you can just take a different route?

Bureaucrats no longer control information flows. The layers between the individual and government are long gone—anyone can drill right through the bureaucracy to get the answers he needs. Those worrying rat stats are available to every city resident, every reporter, every prospective mayoral challenger, and every representative of the Hamelin Exterminator Company. Which is one reason the lousy stats get better so much faster.

Citizens have more access to the inner workings of government than ever before, but, more importantly, they can also play a role in many government decisions. They can comment on all rules before they're enacted and on all legislation before it's voted on. We take it for granted that government officials ask for our input on a whole range of issues, thus providing a powerful counterweight to the special interests that typically dominate such discussions. And government officials take it for granted that the citizenry is engaged, educated about the issues, and worth listening to—there's none of the insularity of an entrenched bureaucratic elite.

Campaigns and elections have changed immeasurably. The Net has enabled candidates and issue groups to target and customize their pitches to voters at a fraction of the cost of mail, TV, or radio. Anyone can get updates on legislation she cares about, and she can participate in a moderated discussion with her representatives or their staff. Nobody writes long thumbsucking articles about "The Death of the Voter" or "The End of Responsive Government."

The billions in annual cost savings generated by IT have been used to reduce tax burdens, invest in infrastructure, transform the educational system, and digitize more government services. Instead of being organized solely around bureaus and agencies, governments are organized around networks and governance webs that knit together responses around problems.

In this future, people find it hard to remember that things weren't always this way—that government used to be remote, unresponsive, slothful, and static. They're used to a government that promotes markets and choices, personalization and citizen participation in decision making. A government that is less burdensome, less costly, more transparent and infinitely more accountable. The end of Industrial Age government will come when a return to the old ways seems unimaginable.

Afterword

In February 2006, President George W. Bush launched a website. The announcement didn't exactly dominate the headlines, however. In fact, almost no one noticed, apart from a few Beltway insiders who get as excited about government websites chock full of performance data as ten-year-olds do about tearing open Christmas presents. This silent launch was too bad, however, because in more ways than one the launch of this particular website, "Expectmore.gov," was a remarkable event—even historic in a sense.

That's because Expectmore.gov is not just another government website with pictures of well-suited politicians in front of the American flag. It's a window into the performance of the federal government. In just a few clicks anyone can see not only all the federal programs that are working (yes, there are federal programs that are working, and politicians aren't bashful about those), but also every federal program that's failing to achieve results commensurate with the tax dollars we send to Washington to keep its doors open.

Click on the "nonperforming programs" icon. Up pops detailed information, without all the government jargon, about each program that is "ineffective" or for which there isn't sufficient data to judge whether it's meeting its mission (according to the White House Office of Management and Budget). Beyond that, the site explains in plain English—something of a shock to those expecting typical government bureaucratese—why it was rated that way and what steps will be taken to fix it.

More adventurous sorts will find detailed performance information on each of the programs, including the strategic plan. The data has even been packaged to allow researchers and academics to slice it every which way. The site's twenty thousand pages of information are a virtual treasure trove of information for any opposition researcher.

This might not seem like a big deal. After all, don't taxpayers deserve to see whether they are getting good value for their money? It seems like common sense.

In theory, sure. But the reality is that no country in the world has ever done this before. With the launch of Expectmore.gov, the Bush administration, widely accused by its critics as being one of the most secretive in American history and facing huge criticism for its handling of Iraq and Katrina, opened up its performance—warts and all—to public scrutiny to an unprecedented extent.

"People can go on to that website and determine whether or not the results are being met for programs," explained President Bush. "We're arming our fellow citizens with the information that will enable them to demand we do a better job—a better job in the executive branch and a better job in the legislative branch."

The question is: why? From a strictly political perspective, there would seem to be only political downsides. Why risk it? I asked this question of Office of Management and Budget Deputy Director Clay Johnson, the architect of the program, who also happens to be President Bush's best friend. First of all, he told me, public shaming sometimes works to fix problems when nothing else will. Second, most of the information was already out there, but just hard to find. The American people deserved to see it, he told me.

"Moreover, I think you get a lot of credit for the candor," he said. "Regular citizens are shocked just to find out that half the federal programs actually work well." Johnson jokingly recounted how as he was making the rounds briefing senior White House officials on the site, people kept saying to him: "You're not really going to put all the bad stuff up there, too, are you?"

The launch of Expectmore.gov represents one of several milestones since *Government 2.0* first hit the bookstores in January of 2005. I finished writing the book right around the time the gloom from the Dot Com bust was starting to dissipate. With the much-hyped "Web 2.0" period well underway, it seems as good a time as any to reflect on how far we've come and where we're going in the transition from Government 1.0 to Government 2.0.

Predictably, not all the news is good. In some areas, progress has been slow—in some cases painfully so. Convincing citizens to complete their government transactions online, which was supposed to be the easy part, has been a tough slog for many governments. Policymakers have discovered that, when it comes to e-government services, even if they build it, citizens won't come—or at least not without a lot of creative marketing and even some economic incentives. There's no shortage of reasons—privacy, security, ease of use, lack of Internet access, insufficient marketing to generate awareness. But the fact remains that as of this writing few governments have really figured out how to enthuse citizens when it comes to getting them to do their business online.

Likewise, technology as currently deployed has turned out to be something less than a panacea for an ailing education system. The main problem is the same as it has been for a decade or more: many teachers and school administrators struggle with how to actually use technology in the classroom. The result: lots of money spent on education technology goes to waste. A 2007 U.S. Department of Education study found almost no difference in learning (as measured by standardized test scores) between students who used education software technology versus those who lacked access. This won't improve much until there are more teachers who really understand—through both training and practice—how to use technology to transform how students learn.

Perhaps most troubling of all: six years after 9/11, intelligence agencies still find it difficult to share information with each other. Progress towards effective, systemic information sharing in most places has been minimal. Many agencies still view information sharing as solely a technology issue and assign it to the IT group. In most cases, however, the real issue is getting people to change their behavior. Dumping the problem on IT won't get it done. Leaders must be directly involved in making this change happen.

But things aren't all gloom and doom in the world of Government 2.0. Progress in many areas has exceeded even what many of us technophiles could have predicted six or seven years ago. Most notably, when it comes to political campaigns the Internet is rapidly displacing television as the most influential medium—and fundamentally altering the rules of the game. (Just ask *former* Virginia Sen. George Allen!) The decline of broadcast campaigns— specifically the scripted monologue that national campaigns traditionally have with their supporters, as opposed to engaging in a real dialogue—is just one of a several important emerging trends, some of them foreshadowed in *Government 2.0*, reshaping both how government institutions operate and how citizens interact with them.

TAPPING INTO THE "WISDOM OF THE CROWDS"

A much talked about book in recent years, James Surowiecki's *The Wisdom of Crowds* explores the delightfully anarchic notion that experts don't come up with the best ideas. Surowiecki's thesis is simple: a large group of people is better at solving complex problems than an expert, no matter how brilliant. There is a rider, of course—the group should consist of independent, self-interested individuals working on a problem in a decentralized way, without any direction from the top.

The ideas embodied in *The Wisdom of the Crowds* have made a big splash in the business world, but also have huge implications for public policy. In countless ways, government agencies can take decentralized, local knowledge and use it collectively to solve public policy problems or improve services. Governments can use collaboration technologies to harness the creativity of their constituents, whether through social networking and e-democracy tools or more traditional focus groups and design sessions. At all stages of the policy process, from elections to policy development and implementation, citizens can be called upon to serve as partners in the innovation process.

The Australian Tax Office's "Listening to the Community" program aims to create a more user-friendly tax system by involving stakeholders at every stage in the design process. Through field visits, focus groups, prototype development, and product testing, citizen input is being used to continually refine this system. The agency has even created a simulation center where users and designers work together to troubleshoot problems and test products.

The next step for governments wanting to improve innovation and decision making in the public sector will be to build mechanisms to aggregate information and knowledge from diverse groups of citizens. Consider the 311 systems discussed in chapter 1. In cities such as Chicago and New York, residents have to call only one number and within seconds they can file a complaint, request a trash pickup, report a pothole, or be connected into a wide range of city services. What if the 311-enabled cities aggregated and analyzed all the millions of pieces of data that came into the 311 systems each month? The collective wisdom embodied in these calls could allow government officials to make better resource decisions and catch problems before they become crises.

The open-source software movement represents another good example of harnessing the power of countless unrelated individuals to build and maintain complex world-class systems, in this case technologies such as the Linux operating system and the Wikipedia online encyclopedia. The Education Ministry in Alberta, Canada, is applying the same open-source concept to education content. As the department develops course modules for online education, it posts them on its website for anyone to download, with the expectation that teachers and any other interested parties will validate and improve the content.

Meanwhile, in April 2006 the Central Intelligence Agency launched "Intellipedia," a top-secret wiki based on the same open-source software that powers Wikipedia. The site allows intelligence analysts and operatives from the sixteen U.S. intelligence agencies to engage in free-flowing discussion across agency silos about everything from terrorism to country economic conditions. Already more than seven thousand intelligence officials now use Intellipedia.

These examples offer only a small window into the possibilities for improving governance and service delivery by tapping into the collective wisdom of citizens and public officials. The biggest limits to the application of this concept will be the limits to our imagination.

PERSONALIZED GOVERNMENT

When I first wrote in chapter 1 about moving from "one-size-fits-all government" to "government you design," the actual application of this concept was still pretty scarce. Governments hadn't really figured out how to bring personalization to bear on the customer experience—or at least not anywhere near to the degree it was being applied in the private sector. It hasn't happened overnight, but change seems imminent.

After years of hype, information technology's ability to deliver personalized services and information at low cost is finally impacting how some public services are delivered. Consider the city of Barcelona's IRIS system for managing incidents and complaints. As with the 311 systems, residents call a toll-free phone number to access services or register a complaint—for example, a pothole on the street or abandoned lot next door. Once a request is resolved, callers receive a personalized reply through their choice of email, SMS, or regular mail. In addition to providing a single personalized point of entry, IRIS also allows access to most of the data local government keeps about the citizen and provides easy entry to many online services.

Self-service web tools like this enable real-time customer segmentation. Based on answers to the questions, agencies can discern various patterns in their customers. This in turn allows them not only to tap into the collective wisdom of users, but also to better tailor their services and channels to individual customer preferences.

More importantly, personalization can transform the debate in major policy areas. In education and health care, for example, the central challenge is how to design more individualized delivery systems. In education this means taking the principle of student-centered learning (enabled by technology) from the nice-but-rare-in-practice idea to mass deployment in schools. Great Britain is on the right track with its stated intention to provide a personalized education for every student.

In health care, the action centers on how to create a patient-centered health care delivery system. A key enabler will be high-tech, user-friendly computer devices that allow many citizens—particularly the elderly—to lead more independent lives. Patients can solicit advice from health professionals in remote medical centers and keep tabs on their own treatment progression from home. Devices customized to individual patient needs can increase patient compliance by prompting them to take their medications and asking them questions to assess their well-being.[1] And the savings are huge: the yearly equipment cost is equivalent to just two weeks of residential care.[2]

ENDING THE MAZE: SERVICE INTEGRATION

Ultimately, personalization will mean providing truly integrated service delivery for citizens—a far cry from the status quo. Now, for example, someone on public assistance needing a variety of related services—job training and placement, child care, food stamps, and drug rehabilitation—would likely access and apply for those services through multiple departments and agencies.

Service integration brings related service offerings together and organizes them around the citizen's individual needs, with services from various departments and agencies combined to address problems from every angle. Ultimately, activities become better coordinated and resources are focused on the real problems citizens face, not just those a particular agency is set up to address. Tax payments are used more efficiently, with fewer resources wasted on redundant activities, unnecessary services, and partial solutions.

Pennsylvania's web-based portal, COMPASS, puts a number of health and human services under one umbrella, regardless of which department administers the relevant programs. The single mom who needs transportation assistance, job training, child health care, and day care assistance doesn't have to travel to several different physical locations and muster the energy, time, and—because visiting government agencies isn't usually regarded as recreation—the motivation to cover all bases. Instead, she can go to one place and receive an integrated services plan customized to meet all of her needs.

The result is a holistic approach to human services. And for those agencies that are trying to help that single parent, integration lessens redundancy and enables a single point of contact, ensuring that all needs are being met. The ability for those in human services to identify needs across a range of areas, put solutions in place more quickly, and save someone from filling out endless paperwork and standing in six different lines at four different locations is efficient. But, more importantly, it can be quite empowering for the agency workers and the people they serve.

MASHED-UP GOVERNMENT

In chapter 2, I wrote about Neighborhood Knowledge Los Angeles (NKLA), an online tool developed by UCLA aimed at improving and preserving the city's neighborhoods. The group used web services to aggregate data from a smorgasbord of public sources in order to help prevent community decay in at-risk communities.[3]

Techies now have a term for this sort of thing: "the mash-up." Mash-ups refer to new online services developed at little cost by using web services to seamlessly blend functions and data from two or more online sources. There's Wikimapia, which mashes up wikis and Google's mapping. Or HousingMaps.com, a popular site that combines real-estate listings from Craigslist.com with Google Maps. Weather Bonk, a mash-up of a host of weather sites and Google Earth, lets you view real time weather information on a map. And, not to be forgotten, "Find the Pink Spoon," a mash-up of Baskin Robbins trivia questions and Yahoo! Maps (some people have more time than others).

Mash-ups are a natural for the public sector. With a little creativity, they enable governments to syndicate their information and services through dozens of different channels—many of which might be a lot closer than the government agencies to the people they hope to reach. Governments can use third-party services such as Google Maps to quickly create new citizen services, such as the electronic map of county voting centers in Larimar County, Colorado.

For the private and nonprofit sector, mash-ups offer at minimal cost a way to enhance the experience of their customers while also helping governments reach more citizens and businesses online. For example, the Australian Business Entry Point (BEP), a government business portal, partners with more than 160 individual businesses and associations to syndicate government information and transactions relevant to businesses. Westpac, Australia's oldest bank, and NineMSN, Australia's top website, are just a few of the partner companies that use BEP's reverse portal service to offer value-added resources for their customers.

Notes government technology guru Paul Taylor:

> The new mashed-up sense of place adds up to a whole new world of collaboration—even among those who have never met—where government does what it is uniquely able to do, and others do the rest.[4]

THE DECLINE OF BROADCAST POLITICS

Lastly, we turn to political campaigns. The speed of technology-driven change is so rapid here that Howard Dean's groundbreaking 2004 Net-roots presidential campaign—pre-YouTube, pre-Facebook—now seems like so much ancient history. Consider just a few snippets of what's transpired since then:

- After launching his campaign, political sensation and Illinois Sen. Barack Obama raised $25 million from 100,000 donors—*in three months*. These numbers would have been science-fiction without the fundraising power and social networking of the Internet.
- A controversial seventy-four-second amateur video that surfaced on YouTube depicting Hillary Clinton as the droning voice of the totalitarian, Big Brother establishment created national attention, sparked more chatter, and garnered more media attention than any candidate ad could hope to achieve.
- Virginia Sen. George Allen, widely expected to be a top-tier Republican presidential candidate in 2008, was unceremoniously tossed out of office by voters after a video turned up on YouTube showing the good senator referring to an American of Indian descent as a "macaca," a reference to a type of monkey and a common racial slur in some European cultures. Pre-YouTube, the incident might have survived a news cycle or two. In the age of YouTube, you could log on and watch it again right now (or maybe a page from now).
- And, in the you-have-to-see-it-to-believe-it category, in the French 2007 elections each of the major presidential candidates devoted *full-time staffers* to operate their *virtual* headquarters in the *make-believe* virtual reality world of Second Life. Virtual campaign staffers, referred to as "avatars," passed out pamphlets, took part in campaign debates, and—perhaps most importantly—guarded headquarters against virtual attacks from opposing campaigns wielding push guns and pig grenades (the exploding pigs won).

By the time you read this, many of these examples might even seem old hat. While technological developments are making the future of political campaigning increasingly hard to predict, one thing at least seems certain: candidates will continue to lose control of "the message" as voters increasingly discount slick, pre-packaged messaging from campaign politicos. Instead, they will pick up bits and pieces of information from their social networking sites and discussion groups, the web, television, newspapers, and news magazines, and process it in very unique ways, a phenomenon *Wall Street Journal* columnist Daniel Henninger refers to as "packet politics":

> Our political thinking is being bent by constant streams of small, value-laden packets of data that we constantly remix into personal hierarchies. . . . No poll can predict how the voting mind is processing the political inbox today.[5]

Candidates unable to adapt to this radically more unpredictable landscape will increasingly find themselves on the losing end at the ballot box.

We have yet to scratch the surface of the transformation of government made possible by today's information technologies. There's no mistaking it: progress is being made. Most governments are at least heading in the right direction. But it is a long road from yesterday to tomorrow. If it's a one-hundred-mile journey, we're on mile ten. But, as some notable singers have reminded us, the best is yet to come.

Notes

All quotes from individuals that are not sourced are the result of one-on-one interviews with the author.

INTRODUCTION

1. Dan Pink, *Free Agent Nation: How America's New Independent Workers Are Transforming the Way We Live* (New York: Warner Books, 2001), chapter 1.

2. In the United States, 90 cents of every federal dollar goes to either individuals in the form of entitlements or to state and local governments and private or nonprofit contractors as grants and contracts. See: Donald F. Kettl, *The Global Public Management Revolution: A Report on the Transformation of Governance* (Washington, D.C.: Brookings Institution Press, 2000), 35.

3. Donald F. Kettl, "What's Next?" *Government Executive*, January 2001, Cover story.

4. For example, digitizing the entire FDA drug approval process could potentially cut the time it takes to approve some new drugs by one-third, saving pharmaceutical companies money which could be passed on in the form of lower drug costs, but more importantly reducing the time it takes for potentially life-saving drugs to get to the market.

5. Joshua Kurlantzick, "Dictatorship.com," *New Republic*, April 5, 2004, 21–25.

6. One way police departments use robot cams is in bomb units, so the officers can keep a safe distance and the machines can take the risks.

7. Stuart Taylor Jr., "How Civil-Libertarian Hysteria May Engender Us All," *National Journal*, February 22, 2003.

CHAPTER 1

1. Julie Hasson, "Code Blue," *FCW.com*, June 25, 2001.

2. Hasson, "Code Blue," June 25, 2001.

3. John Jesitus, "Confronting Medical Errors," *Managed Healthcare Executive*, November 1, 2001.

4. John Breeden II, "Medical Apps Are Flesh and Blood of Hospital Systems; VA's Use of Computer-Based Technologies; Government Activity," *Government Computer News*, September 19, 1997, 30.

5. "Agency Makes Forms Easier to Fill Out," *FederalTimes.com*, April 15, 2003, www.federaltimes.com.

6. The number of hits to the site, already a larger-than-average 6 to 7 million page views per month, nearly tripled after the attack; the number of unique visitors increased fourfold.

7. All these virtual schemes share one goal: to make it easier and more intuitive for citizens and businesses to navigate the public-sector maze. And their strategies for doing so have several similarities: 1) You don't need to know which agency does what; 2) agencies are either deep in the background or totally hidden; and 3) they bear little resemblance to how governments are actually organized in the "real" world.

8. Facilities can receive anywhere from one to five stars depending on how they rank compared to other nursing homes. Facilities that fail to meet, or correct upon minimum standards at the time of inspections are placed on a special nursing home guide watch list.

9. Chester Finn Jr., president of the Thomas Fordham Foundation, suggests taking this concept a step further and creating an educational equivalent of the Generally Accepted Accounting Principles for all schools to follow. Schools and school districts would be required to publicly disclose timely information on academic performance and fiscal soundness, while the state would provide comparative information for each of these categories. All this information would be pushed out to parents and students through emails, newsletters, annual reports, and websites. "Generally Accepted Accountability Principles for Education (GAAPE) affords everyone concerned with a school a picture window through which to see what's actually happening there and how well it's working," explains Finn. "Instead of a brick wall around such information, the school is surrounded by glass." Private schools wouldn't be required to participate, but in time many would probably do so, as a result of pressures from parents who are seeking to ensure that they're getting demonstrable results for their money.

10. Government doesn't even have to provide the navigation services; it just has to make sure someone does. In Texas, nonprofits link to an online database that tracks all child-care customers and providers and assists the nonprofits in matching clients with providers. High-quality child-care providers serving subsidized children are designated "Texas Rising Stars" and given ratings of between one and four stars.

11. Alison Overholt, "Smart Strategies: Putting Ideas to Work," *Fast Company*, April 2004, 62.

12. Stephen Goldsmith, "Keeping Citizens in the Loop," Cutting Edge Column, *Governing.com*, governing.com/manage/edge0104.htm (April 6, 2004).

13. Don Peppers and Martha Rogers, "The Role of Personalization and Privacy in Streamlining Government," Peppers and Rogers Group, 2002, 5.

14. "The Connected World," Institute for the Future, 2003, 5.

15. Ravi Nath, "The Next Generation E-Business," from HIGPA, August 22, 2002, www.higpa.org/events/past/MTHP/nath.pdf.

16. G. Christian Hill, "Dog Eats Dog Food. And Damn if It Ain't Tasty," *eCompany Now* (now *Business 2.0*), November 2000 (cover story).

17. Ira Sager, "Big Blue Gets Wired," *Business Week E.Biz,* April 3, 2000, EB 99.

18. Texas Comptroller Carole Keeton Rylander, "Improve the Medicaid Eligibility Process," from e-Texas: smaller, smarter, faster government, state of Texas, December 2000, 183.

19. Ellen Perlman, "Local Governments: Time is Ripe for IT Investments," *Governing.com*, April 11, 2003, governing.com.

20. See, for example, John Kost, "Understanding True Costs of Self-Service in Government," Research Note, Gartner, April 12, 2003.

21. Bridgette Blair, "E-Filing Efficiencies Allow IRS to Shift Positions to Compliance," *Federal Times*, April 28, 2003, 4.

22. Albert B. Crenshaw, "IRS Reshapes Workforce," *Washington Post*, January 8, 2004, 21.

23. William D. Eggers, "Show Me the Money: Cost-Cutting Strategies for Cash-Strapped Governments," American Legislative Exchange Council and the Manhattan Institute for Policy Research, November 2002.

CHAPTER 2

1. Peter Harkness, "The U.S. Balkans," *Governing*, April 2003, 4.

2. Roger E. Meiners and Andrew P. Morriss, "Property Rights in a Complex World," in *Smarter Growth: Market-Based Strategies for Land-Use Planning in the Twenty-First Century* (Westport, Conn.: Greenwood Press), 183–84.

3. Megan O'Matz, Sally Kestin, Terri Somers, and Maya Bell, "Judge Opens Rilya Files" *Sun-Sentinel* (Fort Lauderdale, FL), May 24, 2002, 1A.

4. Megan O'Matz, Sally Kestin, and Diana Marrero, "Child Tracking System Lacking; Some Kids Listed as Missing in Florida Were under Other States' Supervision." *Sun-Sentinel* (Fort Lauderdale, FL), September 16, 2002, 1A.

5. California's Little Hoover Commission, a state watchdog agency, titled one of its reports on the cluttered and overstressed child-welfare system "Now in Our Hands." In 2003, four years after that report, it issued "Still in Our Hands." The title conveys the appropriate sense that this wasn't a progress report so much as a lack-of-progress report; both problems and proposed solutions had persisted in the intervening years. There is currently no usable national database for states to check to see if a child missing from one state has turned up in another.

6. David F. Carr, "Poor Systems Fail Missing Kids," *Baseline*, March 19, 2003.

7. See O'Matz, Kestin, and Marrero, "Child Tracking System Lacking," 1A.

8. O'Matz, Kestin, Somers, and Bell, "Judge opens Rilya files," 1A.

9. "DCF Eyes New Way to Help Track Kids; Fingerprints, Photos Stored in Digital Form," (from wire reports), *Sun-Sentinel* (Fort Lauderdale, FL), August 20, 2002, 4B.

10. Russell M. Linden, *Working across Boundaries: Making Collaboration Work in Government and Nonprofit Organizations* (San Francisco: Jossey-Bass, 2002), 61–63.

11. The initiative was originally called the National Data Fusion and was run by the Defense Advanced Research Projects Agency (DARPA) before it was moved over to the new Department of Homeland Security.

12. Sydney J. Freedberg Jr., "Homeland Defense Effort Breaks Down Walls of Government," *National Journal*, October 19, 2001.

13. Michael J. Sniffen, "Office Was Cut but Data-Mining Work Continues," *Austin-American Statesman*, February 23, 2004, A6.

14. Privacy advocates warn that they will result in high numbers of innocent people being under suspicion by government authorities due to the large number of "false positives" that inevitably result from such approaches.

15. Seth Mnookin, "A Google for Cops," *Newsweek*, March 3, 2003, 9.

16. "Bantu Selected by Northrop Grumman to Provide Enterprise Instant Messaging for U.S. Department of State's Messaging and Archive Retrieval System." *Market Wire*, February 4, 2004.

17. Leslie Brooks Suzukamo, "Cyber-Crimestoppers," *Pioneer Press*, TwinCities .com, April 22, 2002, www.twincities.com.

18. William Rosenau and Peter Chalk, "Can We Learn from Others?" *Wall Street Journal*, April 15, 2004, A14.

19. In a provocatively titled report called "Why Today's Government Portals Are Irrelevant," the Gartner Group predicts that by 2006 fewer than 20 percent of G2C web transactions will take place through government-managed portals. The rest will take place "through different channels, and managed by external service providers or partners in private or nonprofit sectors," the report said. See: Andrea De Maio, "Why Today's Government Portals Are Irrelevant," Gartner Group, January 29, 2001.

20. Sportsmen will obtain licenses in the course of buying camping gear; realtors will have their real estate licenses automatically renewed when they renew their membership in their local realtors' association; small businesses will handle government licensing and tax-filing requirements on small business portals.

21. Gary Chapman, "Digital Nation: Project Applies Power of Net to L.A. Housing Woes," *Los Angeles Times*, November 22, 1999, C1.

22. To solve this issue, the United Kingdom's government has built an XML-based security and authentication infrastructure for all agencies and a single user credential for all UK e-government services. Government officials envision a time in which a bank offering online tax filing would also provide a digital certificate from an authorized provider to its client. The digital certificate would be sent from the bank to the government agency as a component of the online tax filing transaction, providing the necessary proof of identity.

23. Not all public officials consider Pinder's scenario to be so rosy. Some believe that soon most citizens' awareness of government will come not from their experiences in public buildings or at public hearings but from what they experience online. Start from this view, they say, and the potentially large online traffic reductions that government web services promise to produce aren't an efficiency and convenience boon, but a major problem because it could become much harder for public agencies to get important and accurate information out to the public and engage citizens in public policy without

the prod of having to go to a government site to complete a government trans-action.

While the argument has a certain amount of merit, it ultimately falls short. For one thing, some people will always choose to come to government websites to complete government transactions believing them to be more secure. For an-other, governments can offer other compelling reasons for citizens to come to their sites, such as e-democracy tools that allow for greater citizen engagement. Lastly, the Internet has always been about distributed data, and e-government is likely to prove no exception to that general rule, meaning the ubiquity of certain government e-services could result in even greater popularity for certain gov-ernment sites.

CHAPTER 3

1. "Texas homeschoolers, getting public funds under charter program," *Church and State*, November 1, 2001, 17.

2. The Einstein Academy, the largest cyber school, almost ran out of funds. Legislators sponsored bills to torpedo them.

3. Written in 1951 for a syndicated newspaper page, "The Fun They Had" was later published in *Fantasy and Science Fiction* magazine.

4. Erik Schonfeld, "Wireless Guerillas," *Business 2.0*, April 2002, 99.

5. This depends on the grade level of the student. In the upper grades where parents are less needed to translate and mediate the subjects, the percentage of time spent on the computer will be higher.

6. According to the study, students who spent more time on computers in school scored worse on math tests than those who spent less time on them. Jay Mathews, "Computers Not Used Properly, School Study Says," *Washington Post*, September 30, 1998.

7. William J. Bennett, Chester E. Finn Jr., and John T. Cribb Jr, *The Educated Child: A Parents Guide from Preschool through Eighth Grade* (New York: Free Press, 1999).

8. Seymour Papert and Gaston Caperton, "Vision for Education: The Caperton-Papert Platform," Essay written for the 91st annual National Governor's Associa-tion meeting, St. Louis, MO, August 1999, 7.

9. Todd Oppenheimer, "The Computer Delusion," *Atlantic Monthly*, July 1997.

10. Oppenheimer, "The Computer Delusion," *Atlantic Monthly*, July 1997.

11. One of these things is rich interaction with other students. Survey after sur-vey of students suggests that the lack of that kind of interaction is today the biggest weakness of online courses. Cognizant of this problem, online course de-velopers are developing technologies that will give online courses much richer means of interaction. These tools, however, will require more bandwidth than many schools and homes now possess.

12. In an Education Week survey of students enrolled in Florida's Virtual School (FLVS), the largest and most well-established state-financed virtual high school in the nation, 42 percent said they enrolled in the FLVS in order to take a

course not offered at their school; 21 percent said online courses help them better balance academic and extracurricular activities. Said one student: "I can travel all over all the time for tournaments, and I'm glad I can do my work from any computer at any time." Importantly, 58 percent of students rated the quality of online courses better or much better than regular high school classes, while another 27 percent said the quality is about the same. See: Kathleen Doherty, "Students Speak Out," E-Defining Education Special Report, *Education Week on the Web*, May 9, 2002.

13. Stephanie Sanford, "William Bennett: Education Philosopher," *Converge Magazine*, September 2001.

14. Email from John Bailey to the author, April 16, 2002.

15. Henry Mitchell, "Higher Impulses, Animal Instincts," *Washington Post*, April 8, 1988, D2.

16. David Cohen, "What price a 'proper' education? Albert Einstein, Jessica Mitford, Gerald Durrell—all gifted, passionate, shining—and none of them went near a classroom. What does that tell us?" *Independent* (London), July 30, 1996, 2. Note that the claim about Einstein in the headline is false; Einstein's academic difficulties have been greatly exaggerated. He did quite well in his classes, with the exception of courses requiring a great deal of memorization.

17. Romesh Ratnesar, Sally B. Donnelly, and Aisha Labi, "Lost in the Middle: While America's Schools Focus on the Needs of High Achievers and the Learning Disabled, Average Students are Falling through the Cracks," *Time*, September 14, 1998, 60.

18. Daniel H. Pink, "School's Out," *Reason*, October 2001, 32.

19. Greg Nadeau, "The Conversation in Cambridge," *Converge*, June–July 2002, 33.

20. Toya Lynn Stewart, "Individual Success," *Dallas Morning News*, August 25, 2000, 1M.

21. William J. Bennett, "Technology in Education: This Changes Everything (Except the Most Important Things)," Speech to the Education Leaders Council, spring 2001.

22. James Coyle, "Final Answer?" *Electronic School*, www.electronic-school.com, March 2001.

23. Carol J. Brown, "Online Classroom Assessment Project: Evaluation Report #1," prepared for the Bill and Melinda Gates Foundation by Fouts & Associates, July 1, 2002, 16.

24. Randy Bennett, "Using Electronic Assessment to Measure Student Performance," National Governors Association Center for Best Practices Issue Brief, January 2, 2002, 7.

25. Dan Carnevale, "Union Offers Warning on Distance Education," *Chronicle of Higher Education*, September 14, 2001, 390.

26. Mary Axelson and Lawrence Hardy, "Learning Online: As Web-Based Curriculum Grows, Are Textbooks Obsolete?" *Electronic School*, June 1999.

27. Rosalind S. Helderman, "Homeschooled Away from Home," *Washington Post*, March 26, 2002, B1.

28. Julie Jargon, "Reading, Writing, and Refrigerator Raids," *Denver Westword*, January 31, 2002.

29. "Is Online Education Off Course?" press release, American Federation of Teachers, January 17, 2001.

30. Critics believe this is a distinction without a difference, i.e., that what's on the high-stakes tests will dictate what gets taught.

31. June G. Kronholz, "The Federal Case," *Wall Street Journal*, March 12, 2001, R22.

CHAPTER 4

1. And the problem is only getting worse, as a quick look around the country makes clear. Los Angeles freeways are a giant parking lot. Bill Gates has threatened to move Microsoft out of the Seattle area unless something is done about the region's notorious congestion, and Boeing's executives are already gone, citing traffic as one reason they packed their bags. Some of the worst traffic is in the suburbs. About three-quarters of Northern Virginians rate traffic as "very bad." In New Jersey's Somerset County, the price tag for congestion in lost productivity is estimated to be a whopping $2,110 a year per driver. See Survey conducted by the American Automobile Association's Mid-Atlantic Region, www.aaamidatlantic .com/livenew/about us/pga/pga_dc/021901/leaving_area.asp, and Phillip J. Longman, "American Gridlock: Traffic Is Making Millions Sick and Tired," *US News and World Report*, May 28, 2001.

2. Economic and Social Commission for Asia and the Pacific, "Statistical Abstract of Transport in Asia and the Pacific 2002."

3. David Schrank and Tim Lomax, "The 2002 Urban Mobility Report," Texas Transportation Institute, Texas A&M University, June 2002.

4. Population growth will surely cause an increase in the number of vehicles, however, probably not as large an increase as over previous decades due to a saturation rate of vehicles per adult.

5. "Transportation Planning and ITS: Putting the Pieces Together," prepared by Sarah J. Siwek & Associates for the Federal Highway Administration, U.S. Department of Transportation, 2001, 9–11.

6. Andrew Garber, "For Buses, Green Lights Bring More Than Just Luck," *SeattleTimes.com*, March 29, 2000.

7. This is particularly true in metro regions such as Phoenix and Los Angeles where there are wide arterials and usually a variety of alternate routes.

8. Sometimes providing the information can actually be counterproductive from the standpoint of the transportation network at large, but this is the exception, not the norm.

9. David Rizzo, "What Motorists Really Want from ATIS Providers," *ITS World*, May/June 2001, 28.

10. Another barrier is consumer demand. So far, motorists have been unwilling to pay for traffic information that they feel they can get for free over car radios or the Internet. This is expected to change as fees come down, real-time, customized traffic information improves, and established telematics providers such as OnStar incorporate these services into their systems.

11. Dan Baum, "The Ultimate Jam Session," *Wired*, November 2001, 173.

12. "People Profile," *ITS Daily News*, www.itsinternational.com, Miami, June 2001.

13. Despite the constant fears that each new technology will destroy our privacy, in this case, maintaining privacy is relatively easy. For example, if the traffic managers do not have access to a correlation matrix to identify who owns which transponder, privacy violations are impossible—managers will know where cars are, but not whose cars they are.

14. To be fair, not everyone agrees that you can predict travel times accurately. "Predicting is bull, right out of the gate," says one veteran A.M. news editor. "I'm speaking from a commuter's viewpoint here, from living and dying on the L.A. freeway system. Radio reporters aren't going away for a long time." See: Dana Bartholomew, "Putting a Lid on BAD JAMS," *Los Angeles Daily News*, February 20, 2001.

15. Varaiya disagrees with much of the accepted wisdom about traffic congestion, which is, he says, based on transportation "models" and "deeply-held prejudice learned in engineering schools" instead of hard data. For example, it was long believed that highways carry the most cars per hour at speeds of 35 to 50 MPH, so traffic management models all tried to maintain traffic flow at these speeds. But the actual number, says Varaiya, is 60 MPH. And thanks to PeMS, he can prove it.

16. David Schrank and Tim Lomax, "The 2001 Urban Mobility Report," Texas Transportation Institute, Texas A&M University, May 2001.

17. In response to a new law that went into effect, the transportation authorities turned off the ramp meters for a few months, thus allowing transportation planners to do before and after tests to gauge the effects of ramp metering. The main finding was that without any ramp meters congestion was definitely much worse. When they turned off the ramp metering during rush hour times, throughput declined by 14 percent, travel time increased by 22 percent, travel time reliability plunged 91 percent, and crashes increased by 26 percent. In other words, in almost every category that matters, ramp metering had a positive effect. In fact, researchers estimated ramp metering resulted in $40 million annual savings to the traveling public in the Twin Cities.

The study also came up with some commonsense suggestions for mitigating some of the excesses of the system. First, drivers argued strongly in surveys that the meters needed to change more quickly from red to green. Second, the researchers found that 430 ramp meters operating all at once was too much and actually produced declining returns. The number of meters should be reduced and limited to areas of high traffic congestion. The lessons from Minnesota are fairly straightforward: ramp metering works pretty well in increasing the throughput and safety on highways, but overusing it will start to produce results the opposite of what is intended.

Most ramp metering today is dumb, that is, it's not based on time of the day. Intelligent ramp metering would be able to respond to current traffic conditions, continually adjusting to keep traffic going at the 60 to 70 MPH, which researchers have determined is the speed where you have maximum throughput.

18. Baum, "The Ultimate Jam Session," *Wired*, 172.

19. "Transportation Planning and ITS: Putting the Pieces Together," prepared by Sarah J. Siwek & Associates for the Federal Highway Administration, U.S. Department of Transportation, 2001, 11. According to the study, measured travel-time savings range from 10 percent to 45 percent for incident management sys-

tems; 13 percent—48 percent for ramp metering programs; 8 percent—25 percent for traffic signal systems; 5 percent—8 percent for signal priority systems; and 4 percent—20 percent for in-vehicle navigation systems.

20. Peter Samuel, "Government Hucksters: FHWA Claims Credit for E-ZPass," *Toll Roads Newsletter #34*, December 1998.

21. Peter Samuel, "Port Authority Proposes Radical New Toll Structure," *Toll Roads Newsletter #52*, November 2000.

22. "What Have We Learned about Intelligent Transportation Systems?" U.S. Department of Transportation, December 2000, 40.

23. Peter Samuel, "Electronic Tolling: Triborough Transformed," *Toll Roads Newsletter #35*, January 1999.

24. Melbourne's CityLink tollroad, opened in January 2000, also operates without any tollbooths. The privately financed project is the world's largest open-road tolling system.

25. About 10 to 20 percent of the images have to be verified by people on computer screens and entered into databases.

26. Mark F. Muriello and Danny Jiji, "The Valve-Pricing Toll Program at the Port Authority of New York and New Jersey: Revenue for Transportation Investment and Incentives for Traffic Management," Port Authority of New York and New Jersey Tunnels, Bridges, and Terminals Department, 13–14.

27. Robert W. Poole Jr. and C. Kenneth Orski, "HOT Networks: A New Plan for Congestion Relief and Better Transit," Policy Summary No. 305, Reason Public Policy Institute, February 2003, 2.

28. Conventional methods of collecting tolls also pose significant auditing challenges for time-of-day pricing arrangements.

29. James Fallows, "Freedom of the Skies," *Atlantic Monthly*, June 2001, 48–49.

30. Cheryl Little, "The Intelligent Vehicle Initiative: Advancing 'Human-Centered' Smart Vehicles," U.S. Department of Transportation, Federal Highway Administration, Research, Development and Technology, McLean, Virginia, 1997.

31. Peter Haapeniemi, "Smart Vehicles Have Minds of Their Own," *Safety + Health*, November 1996, 64.

32. Two researchers at George Washington University believe they can dramatically reduce accidents due to drowsiness through the application of neural networks, a form of artificial intelligence, and biometrics, which would entail monitoring eye and head movements. Neural networks are mathematical computations designed to recognize patterns in behavior when we don't know the exact relationship between the different data elements. They are based on biological systems learning. When you learn the walking function, certain brain waves occur that help you learn coordination. Neural networks try to artificially mimic these processes using numbers.

In this case, the car's computer would warn the driver when it detects she's getting drowsy. It would do this by monitoring the angle of the steering wheel (using neural networks it knows which steering wheel movements correspond to drowsiness characteristics) and the movements of the individual's eyes and head (head drops). A camera would simply be embedded in the instrument panel. First deployments will be in vehicles of commercial trucking companies and then mass deployment in automobiles should occur within the next ten years.

33. Implementation of the National Intelligent Transportation Systems Program, Report to Congress, ITS Joint Program Office, Federal Highway Administration, Washington, D.C., 1996.

34. Daniel Whitten, "Collision Warning Protects Eaton's 'Innovation' Truck, *Transport Topics,* American Trucking Association, June 23, 1999.

35. "Staying Out of Trouble," A Maple Publication, 55.

36. Patrick Hook, "All Gain, No Pain," *Traffic Technology International,* United Kingdom, April/May 2001, 29.

37. Hook, "All Gain, No Pain," 28.

38. J. D. Turner, "Mark Factors," *Traffic Technology International,* United Kingdom, April/May 2001, 85.

39. Andrew Tilin, "You Are about to Crash," *Wired,* April 2002, 101.

40. www.tfhrc.gov/pubrds/july97/demo97.htm/.

41. They were able to obtain this lateral control by equipping lanes with radar-reflective tape and a camera-based vision system. Radar was used for detecting vehicles on the side of the car and a laser system was utilized for longitudinal control.

CHAPTER 5

1. "Managing Information Collection and Dissemination," U.S. Office of Management and Budget, Office of Information and Regulatory Affairs, Fiscal Year 2003.

2. W. Mark Crain and Thomas D. Hopkins, "The Impact of Regulatory Costs on Small Firms," A Report for the U.S. Small Business Administration's Office of Advocacy, Washington, D.C., 2000, 6. It costs an additional $21 billion a year for the government to write, administer, and enforce regulations. See: Susan Dudley and Melinda Warren, "Regulatory Response: An Analysis of the Shifting Priorities of the U.S. Budget for Fiscal Years 2002 and 2003," Regulatory Budget Report No. 24, Weidenbaum Center on the Economy, Government and Public Policy, Washington University and Mercatus Center at George Mason University, June 2002, 2.

3. Crain and Hopkins, "The Impact of Regulatory Costs on Small Firms," 6.

4. Peter J. Ferrara and Daniel M. Clifton, "Cost of Government Day Report Calendar: Year 2002," Americans for Tax Reform Foundation, 2003, 13.

5. "Is Anyone Listening?" Campaign 2000: A Special Report, *FSB,* July/August 2000, 106.

6. Quality of life factors are also very important in business location decisions. The general point, however, is that when faced with competition, tax and regulatory burdens are important factors in the start-up business/business location decision.

7. Victor Rivero, "A Ridge to the 21st Century," *Government Technology,* December 1999, 116

8. Rivero, "A Ridge to the 21st Century," *Government Technology,* 116

9. The cities are Freemont, Milipitas, Mountain View, Palo Alto, San Carlos, Santa Clara, Sunnyvale, and later, San Jose.

10. "The Business Case for Streamlining the Nation's Building Regulatory

Process through the Effective Use of Information Technology," National Conference of States on Building Codes and Standards, 2003, www.ncsbcs.org.

11. "Business Case," 2003.

12. Philip K. Howard, *The Death of Common Sense* (New York: Random House, 1994), 14.

13. There is a reason for this. Contrary to the impression many business people have of the agency, OSHA has only about 2,000 inspectors. There are millions of businesses it must police, so only a tiny percentage of businesses will ever actually be inspected by OSHA. This means that the agency must rely on fear of all the bad things that would happen if an inspection occurs in order to induce businesses to voluntarily comply with OSHA health and safety regulations.

14. Email from Edward Stern, Occupational Safety and Health Administration (OSHA), April 9, 2004.

15. There were several practical reasons for this failure. The first is the wide diversity in the demographics of the firms the department regulates. A "mom and pop" firm of a dozen employees or less faces very different issues in complying with regulations than a company of several hundred employees. Designing user-friendly compliance assistance materials to meet the needs of all the different sizes is no easy task because they would have to cover all the topics faced by all the different-sized firms. Second, any information the agency stuck on a pamphlet or handout would be too general to be of much use because businesses typically need specific information and assistance to deal with a particular situation they're confronting.

16. The hardest part about building expert systems is not the technology per se, but the process of acquiring and organizing the needed knowledge base from domain area experts and users and then constructing business rules based on this knowledge. "We have to bottle the knowledge," explains Droitsch. It takes at least six months—and lots of man-hours of senior agency experts—to complete the research, technical, legal, policy, and quality control work needed before an advisor can be put on the web. Getting this kind of time commitment from already overburdened lawyers, technicians, regulatory experts, and economists requires a lot of pleading, persistence, and a strong push from an agency's leadership.

17. Jason Miller, "SBA's New Portal Portrays OMB's Idea of e-gov," *Government Computer News*, January 7, 2002, www.gcn.com.

18. U.S. Small Business Administration, "Business Compliance One Stop Projected Cost Savings," provided by Ron Miller, May 30, 2003.

19. Fred E. Foldvary and Daniel B. Klein, *The Half-Life of Policy Rationales: How New Technology Affects Old Policy Issues* (New York: New York University Press, 2003), Introduction.

20. In addition to publishing the grades, OSHA would publish standards and best practices and provide detailed assistance in the form of the expert advisors on how businesses can make their workplaces safer.

21. Carole Keeton Rylander, "Smaller, Smarter, Faster Government," Recommendations of the Texas Comptroller, *e-Texas Report*, December 2000, Volume 2, 398.

22. The reengineering included redesigning key business processes, integrating software, deploying customer relationship management (CRM) software, and restructuring the department's organization.

CHAPTER 6

1. Caroline Hoxby, "Testing Is All about Openness and Openness Works," *Weekly Essays*, Hoover Institution for War and Peace, www-hoover.stanford.edu, July 30, 2001.

2. Janet Bingham, "Pueblo school changes focus and scores," *Denver Post*, February 29, 2000, 11A.

3. The New E-Government Equation: Ease, Engagement, Privacy, and Protection," report based on a survey conducted by Hart-Teeter for the Council for Excellent in Government, April 2003.

4. "e-government: The Next American Revolution," report based on findings of a survey conducted by Hart-Teeter for the Council for Excellence in Government, January 2001 and August 2000, Washington, D.C., 22.

5. Jim McCay, "Compstat for the 21st Century," *Government Technology*, July 2002, www.govtech.net.

6. "Chicago Topped Nation in Homicides in 2003," Associated Press, January 1, 2004.

7. Lenneal Henderson, "The Baltimore Citistat Program: Performance and Accountability," University of Maryland, May 2003, 21.

8. Mary Jordan, "Mexicans Seek to Lift Government's Veil; Publisher Leads One Campaign: 'How Can We Have Democracy without Daylight?'" *Washington Post*, November 16, 2000, A29.

9. Since Mexico has the lowest tax collection rate of any major country, the effect of greater cooperation could be immense. And a society does not have a stable rule of law when economic policies can change without warning.

10. Jordan, "Mexicans Seek to Lift Government's Veil," 29.

11. Mary Anastasia O'Grady, "Mexican Reformers Seek to Outlaw Government Secrecy," *Wall Street Journal*, October 26, 2001, 15.

12. Julia Scheeres, "The Net as Corruption Disruption," *Wired*, March 26, 2001, www.wired.com.

13. "Triple Play: Three Mexican Governors Describe Opportunities in Their States," Institutional Investor (International Edition), July 1, 2001.

14. Jenalia Moreno,"Catching a Ride on the Digital Wave; Where Few Have Net Access, Cafes Sprout to Bridge Gap in Mexico City," *Houston Chronicle*, October 27, 2001, 1.

15. Keynote remarks by Vice President Al Gore at the Global Forum on Fighting Corruption sponsored by the U.S. Department of State, Washington, D.C., February 24, 1999.

16. Scheeres, "The Net as Corruption Disruption," *Wired*, March 26, 2001, www.wired.com.

17. Cheryl W. Gray and Daniel Kaufmann, "Corruption and Development," *Finance & Development*, The World Bank, March 1998.

18. Claudio Orrego Larrain, "Chile's E-Procurement System: Transparency, Efficiency, and PPP," presentation at the E-Government in Developing Countries: Achievements and Prospects conference, World Bank/Development Gateway, Washington, D.C., June 11–12, 2001.

19. "Philippines Customs Reform," The World Bank Group, January 3, 2001, www.worldbank.org/publicsector/egov/.

20. "April 3, 2000 report on Seoul's OPEN Center for Clean Hands website, www.metro.seoul.kr/eng/smg/corruption/clean.html.

21. Sudip Mazumdar, "Shame, the Virtual Weapon: A Web Site Works Wonders in the Fight against Corruption," *Newsweek*, February 21, 2000, 24.

22. "Central Vigilance Commission Website: A Bold Anticorruption Experiment," The World Bank Group, September 14, 2001, www.worldbank.org/publicsector/egov/.

23. Mazumdar, "Shame, the Virtual Weapon," 25.

24. Citizens who don't trust their government often avoid paying taxes; citizens who can see where their money is going are more forthcoming.

25. This view is not universally held. In a cover story in the *New Republic*, Joshua Kurlantzick argues that authoritarian regimes have found it easy to use the web to stifle, control and co-opt dissent. Kurlantzick's arguments are compelling and likely correct in the short term, but over time the Internet should encourage more openness, particularly in countries like China that are opening up their economies. See Joshua Kurlantzick, "Dictatorship.com," *New Republic*, April 5, 2004, 21–25.

26. P. J. Simmons and Chantal de Jonge Oudraat, *Managing Global Issues: Lessons Learned,* Carnegie Endowment for International Peace, 2001, www.ceip.org.

27. Elizabeth Becker, "Farmers Are Abashed, or Irate, over Subsidy List," *New York Times*, December 27, 2001, A1.

28. "The Post-September 11 Environment: Access to Government Information," *OMB Watch*, November 23, 2001, www.ombwatch.org.

29. Steve Towns, "Jurisdictions Remove Sensitive Data from Web Sites," Government Technology, November 5, 2001, www.govtech.net.

30. Towns, "Jurisdictions Remove," www.govtech.net.

31. Eric Lichtblau, "Rising Fears That What We Do Know Can Hurt Us," *Los Angeles Times*, November 18, 2001.

32. David Colker, "Despite Government Efforts, the Web Never Forgets," *Los Angeles Times*, November 27, 2001.

33. Colker, "Web Never Forgets," November 27, 2001.

CHAPTER 7

1. Robert D. Putnam, "Bowling Alone: America's Declining Social Capital," *Journal of Democracy*, vol. 6, no. 1 (January 1995), 68.

2. Cokie Roberts and Steve Roberts, "Internet Is a Threat to Representative Government," *Times-Picayune* (New Orleans), April 5, 1997, B7.

3. Cass Sunstein, *Republic.com*, (Princeton, N.J.: Princeton University Press, 2001), 199.

4. Rebecca Fairley Raney, "Mailing List Feeds Minnesota's Politically Minded," *New York Times*, Technology/Cybertimes, March 2, 1998.

5. Steve Brandt, "E-mail List Holds a Key to City Hall," *Minneapolis-St. Paul Star Tribune*, October 22, 2001.

6. Brandt, "E-mail list," October 22, 2001.

7. Kevin Featherly, "MN-Politics," Channel 4000, WCCO 4 News, WCCO.com (March 2003).

8. R. T. Rybak, "Yesterday's Incident," post to Minnesota e-democracy forum, March 11, 2002.

9. John Stein Monroe, "Meet Your Mayor . . . Online," *civic.com*, June 4, 2001, 1.

10. Thomas Beirele, "Democracy On-Line: An Evaluation of the National Dialogue on Public Involvement in EPA Decisions," *Resources for the Future Report*, January 2002, 9.

11. Jackie Ashley, "Intent on change, Radical Robin returns to the fray," *Guardian*, January 7, 2002, guardian.co.uk.

12. Rt. Honorable Robin Cook, "Reviving Democracy," speech to the YouGov Democracy Conference, United Kingdom, April 2002, www.yougov.com.

13. Stephen Coleman and Emilie Normann, "New Media and Social Inclusion," Hansard Society, London, United Kingdom, July 2000.

14. Experience in several countries suggests that governments need to clearly lay out at the beginning of the consultation exactly what the process will be for incorporating public input into the final proposal. The lack of clarity leads some participants to doubt whether the input is valued and used.

15. Graham Stringer, speech at the Third Global Forum, Naples, Italy, March 15, 2001.

16. Jay G. Blumler and Stephen Coleman, "Realising Democracy Online: A Civic Commons in Cyberspace," Institute for Public Policy Research, Citizens Online Research Publication No. 2, London, United Kingdom, March 2001, 16.

17. Stephen Coleman and John Gotze, "Bowling Together: Online Public Engagement in Policy Deliberation," Hansard Society, London, England, 2001, 5.

18. Pauline Poland, "Online Consultation in GOL Countries: Initiatives to Foster e-democracy," Government Online International Network, December 6, 2001, 30.

19. Pauline Poland, "Online Consultation in GOL Countries: Initiatives to Foster e-democracy," Government Online International Network, December 6, 2001, 30.

20. Steven Clift, *The E-Democracy E-Book: Democracy is Online 2.0*, Publicus.Net, 2000, 4.

21. Previously, if you wanted the guidance documents that explained the details behind enacted regulations it could cost you hundreds of dollars and take weeks to obtain. Now all this is available free and instantly on the Net.

22. Cindy Skrzycki, "Project Aims for One-Stop Online Shopping for Federal Rules," *Washington Post*, March 30, 2004, E1, and Cindy Skrzycki, "U.S. Opens Online Portal to Rulemaking," *Washington Post*, January 23, 2003, E6.

23. Elena Larsen and Lee Rainie, "The Rise of the e-citizen: How People Use Government Agencies' Web Sites," Pew Internet and American Life project, Washington, D.C., 2. Some observers question these numbers, believing them to be higher than what is actually occurring.

24. Roberts and Roberts, "Internet Could Become a Threat," A-11.

25. Mary Clare Jalonick, "The Best Sites of Campaign 2000," *Campaigns & Elections*, December 2000–January 2001, 70.

26. This term was coined by e-democracy guru Steven Clift.

27. Coleman and Gotz, "Bowling Together," 17.

28. Dennis Johnson, "Constituents and Your Web Site: What Constituents Want to See on Congressional Web Sites," Congress Online Project, *Issue Brief No. 2*, Washington, D.C., October 2001.

29. Nicole Folk and Kathy Goldschmidt, "Congress Online 2003: Turning the Corner on the Information Age," Congress Online Project, A Partnership of the Congressional Management Foundation and George Washington University, March 2003, vi.

30. Jan Hamming, "Being a "Wired" Elected Official," posting to Democracies Online "do-wire," June 25, 2001, www.mail-archive.com/do-wire.

31. William Matthews, "Email Keeps Lawmakers in Touch: Is an Electronic Congress Next?" *Federal Computer Week*, October 29, 2001, 2.

32. Rebecca Fairley Raney, "Email Gets the Cold Shoulder in Congress," *New York Times on the Web*, December 13, 2001, www.nytimes.com.

33. Kathy Goldschmidt, "Email Overload in Congress: Managing a Communications Crisis," Congress Online Project, A Partnership of the Congressional Management Foundation and George Washington University, March 2001, 12.

34. John Stein Monroe, "Meet Your Mayor . . . Online," *civic.com*, June 4, 2001, 3.

35. "Members Are Turning off E-Mail Addresses and Turning on Web Forms," press release, Congress Online Project, Washington, D.C., August 7, 2002.

36. "Crisis Case Study: Model Office Uses Email to Stay in Touch," Congress Online Project Newsletter, November 2001, 3.

CHAPTER 8

1. Howard Fineman, "Pressing the Flesh Online," *Newsweek*, September 20, 1999, 50.

2. "Ventura being admired for his use of high technology in campaign," Associated Press, March 1, 1999.

3. Bill McAuliffe, "Ventura is blazing new political trails with use of the Internet," *Minneapolis Star Tribune*, March 1, 1999, 1A.

4. Phil Madsen, "Notes Regarding Jesse Ventura's Internet Use in His 1998 Campaign for Minnesota Governor," Jesse Ventura for Governor Volunteer Committee (1998).

5. Steven Clift, "DW: Inside Story on Ventura Internet Use," Democracies Online Newswire, December 10, 1998, www.publicus.net/dowire.html.

6. Rita Ciolli, "Reaching Voters Via the Internet," *Newsday*, January 17, 2000, A06.

7. Andrew Ward, "'Netizens' Wooed in South Korea Poll," *Financial Times*, December 18, 2002.

8. Stephen Clift, "Korea's 2nd Net Election," *Democracies Online Newswire*, April 13, 2004, 2.

9. Daniel Jeffreys, "His McCain Site Was Key to Cash Inflow," *New York Post*, March 2, 2000, 37.

10. Sebastian Mallaby, "McCain's E-Politics," *Washington Post*, March 4, 2000, A17.

11. Rita Ciolli, "Internet Is Our Slingshot," *Newsday*, March 2, 2000, A32.

12. Jeffreys, "His McCain Site Was Key to Cash Inflow."

13. Mallaby, "McCain's E-Politics," A17.

14. Ryan Thornburg, "Digital Donors," The Democracy Online Project, George Washington University, November 2001.

15. Michael Cornfield and Jonah Sieger, "The Net and the Nomination," in *The Making of the Presidential Candidates 2004*, ed. William Mayer (Lanham, Md.: Rowman & Littlefield, 2003).

16. Max Fose, interview with the author, May 2002.

17. Fose, May 2002.

18. Elisabeth Rosenthal, "Political Challenge 2.0: Make a Virtual Army a Reality," *New York Times*, December 21, 2003.

19. Linda Tischler, "Joe Trippi's Killer App," *Fast Company*, October 2003, 110.

20. David S. Broder, "When the Web Is Not Enough," *Washington Post*, February 1, 2004, B07.

21. Joe Trippi, "Down from the Mountain," keynote presentation at the O'Reilly Digital Democracy Teach-In, San Diego, California, February 9, 2004.

22. "Anti-Know Your Customer Web Site Gets 37,114 Signatures in First 7 Days," *PR Newswire*, PR Newswire Association, February 23, 1999.

23. Richard A. Knox, "Vt.-Based Mine Foes Awarded the Nobel," *Boston Globe*, October 11, 1997, A1.

24. Melody Simmons, "Internet Helped Activist Push Land Mine Ban," *Baltimore Sun*, October 21, 1998, 3B.

25. Simmons, "Internet Helped Activist Push Land Mine Ban," 3B.

26. Richard Gwyn, "After Land Mines, Challenge Is to Find New Cause," *Toronto Star*, December 10, 1997, A27.

27. MoveOn.org, "'We Will Remember' Campaign Targets Impeachers," MoveOn.org press release, December 21, 1998.

28. MoveOn.org, "We will remember," 1998.

29. MoveOn.org, "MoveOn.org Delivers 30,000 Messages of Support for McCain-Feingold," MoveOn.org press release, March 29, 2001.

30. Miklos Sukosd and Endre Danyi, "Viral Political Marketing: M-Politics in the Making SMS and E-Mail in the 2002 Hungarian Election Campaign," unpublished paper, Central European University, Hungary, 2002.

31. Jill Lawrence, "Think Election Was a Mess? Look at System," *USA Today*, November 14, 2000, 21A.

32. John Fund, "Vote Early and . . . ," *Wall Street Journal*, December 12, 2001.

33. Jackie Ashley, "Intent on change, Radical Robin Returns to the Fray," *Guardian*, January 7, 2002, guardian.co.uk.

34. William Matthews, "Election Day Winner: Online Voting," *FCW.com*, November 10, 2000, fcw.com.

35. Michael Alvarez and Thad Hall, *Point, Click & Vote: The Future of Internet Voting* (Washington, D.C.: Brookings Institution Press, 2004), 129–35.

36. A total of sixteen local authorities ran pilot projects that included elements of e-voting or e-counting; two offered text messaging via mobile phones, and five offered Internet voting. In Swindon, 10 percent of all those who voted did so online, while in two wards in Sheffield, thirty of those who voted did so electronically. See: "In the Service of Democracy: A Consultation Paper on a Policy for Electronic Democracy," Office of the e-Envoy, Cabinet Office, London, UK, July 15, 2002, 49–50.

37. T. R. Reid, "England Votes, but Not Necessarily at Polls; Cell Phones, Internet and Touch-Screen Kiosks Used by Many in Local Elections." *Washington Post*, May 3, 2002, A23.

38. Andy Kelly, "Local Elections: Fraud: E-Voting Makes It Too Easy; Serious Flaws in Election Are Exposed by Daily Post," *Daily Post* (Liverpool), May 3, 2002, 2–3.

39. Todd Weiss, "Pentagon Drops Internet Voting Plans for Military Personnel," *Computerworld*, February 5, 2004, www.computerworld.com/2004/0,4814,89902, 00.html.

40. Alvarez and Hall, *Point, Click & Vote*, 145.

41. Lance Hoffman, "Internet Voting: Will It Spur or Corrupt Democracy?" *Proceedings of the Tenth Conference on Computers, Freedom & Privacy* (New York: Association for Computing Machinery, 2000).

42. Since there are no poll-watchers, it's even more important that the state have good technical assistance available. That assistance needs to be available by telephone (in case the voter's computer crashes) and online (in case the voter is using his only phone line to connect to the Internet). The lack of poll-watchers might also increase the potential for vote-selling and coercion of voters, just as these possibilities are increased by traditional absentee voting.

CHAPTER 9

1. Amy Borrus, "When Right and Left See Eye-to-Eye," *Business Week*, November 5, 2001, 88.

2. Jane Wakefield, "Electronic Government Could Hamper Privacy," *ZDNet UK*, July 16, 1999, news.zdnet.co.uk/hardware/emergingtech/0,39020357, 2072697,00.htm (April 7, 2004).

3. Encryption, anonymous web-browsing software and anonymous emailing services are just three examples of technologies that enhance privacy. Many experts expect the market for privacy protection and anonymous communications— email, Internet, telephone—to grow significantly in the future. This market, in turn, would spawn still more privacy-enhancing technologies.

4. Paul Schwartz, "Data Processing and Government Administration: The Failure of the American Legal Response to the Computer," *Hastings Law Journal*, 43, Part 2 (1992): 1374.

5. Charles Piller, "Web Mishap: Kids' Psychological Profiles Posted," *Los Angeles Times*, November 7, 2001, A1.

6. Charlotte Twight, "Watching You: Systematic Surveillance of Ordinary Americans," *Cato Institute Briefing Papers, No. 69*, October 17, 2001, 34.

7. From September 1999 to February 2001, federal agencies announced forty-seven times in the Federal Register that they were exchanging and merging personal information about American citizens from their databases. See: "Privacy and Federal Agencies: Government Exchange and Merger of Citizens' Personal Information Is Systematic and Routine," privacilla.org, March 2001, privacilla.org.

8. Quoted by Charlotte Twight, "Watching You: Systematic Federal Surveillance of Ordinary Americans," *Cato Institute Briefing Papers No. 69*, October 17, 2001, 25.

9. "Privacy Practices that Work: Eight Federal and Non-Federal Examples," Industry Advisory Council, eGovernment Shared Interest Group, March 2004, 7.

10. "Privacy Practices that Work," 16.

11. The Regulatory Flexibility Act, passed in 1980, requires that each time an agency publishes a proposed new rule in the Federal Register that they describe the impact of the rule on small businesses, organizations, and government jurisdictions.

12. "Privacy Practices that Work," 22–48.

13. Vivienne Jupp and Lis Astall, "Technology in Government: Riding the Waves of Change," Accenture, *The Government Executive Series*, September 2002, 13.

14. "Imperative 5: Protect Privacy and Security," from the Eight Imperatives for Leaders in a Networked World series, The Harvard Policy Group on Network-Enabled Services and Government, John K. Kennedy School of Government, Cambridge, Mass., December 2001, 13.

15. The Defense Advanced Research Projects Agency (DARPA) has several data mining research projects underway that explore the potential of "selective revelation" technologies which minimize personally identifiable information when conducting data searches and looking for patterns of behavior. See: Jeffrey Rosen, *The Naked Crowd: Reclaiming Security and Freedom in an Anxious Age* (New York: Random House, 2004), 118–21.

16. "Privacy Practices that Work," Industry Advisory Council, 18.

17. Chinta Puxley, "Identity Theft Soaring as Victims Face Huge Bills," *Hamilton Spectator*, January 3, 2002, A3. It is estimated that between 500,000 and 700,000 identity thefts occurred in the United States in 2000.

18. See: "Public Advisory: Special Report for Consumers on Identity Theft," U.S. Department of Justice, and "State Trends in Fraud and Identity Threat, Federal Trade Commission, January 22, 2004.

19. See, for example: "E-Government: To Connect, Protect and Serve Us," poll conducted by Hart-Teeter for the Council for Excellence in Government, March 2002. In the poll, the public's leading concern with e-government (65 percent of all those surveyed) is that hackers will obtain government-stored personal information and use it to assume their identity.

20. Maria Atanasov, "The Truth about Internet Fraud," *Ziff Davis Smart Business for the New Economy*, April 1, 2001, 92.

21. Atanasov, " Internet Fraud," 92.

22. Stephen Dinan, "Fraud Let 100,000 Obtain Social Security Numbers," *Washington Times*, May 21, 2002, A3.

23. John Woodward Jr., "Biometrics: Facing Up to Terrorism," Rand Institute Arroyo Center, October 2001, 3.

24. Stephen Coleman, "Biometrics," *FBI Law Enforcement Bulletin*, June 1, 2000, 9. Another proposed probation system would use voice recognition. The probationer would have to carry a pager, which would page him at random intervals. He would then have to go to a telephone and call a toll-free number. His voice would be matched with a previous recording, and Caller ID would verify his location.

25. Susan Stellin, "Business Travel: A Road Less Traveled through Immigration Lines," *New York Times on the Web*, March 16, 2004, www.nytimes.com.

26. Richard Simon, "Border Crossing Made Easy," *Los Angeles Times*, June 29, 1997, B2. Only travelers willing to be fingerprinted and carefully screened are able to take advantage of the conveniences the system brings.

27. "Border Update Alert," American Chamber of Commerce in Canada, February 2004.

28. This approach, "one-to-one" verification as opposed to "one-to-many" verification, explains Jeffrey Rosen would allow an individual to confirm she is who she says she is without allowing the government to pick her out of the crowd. Writes Rosen: "Assuming (and this is a big assumption) that the fingerprints aren't stored anywhere, individuals retain complete control over how much information about themselves to control." See: Rosen, *Naked Crowd*, 117.

29. Doug Tsuruoka, "Will Cautious Business Traveler Like Fast-Pass Airport ID Card?" *Investor's Business Daily*, April 29, 2002, A18.

30. Matthew Reed Baker, "Welcome to the Fast Track," *Forbes.com*, www.forbes.com/fyi/2004/0329/066, and Robert Poole Jr., "To Speed Up Airport Security, Issue I.D. Cards," *Wall Street Journal*, January 17, 2002.

31. Shane Harris, "Private Eye," GovExec.com, www.govexec.com (March 16, 2004).

32. Jay Stanley and Barry Steinhardt, "Bigger Monster, Weaker Chains: The Growth of an American Surveillance Society," ACLU Technology and Liberty Program, Washington, D.C., January 2003, 1.

33. Martin Kasindorf, "Big Brother" cameras on watch for criminals," *USA Today.com*, August 2, 2001, USAToday.com.

34. "ACLU Blasts Facial-Recognition Technology," *Government Technology*, January 8, 2002.

35. Lance Gay, "Face-Recognition Machines Coming to Airports," *Scripps Howard News Service*, January 8, 2002.

36. David McGuire, "ACLU Report Rips Face Recognition Technology," *Newsbytes.com*, January 4, 2002.

37. Larry Jacobs, "An About-Face for Facial Recognition," *ABC News*, September 5, 2003, abcnews.go.com/sections/scitech/US/cybershake030905.html.

38. Dan Farmer and Charles C. Mann, "Surveillance Nation: Part One," *Technology Review*, April 2003, 36.

39. Wilson P. Dizzard III, "Homeland Security Rolls out Tactical Response Network," *Newsbytes News Network*, February 24, 2004.

40. Jesse Bravin, "Washington Police to Play 'I Spy' with Cameras, Raising Concerns," *Wall Street Journal Online*, February 13, 2002.

41. John Schwartz, "New Side to Face-Recognition Technology: Identifying Victims," *New York Times on the Web*, January 15, 2002, www.newyorktimes.com.

42. Mark Rice-Oxley, "Big Brother in Britain: Does More Surveillance Work?" *Christian Science Monitor*, February 6, 2004, www.csmonitor.com.

43. Carl Honore, "Britain's Big Brother," *HoustonChronicle.com*, April 12, 2004, www.chron.com/cs/CDA/front/24999854.

44. Brandon C. Welsh and David P. Farrington, *Crime Prevention Effects of Closed Circuit Television: A Systematic Review*, Home Office Research Study 252, August

2002, vi, www.homeoffice.gov.uk/rds/pdfs2/hors252.pdf. The review found that CCTV had no effect on violent crimes, crimes on public transport or crimes in city center settings. The only crime category it had a noticeable effect on was reducing vehicle thefts in parking lots.

45. Jed Rubenfeld, "Privacy Exposed," *Washington Post*, October 26, 2001, A35.

46. Charles Piller, Josh Meyer, and Tom Gorman, "Criminal Faces in the Crowd Still Elude Hidden ID Cameras," *Los Angeles Times*, February 2, 2001, A1.

47. Charles Mann, "Homeland Insecurity," *AtlanticOnline.com*, September 2002, www.theatlantic.com.

48. April Witt, "Maryland Weighs Taping Police Interviews," *Washington Post*, February 12, 2002, B4.

49. Robert O'Harrow Jr., "Intricate Screening of Fliers in Works," *Washington Technology*, February 1, 2002, A1.

50. Jay Boehmer and Jay Campbell, "CAPPS II Curbed, 'Trusted' Traveler Test Gets Okay," *BTNonline.com*, March 29, 2004, btnmag.com.

51. Boehmer and Campbell, "CAPPS II Curbed," March 29, 2004.

52. Dan Farmer and Charles C. Mann, "Surveillance Nation: Part One," *Technology Review*, April 2003, 39.

53. Drawing upon triangulation technology used by global positioning system devices (GPS), a fifteen-year-old student at the University of California at San Diego has developed PDA location-tracking software that allows his fellow students to track each other's movements around campus.

54. Adam L. Penenberg, "The Surveillance Society," *Wired*, December 2001, 157.

55. Jesse Bravin, "Washington Police to Play 'I Spy' with Cameras, Raising Concerns," *Wall Street Journal Online*, February 13, 2002, wsj.com.

56. William Mathews, "Commercial Database Use Flagged," *FCW.com*, January 16, 2002, fcw.com.

57. Penenberg, "Surveillance Society," 157.

58. Penenberg, "Surveillance Society," 157.

59. David Gelernter, "Will We Have Any Privacy Left? Visions of the 21st Century," *Time.Com*, February 21, 2000, www.time.com.

60. Harris, "Private Eye," March 16, 2004.

61. In some respects, the newly public information would force even anonymous city-dwellers to take on the risks of a small town, without the advantages. Everyone would know your name and your business—but they wouldn't necessarily know you well enough to decide you should be forgiven for your youthful lapses. They'd know your criminal record, but not your parents or your friends; they'd have that fiery article you wrote two years ago opposing immigration, but not the knowledge that your husband and your best friend are both immigrants.

62. Paul Rogers and Elise Ackerman, "Oracle Boss Urges National ID Cards, Offers free software," *Mercury News*, September 22, 2001, www.SiliconValley.com.

63. Penenberg, e-mail to the author, April 19, 2002.

64. Rosen, *The Naked Crowd*, 210–15.

65. David Brin, *The Transparent Society: Will Technology Force Us to Choose between Privacy and Freedom?* (Redding, Mass.: Perseus Books, 1998), 332.

CHAPTER 10

1. Tod Robberson, "Plan for Student Database Stirs Opposition in Fairfax," *Washington Post*, January 9, 1997, A1.

2. "E-Government: To Connect, Protect and Serve Us," conducted by Hart-Teeter for the Council for Excellence in Government, Washington, D.C., 2002.

3. Bob Drogin, "Yearlong Hacker Attack Nets Sensitive U.S. Data," *Los Angeles Times*, October 7, 1999, A1.

4. Drogin, "Yearlong Hacker," A1.

5. Drogin, "Yearlong Hacker," A1.

6. "Rolta Gears Up to Cash In on Demand for E-security Services," *Financial Times*, March 10, 2004.

7. Bara Vaida, "OMB Orders Agencies to Boost Spending on Computer Security." *Government Executive Magazine*, December 4, 2001.

8. Karen Robb, "Slow Progress on IT Security, OMB Says," *Federal Times*, March 15, 2004, 5.

9. Alan Paller, "The Unsung Heroes of Information Security," *GovExec.com*, June 1, 2001, www.govexec.com.

10. For many years, insiders were the most prevalent perpetrators of computer attacks, however this is changing as attacks via Internet websites become more frequent.

11. Ellen Perlman, "Staying Ahead of the Hackers," *Governing.com*, from *Governing* magazine, January 2002, www.governing.com.

12. Simply targeting the fifty most common security vulnerabilities enabled NASA to reduce their overall vulnerability to attack by 96 percent.

13. Joshua Dean, "Mounting a Defense," *GovExec.com*, June 1, 2001, www.govexec.com.

14. James P. Lucier Jr., "E-Security and Homeland Defense: The World's Largest IT Purchaser Gets Serious about Security and Integration," Legislative Update, Prudential Financial, May 15, 2002, 4.

15. Dan Verton, *Black Ice: The Invisible Threat of Cyber-Terrorism* (Emeryville, Calif.: McGraw-Hill/Osborne, 2003), xxiii.

16. Verton, *Black Ice*, 236.

17. James Adams, "Virtual Defense," *Foreign Affairs*, May/June 2001, 98.

18. Michael C Sirak, "Threats to the Nets," *Air Force Magazine*, October 2001.

19. Joshua Dean, "Nation Unprepared for Cyber War, Experts Say," *GovExec.com*, December 19, 2001, www.govexec.com.

20. Barton Gellman, "Cyber-Attacks by Al Qaeda Feared," *Washington Post*, June 27, 2002, A10.

21. Almost ten years later, Chinese hackers nearly gained access to California's power grid.

22. Gellman, "Cyber-Attacks by Al Qaeda Feared," A10.

23. It is only in recent years that energy, power, oil, and water systems have been connected to the Internet and become vulnerable to cyber attack. Previously, they were completely isolated from other computer systems, making hacking into them from the outside nearly impossible.

24. Charles Pillar, "Hackers Target Energy Industry," *Los Angeles Times*, July 8, 2002, www.latimes.com.

25. Gellman, "Cyber-Attacks by Al Qaeda Feared," A10.

26. Verton, *Black Ice*, 234.

27. Verton, *Black Ice*, 21–22.

28. Most private companies, including even security conscious banks and brokerages, don't tell the government when their systems are successfully attacked.

29. Shane Harris, "FBI Director Says Industry Must Do More to Prevent Cyberattacks," *GovExec.com*, October 31, 2002, www.govexec.com.

30. Diane Frank, "Intrusion-Detection Net Revived," *FCW.com*, May 27, 2002.

31. Karyl Scott, "Zeroing In: Cyberspies May Meet Their Match in Security Researchers with bright ideas," *InformationWeek*, November 5, 2001, 51.

32. Scott, "Zeroing In," 51.

33. Scott, "Zeroing In," 51.

34. Scott, "Zeroing In," 51.

35. Charles Mann, "Homeland Insecurity," *The Atlantic Online*, September 2002, www.theatlantic.com.

36. Jim McKay, "Evolving Cyber Security," *Government Technology's Crime and the Tech Effect*, e-Republic, April 2002, 8.

37. William Jackson, "Feds Come Out from Hiding at Hacker Show," *Government Computer News*, August 7, 2000, 1.

38. James Adams, "Virtual Defense," *Foreign Affairs*, May/June 2001, 98.

39. Jesse Holland, "Bush Advisor Warns Cyberterrorists," *Washingtonpost.com*, February 13, 2002, www.washingtonpost.com.

CHAPTER 11

1. Katy Saldarini, "GSA to Proceed with Warehouse Closings," *GovExec.com*, September 23, 1999, www.govexec.com.

2. In addition, 101 employees retired or were resigned; seventy-six employees were reassigned to other positions and all sixty-three employees who were laid off were given severance benefits. Source: Kent Latta, Director, Logistics Operations Center, Federal Supply Service, General Services Administration, interview with the author, June 30, 2002.

3. John Buntin, "Assertive Policing, Plummeting Crime: The NYPD Takes on Crime in New York City," Kennedy School of Government Case Program, C16-99-1530.0, 1999, 6.

4. Buntin, "Assertive Policing," 17.

5. Cultural change in government doesn't happen quickly; it can take many years or even decades to change.

6. Jason Miller, "Status Quo Is a Barrier to OMB's e-gov Plans," *Government Computer News*, vol. 21, no. 1, January 7, 2002, 1.

7. Karen Robb, "Bush's IT Agenda Sputters," *FederalTimes.com*, November 10, 2003, federaltimes.com/index.php?S=2378353.

8. Karen Robb, "OMB Prepares to Shutter Duplicative IT Projects, Redirect Funds," *FederalTimes.com*, March 11, 2002.

9. Speech at the John F. Kennedy School of Government's "Making Good on the Promise" conference, e-Government Executive Education Project, February 7, 2003.

10. New Jersey has gone from six data centers to one and South Carolina from eleven to one.

11. Tod Newcombe, "The Disappearing Data Center: Government Consolidates Big Iron," *Government Technology*, January 1999.

12. Robert T. Garrett, "Democrats Criticize Plan to Streamline Aid for the Needy," *Dallas Morning News*, May 24, 2004, www.dallasnews.com.

13. Lisa Terry, "Dot-coms Build Clientele as E-Permitting Comes of Age," *Washington Technology*, vol. 15, no. 5, June 5, 2000, 30.

14. Statement of Witold Skwierczynski, Testimony before the Subcommittee on Social Security of the House Ways and Means, March 16, 2000.

15. Shawn Zeller, "Death of a Website," *GovExec.com*, June 2001, www.govexec.com.

16. J. Christopher Mihm, "Succession Planning and Management is Critical Driver of Transformation," General Accounting Office, GAO-04-127T, October 1, 2003, 1.

17. Mihm, "Succession Planning," 1.

18. Shane Harris, "Rebooting the Bureau," *GovExec.com*, August 1, 2002, www.govexec.com.

19. "Before 9/11, the FBI's computers were less sophisticated than the one I bought for my son for $1,400," said New York senator Charles E. Schumer (D-NY) who convened hearings on the issue. Source: Bill Miller, "Outdated Systems Balk Terrorism Investigations," *Washington Post*, June 13, 2002, A12.

20. Requesting these records would have been made more difficult by the fact that she likely didn't have the ability to send emails outside her building.

21. Harris, "Rebooting the Bureau," www.govexec.com.

22. See: Ronald Kessler, "FBI Needs More Manpower, More Skillful Managers," *St. Paul Pioneer Press*, June 19, 2002, 17A, and Shane Harris, "Rebooting the Bureau," *GovExec.com*, August 1, 2002.

23. Dante Chinni, "As FBI Woes Deepen, Freeh Gets More Flak," *Christian Science Monitor*, www.csmonitor.com, July 24, 2001.

24. Michelle Gamble-Risley, "Governor Angus King," in the Arena profile, Center for Digital Government, July 2002.

25. By strong leadership I mean a clear vision for the future, an ability to communicate the vision, a willingness to invest political capital in realizing the vision, and the management skills to make the vision a reality.

AFTERWORD

1. "Viterion Telehealthcare Tapped by Kent County Council Social Services to Support Largest Home Health Evaluation Initiative in U.K. History, " Viterion Telehealthcare LLC, March 4, 2005.

2. "Shared Ambition: Peter Gilroy, departing Kent social services to take the council's helm, tells Peter Hetherington about his vision of a brave new world for county hall," *The Guardian*, April 6, 2005.

3. Gary Chapman, "Digital Nation: Project Applies Power of Net to L.A. Housing Woes," *Los Angeles Times*, November 22, 1999, C1.

4. Paul W. Taylor, "New Sense of Place," *Government Technology*, March 1, 2007, (www.govtech.net/magazine/story.php?id=104202).

5. Daniel Henninger, "Packet Politics," *The Wall Street Journal*, March 29, 2007, A16.

Index

WEOs, 156–59. *See also*
government–citizen relationship
civic engagement, 143, 144
civil libertarians, and privacy, 184
Clarke, Richard, 221
Clift, Steven, 147–48, 152
Clinger–Cohen Act, 232
Clinton, Bill, 63, 165–66, 171
Clinton, Hillary, 196
closed circuit surveillance cameras,
201–2, 263–64n44
Coleman, Stephen, 150, 156
Colorado, literacy standards, 129–30
Colorado Student Assessment
Program (CSAP), 129–30
Colorado Virtual Academy, 75
Comcar Industries, 95
commuters, alternate routes for, 84,
251n8
compliance: costs of, 114, *115*;
electronic compliance assistance,
113–14; Expert Advisors system,
112–13; government role in, 103,
103; with OSHA regulations, 109–10
Compstat system, 130–31
Computer Assisted Passenger
Prescreening System (CAPPS II),
204
Computer Curriculum Corporation's
(CCC) SuccessMaker, 69
Computerized Patient Records System
(CPRS), 15
computer phobia, 61–65
computer systems: and artificial
intelligence, 67; pre-September 11,
237–39, 267nn19–20; viewed as
deterrent to education, 62–63
Congress, digital responsiveness of,
157–59
Congressional Record, 192
Congress Online Project, 156–57
Connecticut, state debt, 126
Conoco Industries, 118
Conover, Gerry, 96
construction projects, and online
consultations, 150
consumers, and online transactions, *106*

Cook, Robin, 149, 174, 240
cookies, 183–84
Cookson, Peter, 75
coplink, 45
Cornfield, Michael, 164, 165
corruption: anticorruption websites,
135–36; India, 136–37; information
as enemy of, 134–39; Philippines,
135; Probidad, 137; South Korea,
135–36; and transparency in
Mexico, 133–34; and watchdog
groups, 137–38
Cory, Andrew, 102
council meetings, web casting of, 150
court filing systems, 52
Coyne, Jim, 71
Craig, Murray, 137
credit card fraud, 192
crimes and criminals: child
pornography, 200; concern for
hacking of personal information
from government, 192, 262n19;
criminal background checks, 41–42;
homicides, 131; identity fraud,
192–93; prisoner escapes, 28;
probation systems, 193, 262n24;
reduction of, 46–47, 228–29;
tracking of in New York City,
130–31; and use of surveillance
cameras, 199–200. *See also* law
enforcement; police
Critical Infrastructure Protection
Board, 218
crops, markets in India, 20
Crosby, Tom, 213
cruise control systems, 95
curriculum: and accountability, 78;
extracurricular activities, 77–78;
PAVCS, 59–61; religious, 77;
SuccessMaker, 69
customer relationship management
(CRM), 23–25, 255n22
customer service, reduction of costs in,
17, 28
customs, and corruption, 135
cyber attacks and cyberterrorism, 212;
costs of, 215; on dams, 217;

emergency response time, 87–88

Employment Laws for Workers and
  Small Businesses website, 112–13

encryption technology, 213, 219

Energy Department, 140, 211

energy industries: California, 27; cyber
  attacks on, 214, 217, 265n23; facility
  specifications, 139; Texas, 19

eNeuralNet, 137

Engaging and Empowering
  Citizenship (E2C), 48–49

Engler, John, 228

environmental issues, and information
  sharing, 47–51

Environmental Protection Agency
  (EPA), 48, 49, 50, 148

Environmental Working Group
  (EWG), 138

epol, South Korea, 13

e-procurement, 135

e-Proximity, 96

Erbschloe, Michael, 216, 219

Erwin, John, 236

Estonia, 150, 178, 197

ethics, and hack attacks, 220–21

Evans, Karen, 231

Everson, Mark W., 30

e-voting, 173; and absentee voters, 179,
  261n42; advantages of, 174;
  Arizona, 175; and authentication,
  176–77, 178, 179; and denial of
  service attacks, 177; experiments in,
  174–75; military personnel, 177; and
  online identity, 179; pilot projects in
  UK, 260n36; PIN numbers, 176;
  problems with, 175, 176–77; tips for
  practitioners, 179–80

Expert Advisors, 112–14, 255n20

expert systems, *111*, 112, 255n16

extensible market language (XML), 43,
  53, 205, 248n22

extracurricular activities, and cyber
  schools, 77–78

E-ZPass system, 90

face-recognition technology, 198–99,
  201, 202, 203

Fairfax County, Virginia, 210–11

farm subsidies, 138

federal assistance, for drought victims,
  229

Federal Aviation Administration
  (FAA), 141–42, 234

Federal Bureau of Investigation (FBI),
  41, 218–19, 237–39, 267nn19–20

Federal Deposit Insurance
  Corporation (FDIC), 169–70

Federal Emergency Management
  Agency (FEMA), 54

Federal Energy Regulatory
  Commission, 139

federal government: information
  sharing initiatives, 231–32; public
  sector portals, 19; reform in IT
  projects, 230–33; retirement of civil
  servants, 236–37; rulemaking
  websites, 153–54. *See also* e-
  government; government

Federalist, 63, 155

Federal Labor Relations Authority, 225

federal officials. *See* government
  officials

Federal Register, 113, 170, 187, 261n7

Federal Trade Commission, identity
  fraud, 192

Federation of American Scientists, 141

feedback mechanisms, 20, 70–71,
  149–50

Feigenbaum, Ed, *111*

Feldman, Sandra, 77

Fielding, Pam, 157

fingerprinting, 41–42, 194, 196, 263n28

Finland, 197

Finn, Chester, Jr., 65, 246n9

firewalls, 213, 220

FirstGov.com, 224

Fleming, Daryl, 90, 92, 93

flexyourpower.ca.gov, 27

Florida: budget process, 127, 128, 129;
  Department of Business Processing
  and Regulation, 119; Department of
  Children and Families, 38–40, 40;
  digital politics, 158; federal
  assistance for drought victims, 229;

voters and voting: 2000 presidential
election, 172–73; absentee ballots,
173, 179, 261n42; fraud in, 173, 176;
military personnel, 174; registration
of, 52; targeting of, *168*; turnout,
175–76; vote brokers, 173. *See also* e-
voting
voting machines, 177

Wade, Holly, 109
The Wall Street Journal, 134, 164
warehouses, closing of, 223–25
Warner, Chris, 48–49, 240
Warner, Mark, 233–34
Washington, D.C., use of surveillance
cameras, 199–200
Washington Metropolitan Police
Department, 200
Washington State, 18, 73, 153, 228
The Washington Times, 200, 225
wastewater treatment systems, cyber
attacks on, 217
water quality, 50
Wayman, Jim, 202
web logs, 145
welfare recipients, 32
welfare system, accountability via
websites, 131
Wennerstrum, Brian, 66
Westen, Tracey, 155
Western Pennsylvania Cyber Charter
School, Midland, 77–78
Westin, Alan, 207

West Virginia, driver's license
applications, 193
whistle-blowers, 136
White House, Drug Control Office,
183–84
white knight hackers, 214
Whitman, Christine Todd, 48
Williams, Jody, 170–71
Williams, Michael, 117–18
Wilson, Rilya, 39, 41
Wilson, Woodrow, 1
Winona, Minnesota, 146–47
wired elected officials (WEOs), 156–59
wireless technologies, and teaching of
biology, 62–63
Wisconsin, child welfare system, 39
Wood, Jere, 148
Woodward, John, 202
workplace safety, 116–17
World Trade Organization, 172
Wulf, William, 220

XML. *See* extensible market language
(XML)
x rays, 15

Yahoo Groups, 46
Yavapai Elementary School,
Scottsdale, Arizona, 75
Yermack, Larry, 82
"You Called It," 159

Zier, Jason, *26*

About the Author

William D. Eggers is senior fellow at the Manhattan Institute and global director, Public Sector for Deloitte Research in Washington, D.C. He is the coauthor of *Revolution at the Roots: Making Our Government Smaller, Better, and Closer to Home*, which won the Sir Anthony Fisher International Memorial Award for the book "making the greatest contribution to the understanding of the free economy during the past two years." He splits his time between Austin, Texas, and the Washington, D.C., area.